This Diary Belongs To

Our Diaries, Ourselves

ALSO BY BETSY RUBINER

Fun with the Family in Iowa:
Hundreds of Ideas for Day Trips with the Kids

Our Diaries, Ourselves

HOW DIARISTS CHRONICLE THEIR LIVES AND DOCUMENT OUR WORLD

Betsy Rubiner

BEACON PRESS, BOSTON

Beacon Press
24 Farnsworth Street
Boston, Massachusetts 02210
www.beacon.org

Beacon Press books
are published under the auspices of
the Unitarian Universalist Association of Congregations.

Printed in the United States of America

29 28 27 26   8 7 6 5 4 3 2 1

This book is printed on acid-free paper that meets the uncoated paper ANSI/NISO specifications for permanence as revised in 1992.

Text design and composition by Kim Arney

Library of Congress Cataloging-in-Publication Data is available for this title.
ISBN: 978-0-8070-1492-9
e-book: 978-0-8070-1493-6; audiobook: 978-0-8070-2291-7

The authorized representative in the EU for product safety and compliance is Easy Access System Europe 16879218, Mustamäe tee 50, 10621 Tallinn, Estonia: http://beacon.org/eu-contact.

For Dirck
and our family

"A diary means yes indeed."

—GERTRUDE STEIN

"I have a sneaking suspicion
someone's looking in this diary."

—BETSY, age fifteen, 1974 diary entry

Contents

About the Diary Excerpts xi
Preface: Me-Me-Me xiii

PART 1: QUESTIONING ASSUMPTIONS

1. Days of Our Lives: What Is a Diary Now? 2
2. Born Digital: When Do Social Media and AI-Assisted Entries Count? 21
3. About a Girl: Are Diaries *Really* a Woman's Thing? 36
   FROM MY DIARY: Some of what I kept and read 56

PART 2: WHY WE WRITE

4. Self-Help: Are Diaries *Really* Good for Us? 58
5. Memorable: Do Diaries *Really* Help Us Remember? 73
6. Creatives: Do Diaries *Really* Help Us Create? 88
7. Hindsight: Should We Read or Burn Our Diaries? 104
   FROM MY DIARY: My life on May 12, as chronicled from ages 14 to 62 118

PART 3: WHY WE READ OTHER PEOPLE'S DIARIES

8. Other Eyes: What Do We Learn? 120
9. Ordinary People: Why Save Diaries by Us All? 141
10. Herstory: How Do Diaries Help Write Women into History? 156
    FROM MY DIARY: Our times and world, as documented from 1973 to 2020 (at ages 14 to 61) 169

11. Reader Experiences: What Else Do We Gain? 170

12. Self-Exposure: Should We Let Strangers Read *Our* Diary? 186

Appendix: An Informed Donor Is a Smart Donor: Advice on Donating a Diary 203

Acknowledgments 206

Notes 208

Index 248

About the Diary Excerpts

One luxury (and joy) of diary writing is not having to care about proper spelling, punctuation, or grammar. Unfortunately, this doesn't always make for easy diary reading, so I have trimmed some entries for easier reading, using ellipses to indicate this. In a few entries, I have used brackets to indicate when a word was added for clarity or noted when a name was changed for privacy purposes. Most of the entries are as found.

Preface

Me-Me-Me

For decades they have languished in a drab-gray fireproof filing cabinet in my home: a slowly expanding jumble of diary volumes with more than fifty years' worth of entries about me-me-me. Rummaging through them as I neared sixty, I unearthed my oldest survivor, a battered one-year "Page A Day" model with a beige faux-leather cover. The size of a greeting card but an inch thick, the diary has a tiny lock, now busted, and the wrap-around clasp is long gone. It's from early childhood when I wrote sporadically, not yet daily, when I was finding my way and my voice.

Gingerly opening the diary, I am greeted by a girl's erratic scrawl: "1967, 8 years old." Soon after, I find a page sternly labeled IDENTIFICATION, with prompts, followed by fill-in-the-blank lines: Name, Address, Phone, Color of Hair, Color of Eyes . . . I zero in on My Weight is . . . where I spot a dark scribble on the line, followed by 59 written in pencil. Looking closer at the scribble, I see 60 written in pen beneath it, vigorously crossed out in pencil. I smile, recognizing my lifetime habit of fudging my weight. This is me.

Truth is, although I've kept a diary for most of my life, I've rarely gone back to revisit any of the eighty-two volumes, to date, that I've written—first in preformatted diaries, then in less confining blank-page notebooks. Reading old entries didn't seem healthy or necessary—until recently, when I started thinking about letting strangers read them, although not anytime soon, I hope. I've pledged that after I die, my diary will go to a women's archive in Iowa, where I lived and worked as a journalist for thirty-two years before moving to Chicago.

I grabbed onto donating as a simple solution, or so I thought, to a question that bubbled up in my late middle age when I conceded that, yes, someday I will die: Where will my diary go when I'm gone? Like many people, I have filled volume after volume with my thoughts (including some of my deepest and darkest), but I never seriously contemplated sharing them. The idea of my family and friends reading my occasionally very personal writing about myself—and, sometimes, about them—made me nervous. I worried they would judge me poorly—or worse, be hurt by what I wrote in my diary, or journal, as I've sometimes called it, thinking *journal* sounds less girlish, more sophisticated. (I later learned that *diary* and *journal* are commonly used interchangeably.)

I considered destroying my diary, as many women do. One friend told me that she threw away the diary she'd written in the early throes of parenting twins. "Too hormonal," she said. I tried to imagine lugging my old dears from the filing cabinet to the recycling bin. Or tossing them into the firepit we bought during the COVID-19 pandemic. Or shredding them to make garden mulch. Couldn't do it—I am too emotionally attached. I need them nearby. They literally let me hold onto my past.

Women's archives to the rescue! After discovering that these gender-specific archives exist, I found out that they preserve women's diaries and other personal documents so future researchers can use them to learn about women's lives and times. I was amazed to find the Iowa Women's Archives at the University of Iowa, only a two-hour drive east from my then home in Des Moines. Here was a place where my words and memories might safely outlive me—and be put to good use! If we can donate our bodies to science, why not donate our thoughts to history? "Our" assumed new meaning when I learned that archives have traditionally been male-dominated, preserving relatively little material by and about women. Too often, institutions entrusted with safeguarding important papers have dismissed women's diaries and other life writing as trivial and dull, ignoring their power to shed light on women's ideas, roles, contributions, and world, adding "herstory" to history.

Yet, as the idea of donating became more real, I began to worry about other eyes on my diary. Would my do-good impulse do harm by violating my privacy and, more importantly, the privacy of my nearest and dearest? Would the diary reveal too much to strangers? Would it be posted online? My journalist's curiosity kindled, I started asking questions to figure out how best to donate. These questions led to other questions, to insights, doubts, and ultimately, to writing this book, which became a vehicle for discovery about diary donating—and so much more. I realized that although I have written in a diary almost every day since I was thirteen, I have never thought, *really* thought, about what I am doing or creating. Why did I keep stuffing my diary into suitcases, backpacks, and nightstand drawers? Why did I dig out my diary to write in a tent in the Michigan woods? In a noisy youth hostel, a hotel room on my wedding night, a bumpy train from Fez to Marrakesh, during a snatched moment after my babies were asleep? Why are diarists like me so driven to chronicle our thoughts and experiences? I began questioning common assumptions about the diary—That it's private! Handwritten on paper! Truth! For girls! Good for us! A memory saver! A tool for creative expression!—and finding disagreement among diary experts and diarists on whether these hold true.

During this adventure, I stumbled into a space I've come to call Diaryland, which proved to be populated not only by a motley crew of diary writers but also by readers of diaries written by others. To find out why, I talked to family historians saving their ancestors' diaries, to scholars studying diaries, to creatives using diaries for their art, and to diary collectors. I visited American women's archives and European diary archives. I learned more about the pandemic journaling projects that sprang up in 2020, encouraging us to record our experiences for our mental health and for posterity.

As I listened to diary writers and diary readers (paper and digital), I hoped to understand the distinctive appeal that a diary offers. Is it that the diary grants us permission to write about ourselves in some unique way? To my surprise, some interviews got intense, even emotional, leading to conversations about life, mortality, memory loss, legacy; about holding onto our past and understanding our former selves; about what we should leave behind and what we owe others, especially people we love. Gradually, the book took shape as a mix of reporting and reflection. Part 1 explores common assumptions about what a diary is. Part 2 explores why diarists write. Part 3 explores why we read other people's diaries—and returns to my initial donation questions. Mulling all this over, I had some sleepless nights as I tried to sort out my personal responsibilities, my donation plan, and my evolving views about "diary keeping"—meaning both *writing* a diary and *saving* it. One thing was clear: what I learned proved too compelling to keep to myself, in my diary.

PART 1

Questioning Assumptions

1

Days of Our Lives

What Is a Diary Now?

When I started exploring Diary-land, I thought of it as a metaphorical space without physical locations, let alone hotspots—until I discovered Italy's "City of the Diary," otherwise known as Pieve Santo Stefano, a small Tuscan town with a big roadside sign declaring itself the Città del Diario. Pieve Santo Stefano is home to Italy's impressive Archivio Diaristico Nazionale (National Diary Archive) and to a clever diary museum proudly highlighting the archive's crown jewels. Since 1984, this archive has collected more than ten thousand unpublished autobiographical texts, most Italian, most that would otherwise have been lost. The town also hosts an annual four-day festival that celebrates ordinary people's unpublished writing about themselves and awards one lucky life writer a prize of one thousand euros, plus publication of their submission.

But I soon realized there was a catch: Italy's City of the Diary is not only about diaries. The Archivio Diaristico Nazionale also collects unpublished memoirs, autobiographies, and personal letters. So do several other "diary archives" throughout Europe.

Regardless, I was in diary-nerd heaven during the Premio Pieve festival in September 2023, amazed to see hundreds of writers and readers of diaries (and the like) who had traveled from across Italy to this town of some three thousand people. Visitors lined up for diary museum tours, bought diary archive merch, and attended free events and exhibits. On the final afternoon, we packed into a pavilion for the closing ceremony, emceed by an Italian journalist and broadcast on the radio. For over two hours, the audience listened intently as the eight finalists vying for the annual Pieve Prize for the best autobiographical writing were interviewed onstage, talk-show style. Actors performed dramatic readings of each submission, accompanied by live music.

The winner turned out to be the author of an unpublished memoir. No shock there. Five of the eight finalists had submitted a text other than a diary. (A diary *did* win a special mention.) But I left Pieve Santo Stefano wondering even more about Diary-land's turf: What *is* a diary today? How do diaries differ from their near neighbors: memoirs, autobiographies, and letters? How has digital technology expanded Diary-land? Do posts on Facebook, Instagram, and X (or, earlier, Twitter) count as diary entries? What about YouTube and TikTok videos, Fitbit reports, websites, blogs, online newsletters, and entries produced via digital journaling apps, some trumpeting assistance from artificial intelligence (AI)?

Like many people, especially other diarists, I thought I knew what a diary was. Yet the more I discovered about the diaries of today—and yesterday—the more I realized that the diary is a shapeshifting and much-debated form. And the more I felt duty-bound to come up with a workable definition that felt current and inclusive. Slowly, I began to see diary writing as a unique practice and the diary as a unique product. But defining something I've written for so long proved unexpectedly difficult.

∞∞

I knew that my old-school diary writing—pen on paper—is not the only way. My go-to mental image of a *diary*—a once-blank book filled with messy longhand—is not what pops into everyone's mind. What do you see? A bullet journal's dot grid? A journaling app icon on a tablet's touchscreen? A post on X? "People tend to agree on the general idea of it—you know *diary* doesn't mean novel or podcast," Canadian scholar Julie Rak told me. But, when people try to be precise, she said, "we don't have good agreement." Some definitions that I found contradicted each other, or seemed out-of-date, too rigid or too vague. The late British scholar Robert Fothergill, who, in 1974, was among the first to deem the diary a literary form, argued that a diary is whatever a diarist says they're writing. Monica Soeting, cofounder of both the Nederlands Dagboekarchief (Dutch Diary Archive) and the International Autobiography Association's European section, suggested that I refer to "diary" more broadly as "life writing."

Rather than concoct a dictionary-like definition that might be too broad or narrow, I became hell-bent on figuring out what diaries share in common, despite their differences, and what makes a diary a diary, not a memoir or some other form of life writing. I started with a list of potential descriptors that might define all (or most) diaries and might set the diary apart from other forms: *writing*, *me-me-me*, *personal*, *private*, *secret*, *daily*, *truth*, *candid*, *authentic*, *honest*. But the more I explored Diary-land, the more I discarded descriptors like useless gear dumped during a strenuous hike—and the more I understood that my struggle to define the diary was due to challenging conditions on the ground.

Because many diarists and diaries remain out of public view, Diary-land is mysterious. We can't know how many people practice this stealth activity, scribbling thoughts in a once-blank book or tapping into a cellphone while standing in a grocery store line. Hyper-attuned to all things diary, I *did* start noticing diary mentions everywhere—a sign, perhaps, that the diary is also a stealth part of our daily life or culture. Or is Diary-land its own culture, hiding in plain sight?

In newspapers and magazines, I kept stumbling upon "diary stories": A Russian dissident's prison diary published soon after his death. A British writer using his late mother's diary to write a novel. A Palestinian reading her Gaza audiodiary on BBC radio. A summer 2025 newspaper story about "journaling clubs" held across the US in private homes, public parks, bookstores, and via video calls. Canadian American actor Sandra Oh sharing that she thought first of saving her diaries, should she have to evacuate during the 2025 Los Angeles fires. "Do I take the first ones . . . the past 10 years? It just makes you think, What are the things that are very, very important to you?" Oh told an interviewer. I read an evangelical pastor's diary entries documenting his struggle to reconcile "his God and his gay son"—shared by that son with a newspaper. "I think deep down, I hate homosexuality," the pastor writes on May 25, 2013. "I see the isolation, the craving, the insecurity. Father, you have to spare Timothy from that." By January 26, 2019, he writes: "Father, thank you that you created our son gay. Forgive me for how poorly I received this gift." I read about a North Dakota woman who has written a diary daily for ninety years, as of 2025. "Grandma's were at our place. Clarence walked from Aunt Alma's this morning," reads her first entry, in 1936, written in a ten-year-old's wiggly cursive. (She was still writing in cursive, at age one hundred.)

Beyond diary-based memoirs and histories, the diary is everywhere in popular culture: A closeted transgender woman's diary entries shared in the 2024 documentary *Will & Harper*. Arresting entries from lifestyle entrepreneur Martha Stewart's "prison diary," shared in the 2024 documentary *Martha*. The fourth Bridget Jones movie (2025), inspired by the fictional diary series from 1996. Even dancers holding diaries while leaping across the stage in the 2024 Tony-nominated musical *Illinoise*. Smart online publications are into studying diaries, from Maria Popova's website/blog *The Marginalian* ("a sort of public diary of learnings") to Jillian Hess's Substack newsletter, *Noted*, about "the world's best note takers." So are social media users—in 2024, millions of TikTokers were reading a Jewish New York City teenager's 1945 journal entries, posted by a twenty-five-year-old Brooklyn woman who bought the journal at an estate sale. "I am obsessed with this kind of history," wrote one of the 2,821 commenters.

By chance or word of mouth, I kept finding diarists—often women over age sixty (like me) but also men and younger people. So many times, when people got wind of my diary project, they'd confide, "I have a diary." Or say wistfully, "I *had* a diary." Or say regretfully, "I *wish* I had a diary." At small social gatherings, people swapped diary stories with me: Out of seven older people at a Chicago dinner party, three (all women) wrote diaries as kids. One woman originally from central Missouri destroyed her diary during the 1960s after her brother threatened to read it. A man in his early eighties spun a good yarn about traveling to Scotland in 1978 with the 1881 diaries of two of his great-great-grandparents, both Scottish immigrants to Wisconsin who'd written entries during their return visit to Scotland. "How should I save them?" he asked me.

Around another dining table, I met a Chicago journalist who, randomly enough, had cowritten a travel journal with my Iowa newspaper friends thirty years earlier. Soon after, one of those friends (thank you, Jane Burns) sent me the shared journal—a worn spiral notebook with entries written by a succession of *Des Moines Register* staffers who had traveled in separate groups to Paris in 1992. Each journal writer had added observations and tips before passing it along. Three decades later, reading old friends' words, I recognized their wit, sarcasm, or attention to detail. The journal read like a relic, with mentions of francs and pay phones.

Acquaintances urged me to talk to their diary-writing friend or relative, which is how I found forty-year-old Robert Ryan of New York City, who writes a journal for himself and a separate journal for each of his three young children to give them when they're eighteen. The children's journals serve as a record of "events, contexts, what was going on in our lives," and a record of who the children and their father were. When I mentioned this to my thirty-seven-year-old Chicago neighbor Dimitri Gordon, he volunteered that *he* writes a journal for his young son.

Although I knew my mother had kept a travel diary—we found the volumes after her death in 2004—who knew that *her* mother wrote a diary too? My mother's sister knew. With a slight smile, my aunt Mary Ann gingerly handed me the fragile, unbound pages of Grandma Betty's brief diary, written from an Easton, Pennsylvania, maternity ward in 1931 after the birth of her first child. In lieu of looseleaf paper, Grandma wrote on now-yellowed sheets of paper labeled "Nurses' Case Report." Her voice and handwriting were instantly familiar to me. "She sure is a peach of a girl," Grandma wrote about a nurse.

My diary discoveries continued online. On the discussion platform Reddit, I found r/Journaling, a community for people "who keep a written journal" with 2.1 million members, landing it in the top 1 percent of Reddit communities by membership (behind r/fantasyfootball and r/selfimprovement but ahead of r/forbiddensnacks and r/TattooDesigns). On Facebook, my seventy-something friend Tom Alex posted a photo of a handwritten page of his grandfather's diary referring to the infant Tom as "the big baby." Tom wrote above the photo: "This entry from July 23, 1948, made me grin." My sixty-something friend Veronica Lorson Fowler posted a photo of journals discovered in rural Kansas, written by "older women relatives from the 1940s on." The journal covers are splotchy and color-faded, with vintage brand names: "Dailyaide: The Silent Secretary 1958," "Daily Desk Diary 1962," "Daily Reminder 1968," and "Big 1¢ Pencil Tablet." "They're such a gift," Veronica told me. "They let me reach back into history and understand my roots—and make me grateful for the internet, birth control, higher education for women, and central heating."

Beyond personal testimonials, I sought secondary sources to better define Diary-land's contours. What I found in news dispatches, surveys, and studies was often eye-catching but raised unanswerable questions:

- Thousands of people contributed to journaling projects that cropped up during the COVID-19 pandemic. But did they keep writing after the early pandemic? How many other diarists wrote on their own during those long, anxious days?
- In the United Kingdom, almost 30 percent of young people ages five to eighteen kept a diary in 2022, according to a National Literacy Trust survey of seventy thousand people. Far more girls (41 percent) than boys (16 percent) were diarists, and they reported that writing in a diary helped them feel creative and express themselves. But a follow-up 2024 survey found that children's and young people's frequency and enjoyment of writing (not diary writing specifically) during their free time was at an all-time low. What to make of this? What about other countries and cultures?
- "The Internet has arguably made everyone . . . into a life writer of sorts," declared a 2023 Stanford University Press digital publication on "ego media," aka new or social media, "from chatbots to war blogs to mommy vlogs and beyond." A life writer or a diarist?

∞∞

Because diary writing lacks hard-and-fast universal rules, Diary-land is full of rugged individualists. Although there is no shortage of diary how-to guides, workshops, and TikTok tutorials, diarists don't need to *learn* how to keep a diary. We just do it, creating our own rules or habits that change over time as we change or our world changes. (For me, this soon meant writing every night and gradually switching from a preformatted diary with lined and dated pages to a less dictatorial blank notebook but *not* to a computer file.) Often described as a particularly "democratic" writing form, diary writing today is inviting and inclusive, a no-pressure or low-pressure activity, thanks to its refreshing dearth of dictates and literary airs. Anyone who has the necessities—time, ability, freedom, materials—can produce a diary that is as one-of-a-kind as its author. Diarists start at different points in life, using different mediums (on paper or online; in words, illustrations, photos, audio, video), establishing different routines (one-line-per-day, one-page-per day; in the morning or night). We write for different reasons (recording, reckoning, remembering, to be remembered; for posterity, therapy, creativity, gratitude, a love of writing). We write about different topics (daily life, nature, war, travel, parenting) for different audiences (self, descendants, strangers, who knows).

Diarists—especially women—often told me they started diaries as teens or young adults, during a major turning point when they faced a big decision, relationship issue, or emotional upheaval. Author Lucy Sante started a diary in her early sixties while contemplating a gender transition after living, often uncomfortably, as a man. "I'd never kept a diary or journal, but during this whirlwind I started taking notes, just by way of touching ground every now and then," Sante recalls in her 2024 memoir. "I went in for proclamations: 'I have finally found my soul.' 'I'm already past the point of no return' . . . Then there was the inevitable counterpoint: 'Do I deserve this?'" One woman told me she'd recently started journaling after hearing it was a healthy midlife activity. Betsy Edgerton, a fifty-something journalism professor, told me she quit journal writing after her twins were born, lacking time and privacy. She wants to restart: "I think about that several times a week and I never do it."

Diary *readers* also do their own thing. When an unpublished diary is read by someone other than its author, it morphs from personal manuscript to semi-public text. Depending on the reader and the text, the diary becomes a treasured family heirloom, a historical document, a cultural artifact, creative inspiration, or literature (substandard literature, some sniff). Although literary critics, historians, anthropologists, and social scientists have long used diaries as sources, the study of the diary *as* a diary has blossomed since the 1970s, with newly recovered diaries ushered into public view and analyzed, every which way. Scholars from a broadening range of fields (including relative newbies such as digital studies) scrutinize diaries.

I was thrilled to discover a two-inch-thick anthology of diary scholarship shortly after it was published, in 2020. *The Diary: The Epic of Everyday Life* soon became my cherished "diary tome." The impressive anthology's twenty-seven international scholars tackle a dizzying array of topics: diary theories; diary canons in Britain, France, America, and Brazil; thorny issues regarding diary editing, publishing, and digitizing. (Digitizing means turning a physical document into a digital one, not what may follow: posting the digitized document online to make it accessible to readers.)

The Diary also created diary categories (travel, private, online) that accented differences, which I feared might hinder my quest to find commonalities. I thought differently when I looked more closely at one particularly broad category: "The Diary in Political Conflict." This section includes subcategories whose particulars differed wildly: Confederate women's diaries, French soldiers' World War I diaries, Holocaust diaries, Estonian women's deportation diaries. What did they all have in common? They were written by people who faced a similar predicament (political conflict) and, tellingly, felt compelled to write then and there.

Because its basic lingo lacks consensus language, Diary-land is a tricky place for conversation. Scholars generally agree on using *diary* and *journal* interchangeably (as I've opted to do) because the difference between the two terms has become so fuzzy. Yet some people cling to the traditional distinction—that a diary is for recording a day's events, while a journal is for introspection. One longtime diarist, or so I thought, clarified mid-conversation that she writes a *journal* (for addressing "concerns" in her life) not a *diary* (for chronicling "on this day, this happened"). Furthermore, although she has a journal, she would not say she is *journaling*. That "smacks" of the self-help movement, she told me. Meanwhile, others argue that diaries have long been used to express concerns and feelings, especially by women, further fueling the common assumption (or misassumption) that women write diaries and men write journals.

Views vary on what to call a diarist's collective output: *diary* or *diaries*? I opted for *diary* and for *diary volumes* to denote the individual books that a diarist filled. Views also vary on which nonfiction category best fits the diary. In the 1990s, feminists embraced *life writing* (often informal, unpolished self-narratives associated with women) rather than the 1970s-era *autobiographical writing*, which was deemed too narrow and too male, Desirée Henderson, an English professor at the University of Texas at Arlington, told me. Life writing is also feminists' preferred way of describing diaries and describing the academic field studying diaries. Historians tend to call diaries *autobiographical writing* rather than *life writing*, the term some literary scholars prefer. People sometimes replace *life* with *self* or *personal*. (I've grown fond of *self writing*.) *Narrative* sometimes replaces *writing*, as a nod to entries that are *not* written. Europeans seem keen on *ego-documents*, related to *ego media*, which, to me, sounds awkwardly close to *egotistical*.

ooo

"Diaries are so multifaceted that every broad claim made about the genre within these pages should be understood to be provisional and will not apply to all diaries," writes Henderson in her thoughtful 2019 book, *How to Read a Diary*. Furthermore, her "genre-level" claims are "open to question and subject to revision."

Don't I know it, Desirée! I struggled to generalize, given the wide variety of diaries/journals, their changing nature, and debate over whether common assumptions about diaries *and* diarists are accurate. I had to sort through competing claims by diary experts and diarists about the diary/journal's intrinsic nature or defining characteristics. Finally, I chose two broadbrush diary descriptors—*dailiness* and *self*—because they felt truest about diaries *and* truest to me as a diarist. Each *day* that I write, I start by entering the date, followed by my latest *self* report, producing individual dispatches that gradually become a Book of Days and a Book of the Self. Marking time's passing and baring one's self (or soul) are classic diarist behaviors. The diary is "day-to-day writing; a series of dated written records," declares renowned French diary theorist Philippe Lejeune, writing with colleague Catherine Bogaert in *The Diary*. With *self*, things get deep: "A diary is a space where the self momentarily escapes from social pressures, takes refuge within a bubble, or a sealed chamber, where it can unfold without risk, before returning, relieved, to the real world."

By choosing *dailiness*, I hope to reassure diarists who tell me they're not the real deal because they don't write or chronicle *every day*, which is how some interpret *daily* or *day-to-day*. But they *are* diarists and, I'd guess, typical ones. *Dailiness* doesn't infer a daily writing requirement. To me, it means writing that is anchored *in* time (specifically *the day*) but is not necessarily *about* the day. *Dailiness* produces a distinct quality. Each entry has a stand-alone immediacy. When combined with other entries over time, the net effect is a diary that often reads as choppy, not flowing, more staccato than legato. The diary is a series of "traces"—a written trail of the diarist's existence, Lejeune and Bogaert suggest. The diarist is marking a chunk of time with reference points. *Dated* entries are further proof that the diarist is anchored in the given time/day. And they're a diary must-have, they insist, although the dating need not be precise and can be spaced out.

By choosing *self*, I don't mean that diarists must write nonstop *about* themselves, although that happens. The diary's *selfiness* (I made up this word, for lack of a better one) can also mean a diarist writes *to* and *for* their self, in the moment, on the page. They may write for self-awareness/conversation/care/analysis/regard/preservation/documentation, even self-creation, producing personal writing that declares: *This is me*, *I exist*, or *I was here*. "In the journal I do not just express myself more openly than I could to any person; I create myself," author Susan Sontag wrote on December 31, 1957. "The journal is a vehicle for my sense of selfhood."

The diary's dailiness sets it apart in the self-writing sea. While a memoir or formal autobiography aims to offer a retrospective story, the diary typically doesn't, or can't, because it is written from the middle of an unfolding life. It inches forward by the day. An autobiography is "turned to the past," while the diary "sculpts life as it happens," explains Lejeune. Because memoirists and autobiographers, unlike diarists, often know the end of the experience that they're writing about, they can organize it to craft a story, impose a meaning, and develop themes or conclusions.

Because memoirs and autobiographies, as well as letters, are more overtly or commonly written *to* or *for* outside readers than diaries, their writers may offer more reader-friendly touches, from context to proper spelling, than self-oriented diarists do. Mindful of other readers and of posterity, they may be more self-conscious or cautious when writing about themselves and others, producing labored prose that hedges, dodges, or fuzzes particulars, that may self-justify or self-enhance. Diarists are prone to repetition, something I've noticed while reading other people's diaries and my own. Many a time, when writing a fresh entry, I've thought, *This sounds familiar, and not so fresh*. Sure enough, I find a similar recent entry—less a sign of a poor memory (I like to think) than of being so rooted in the day at hand. A diary often feels unfinished, ending suddenly when the diarist opts to stop writing or can no longer write.

For some, the diary feels inferior to other me-me-me forms. "I'm lamenting that my book, originally an autobiography with an intriguing thriller about uncovering an assassination attempt using chemical weapons, has turned into a prison diary. It's a genre so saturated with clichés that it's impossible not to write them," wrote Russian opposition activist and political prisoner Alexei Navalny in an October 21, 2021, diary entry featured in his posthumously published 2024 memoir. The book reads like a hybrid memoir-diary, switching midway from smoother memoir text (begun in 2020) to incremental dated prison diary entries starting in 2021 (which I found especially vivid and gripping). His death in a Russian Arctic penal colony was reported on February 16, 2024.

A diary's blunt, unguarded immediacy can offer readers a singular adventure. "Unlike memoirs or letters, a diary doesn't alter its story in hindsight. Instead, readers get to experience life as the writer does," writes Paula Vene Smith, an English professor at Grinnell College in Iowa. "The diary's day-by-day structure, with its constant uncertainty about the future, allows us to share in the writer's discoveries, life-changing experiences, and new understandings as they unfold." The diary also offers a one-of-a-kind source for historians. Irving Finkel, cofounder of the Great Diary Project, a British archive, writes: "No other kind of document offers such a wealth of information about daily life and the ups and downs of human existence."

"What Did the Stars Foretell at Your Birth?" reads the printed material in my 1967 diary. The stars foretold a mixed bag for young Betsy. As a Taurus, I might "develop an inferiority complex." On the bright side, I was "Muscular, [with] endurance almost superhuman." However dubious, this horoscope—plus dated pages and a one-year structure—are time-related features in my preformatted diary that descend partly from the almanac, first printed in Europe in 1457 and in colonial North America in 1639. (*The Old Farmer's Almanac* has been published in the US since 1792.) Looking for the roots of the diary's dailiness, I followed British diary scholars who land on the almanac as a precursor of the calendar, appointment diary, and "the personal diary." The almanac hails from the beginning of astronomy, in roughly 1400 BCE, when Babylonians inscribed clay tablets with dated charts to predict the movements of the sun, moon, and stars. Printed almanacs often feature astronomy and astrology (horoscopes!), which are both related to time (in varying ways). Although almanacs were designed to forecast what *will* happen, people gradually started writing in an almanac's wide margins and blank pages about what *had* happened, in diary-like fashion.

On the etymology front, the words *diary* and *journal* stem from *day* (*dies* in Latin, *jour* in French). The French use *journal intime* (intimate) to avoid confusion with *journal*, which is French for newspaper, aka journalism. The diary also has been connected to the advent of time-keeping devices—the clock, watch, pendulum, train table—which reflect our desire to track time in ever more granular detail.

As for the diary's selfiness, standard diary history attributes this to a major cultural shift in Western thinking, beginning in the sixteenth century and in full swing by the eighteenth-century Enlightenment, which centered on the individual and individualism, on having the ability and the right to set one's own course in life. No longer was this determined primarily by, say, property ownership, class, or religion. The diary emerged as a vehicle of expression for the new modern individual (with a strong sense of self), whose story surely deserved to be told. Other contemporary forms of autobiography and biography also sprang up. Puritans, Quakers, Baptists, Methodists, and, later, Mormons promoted diary writing for spiritual and earthly reasons. The nineteenth century saw the golden age of the diary, flourishing among a Victorian bourgeoisie characterized by individualism, introspection, leisure time, and a yearning for privacy, according to historian Peter Gay.

Scholars also link diary writing to Italian merchants circa 1300–1500, whose business accounting spawned the *ricordanze*—or home account book—which began to include more personal diary-like notes recording family history and one's own deeds to share with descendants. Florentine apothecary Luca Landucci's landmark diary diligently chronicled his city's unfolding history from 1450 at age fourteen until his death in 1516. Eighteenth-century New England farmers, shopkeepers, ship's captains, craftsmen, housewives added personal notes about work or family events to their household-accounting "daybooks."

ooo

When did the modern diary that we know today, with an ordinary diarist's inner voice recording worldly *and* personal events, debut and become common? Scholars land somewhere between the 1500s and 1700s. How did this happen? Beyond a mounting fascination with time and self, other changes in society, technology, and culture spurred diary writing. During the 1600s and 1700s these included political and religious upheavals, prompting inward reflection; increased foreign travel, offering new material to write about; increased literacy and the arrival of print culture, pocket almanacs, and the popular novel, which sparked interest in ordinary people's lives; and more leisure time. During the 1800s came ready-made dated diaries in Britain, designed for jotting down future appointments but soon also used for reflecting on the past day. These manufactured diaries helped turn "diary-keeping into a mainstream occupation for the first time in human history," writes British author Roland Allen. Between 1900 and 1936, the number of diary sales made by the British company Letts grew by a factor of twelve, to three million annually.

Also driving diary keeping was the nineteenth-century publication of diaries by Englishmen Samuel Pepys and John Evelyn (written in the 1600s) and by Russian French diarist Marie Bashkirtseff, whose late-1800s diary inspired women to start diaries. In more recent decades, the digital revolution, the memoir boom, the genealogy craze, the wellness industry, podcast mania, and our "confessional culture" have encouraged diary keeping.

One caveat: critics of this shaping of diary history fault it as too Western-centric and too male-centric, notes Desirée Henderson. Diary precursors or diary-like texts have been found in non-Western cultures: from ancient Egyptian hieroglyphics on papyrus to the eleventh-century Baghdad scholar

Ibn Banna's record of dreams and daily life. However, non-Western forms that, say, mix self writing with poetry or prose, don't fit the Western concept of a diary. Among the Middle Eastern and Asian texts that some deem early diary-like examples is the tenth-century "pillow book" of Sei Shōnagon, a Japanese lady-in-waiting to the empress in Kyoto. She recorded her daily life, personal reflections, and court gossip in a book reportedly kept bedside, near her pillows. She sounds like my kind of gal, compiling lists like "Unsuitable Things" and "Things That Irritate Me."

∞∞

"Why is this a 'diary'?" asked my brother-in-law Steve, a veteran daily newspaper reporter, forwarding me an article headlined "Trial Diary." The story turned out to be more memoir than diary—and an example of how the not-so-accurate use of the word *diary* complicates efforts to define it. *Diary* is frequently used as a catch-all for related genres or used interchangeably with *memoir*. *Diary* is often plopped misleadingly into the titles of articles, books, movies, or blogs that are non-diaries—done as a marketing tease, I suspect, tapping into the assumption that diaries ooze with juicy secrets.

Granted, the line between the diary and its autobiographical near neighbors can blur. Beyond the memoir/diary, published by, say, Alexei Navalny, some diaries have memoir-like moments, looking back in anger, affection, dismay, pain, regret, or pride. An individual diary entry is often retrospective, recalling the day or earlier days. "The difference with a diary is it hasn't been reconstructed as a story, all at once," explained Laurel Thatcher Ulrich, author of the Pulitzer Prize-winning *A Midwife's Tale*, based on an early American diary.

Diaries often read like a letter, sometimes addressed to a prospective reader. Rock star–poet Patti Smith described her journal as "an imaginary friend." That most famous of diarists, Anne Frank, addressed her entries to friends, most imaginary (*Dear Kitty*, *Dear Pop*, *Conny*, *Lou*, *Emmy* . . .) but some real (*Dear Jacqueline*). Later, some of the many teenage diarists inspired by Frank's posthumously published teenage diary addressed *their* entries to Anne. I never wrote a *Dear Anne* entry in my diary, although she helped inspire me too.

I opted to use *diaristic* or *diary-like* to describe near diaries, as a way of welcoming them into Diary-land. One near diary, to me, is the wildly popular bullet journal (or "bujo"), launched online in 2013 by a designer with ADHD to help him focus and organize. The bullet journal's initial purpose—for "decluttering" the mind—differs from the traditional diary's purpose, as Julie Rak, a University of Alberta English and film studies professor, pointed out to me. Rak also co-edited *On Diary*, a 2009 English translation of French scholar Philippe Lejeune's work. With tidy logs and to-do lists composed of quickly written "bullet" sentences, the bullet journal can feel more like an intricate, forward-looking daily planner than a tool for self-chronicling on the day. The "bullet journal method" bills itself as "part productivity system, part mindfulness practice," offering techniques to "track the past, organize the present, and create the future." However, some bujo do-it-yourselfers *do* include diaristic entries about themselves.

Distinguishing between a diary and a notebook (a book for writing notes) is tricky. Discussion of either a diary or a notebook inevitably touches on the other, charts a similar history, and may describe a similar purpose, especially as a tool for thinking and creativity. Some diarists use *diary* and *notebook* interchangeably, often because they write in a product called a notebook. The notebook has different forms, formats, and purposes, from ship's logs, explorer journals, and lab observations to artists' sketchbooks and police logbooks. A notebook used to mark time passing and address the self qualifies as a diary, in my view, especially if it has dated entries. But if it's used primarily to gather miscellaneous undated jottings, record data, or capture fleeting thoughts, it seems near (or not) diary. Since medieval times, artists, writers, musicians, scientists, and mere mortals (Leonardo da Vinci, Charles Darwin, Geoffrey Chaucer, Agatha Christie, Bob Dylan, me) have written notes for their works in progress. Roald Dahl kept an "idea book" that seeded novels including *Charlie and the Chocolate Factory*.

Author Joan Didion reports writing what, to me, sound like some diary-like entries in her *notebook*—which she insisted was not a *diary*. "At no point have I ever been able to successfully keep a diary; my approach to daily life ranges from the grossly negligent to the merely absent," she explains in her 1960s essay "On Keeping a Notebook." A diary is an effort to dutifully "record a day's events" and produce "an accurate factual record" of one's actions and thoughts, Didion suggests. Her notebook, instead, is "an indiscriminate and erratic assemblage" of impressions, facts, quotes, overheard dialogue, even a recipe. While it may seem that she's notebook writing about other people, Didion adds, she's writing about *herself*, about her impressions, about how things felt to her. "*Remember what it was to be me*: that is always the point," she writes.

Didion seems to define the diary's purpose more narrowly than I do, yet her notebook's purpose (the *me-me-me* part) resembles my diary definition. To complicate matters, in 2025, a newly published collection of highly personal writing by Didion (who died in 2021) was billed by some as her *journal* or *diary*. (Another marketing tease perhaps?) The book, however, is titled *Notes to John* and composed of Didion's recaps of her psychiatric sessions, begun in 1999 at age sixty-five. They are addressed to her husband, John Gregory Dunne, who died in 2003. For me, Didion's detailed "I said/he said" entries sometimes read differently than a typical diarist's internal monologue—more akin to painstaking notes by a patient or by the journalist Didion was. Then again, she produced dated self-reports, meeting my loose diary definition. And Didion appears to be dutifully recording to produce an accurate factual record, corresponding with what seems to be *her* diary definition. "I said I wasn't sure where we left off. Dr. MacKinnon said why not begin where you are now. I said I wasn't sure where I was now," Didion begins a 1,495-word entry on February 16, 2000.

Scientist Marie Curie documented her professional work in her notebooks and workbooks but filled her diary with her sorrow after the sudden death in 1906 of her forty-nine-year-old husband and research partner, Pierre. (Together, they won the 1903 Nobel Prize in physics.) Writing in both the workbooks and diary reflects Madame Curie's "compartmentalized personality," argues a Curie biographer. "I want to tell you that I do not like the sun and the flowers anymore, looking at them makes me suffer," Curie wrote in her diary to her late husband. "I feel better in dark weather, like on the day of your death." In 1911, she won a second Nobel Prize, this time for chemistry. Thought to be radioactive, her diary and other papers were sealed in lead-lined boxes after her death in 1934.

∞∞

Writing and *private* were the hardest diary descriptors to dump. *Writing* had to go, given the diaries composed of photos, videos, and audio. As for *private*, many diarists insist they are producing a private document, meant to remain private, and that because they seek no outside audience, they can write more truthfully about what is in their heart and head—their confessions, fears, regrets, embarrassments, and fuckups. They are free to be candid and rude, to write what they'd never say out loud. No need to engage or explain. They can be repetitive or nonsensical. Proper spelling, completed sentences, legibility, finished thoughts, context, decorum, lucidity: not required. Some scholars also describe the diary as private literature that even if published shares the diarist's private self, thinking, and experiences. As such, many private diarists are horrified by the thought of outside readers, about going public, about publication. (I get it.)

I dumped *private*, in part, because I'd come to believe that very public, audience-seeking social media posts, including blogs, can qualify as diaries, acing the *dailiness* and *selfiness* tests. An argument by American scholar Lynn Z. Bloom was also persuasive. "Contrary to popular conception, not all diaries are written—ultimately or exclusively—for private consumption," she writes in a 1998 essay titled "'I Write for Myself and Strangers': Private Diaries as Public Documents." Diarists often revise or edit their entries so their "superficially private writings become unmistakably public documents, intended for external readership," noted Bloom, now a retired English professor. And some diaries are intended for an outside audience and, as such, can be public, semi-public, or simultaneously public and private.

The contemporary assumption that the diary is a "secret" record of a private inner life dates to the 1880s, wrote the late American diary scholar Margo Culley. Before then, the diary was more public, with diarists—especially women—commonly exchanging brief diary entries during gatherings of friends and relatives. The German composers Robert and Clara Schumann started a joint "marriage diary" after their wedding in 1840. "When a man composes a symphony . . . even his wife must accept herself as set aside!" wrote Clara. In France, the brothers Edmond and Jules de Goncourt gossiped in their cowritten journal about Paris's art and literary stars. "The journal is our nightly confession, the confession of two lives never separated in pleasure, in work or in pain," reads the preface to their entries, first published in 1886, while Edmond (though not Jules) was alive.

Around the same time, rural Iowans Emily Hawley Gillespie and her daughter Sarah were reading each other's diaries, with Emily occasionally commenting *in* Sarah's diary. On February 6, 1886, Sarah wrote: "Pa came for us about 4:30—Was mad—when he came in he shook his fist in Ma's face and said in a tremulous & savage tone, 'Emily you treat me worse than I do my cattle.' . . . Ma nearly fainted away. . . . I believe Pa is insane." Though Emily described marital dysfunction in her own diary, she wrote comments in her daughter's diary that minimized disturbing incidents, referring to them as "silly upset[s]" in an apparent attempt to calm Sarah and preserve appearances.

More recently, in 2010, a Maryland mother-daughter duo published a preformatted journal designed for sharing called *Just Between Us: Mother & Daughter: A No-Stress, No-Rules Journal.* The digital journaling app Day One's online pitch for its "Shared Journal" feature reads: "Experience the joy of collective journaling and grow closer than ever before . . . Invite others to view, comment or add entries of their own." Then there are the politicians, celebrities, war criminals, religious and business leaders who write diaries to set the record straight, burnish reputations, settle scores. Their diaries are used as raw material for memoirs, autobiographies, biographies, even television shows. British cabinet minister Richard Crossman's famously published 1960s diary produced lines reportedly used as dialogue in the popular 1980s satirical sitcom *Yes Minister.*

"I very foolishly tried to talk to Joe today," Arkansas Democrat Hattie Caraway, the first woman elected to the US Senate, wrote about a colleague in her 1930s journal. "Never again. He was cooler than a fresh cucumber and sourer than a pickled one." A mother of three sons who assumed her husband's Senate seat in 1931 after his death, Caraway went on to win a special election in 1932 and then a reelection, serving until 1945. She hoped that publishing her diary might provide extra income. Sadly, it wasn't released until 1979, long after her death in 1950. Titled *Silent Hattie Speaks,* it speaks of congressional fashion and hairstyles, as well as Caraway's struggles as a woman in a men's club. The "die is cast," she wrote in her journal after her historic decision to seek election to a full term. "All I can do is sit tight and take whatever . . . comes from such a blow to tradition."

Back to those descriptors: I also had to ditch *truth*, along with others in its orbit—*candid*, *authentic*, and *honest*. Diaries do offer "the authenticity of the moment," Lejeune and Bogaert argue. In 2023, the *New York Times* seemingly sought to add authenticity to a special report on girlhood by asking thirteen-year-old girls to write a diary and publishing excerpts. One girl wrote: "My mom doesn't let me do anything. Like I'm ALWAYS reminded to do the dishes and my homework. Whatever happened to not being so OVERPROTECTIVE. LET ME LIVE."

But I was swayed by the argument that diarists inevitably self-curate, choosing what to reveal or withhold, what to magnify or minimize, sometimes writing what they want to believe or want others to believe, reinventing or fudging details, as eight-year-old Betsy did about her weight. As a historical source, diaries offer an invaluable "kind of truth" not found elsewhere, argues Margo Culley, but adds: "all diarists are involved in a process, even if largely unconscious, of selecting details to create a persona." Diarists may write to their own selves, current or future; or to a hurt inner child; to a spouse, friend, or lover—real, imagined, or anticipated. Sometimes they imagine their diary being read by others or even published someday. Avery Rowling, a college student and diarist, told me: "This is terrible but I'll just lie," adding that her more "performative" journal entries exaggerate "to make my life seem cooler than it is" to herself and possible future readers.

So goodbye, *writing*, *private*, *truth*, and the rest. Hello, *dailiness* and *self*, which creates a big enough tent to fit the many diverse diaries and diarists through the ages. The process of evaluating and dumping descriptors helped me identify the diary's common ground and how the diary differs from its neighbors. But another important consideration—what qualifies as a diary in our digital age—required a separate grappling. Stay tuned.

2

Born Digital

When Do Social Media and AI-Assisted Entries Count?

When I was a kid, I was fascinated by people's stories about the olden days—before the arrival of the telephone, automobile, radio, and television. When would some yet-to-be-invented gizmos make *me* someone from the olden days? I didn't have to wait long. By 1981, as a new college graduate and a cub newsreporter, I had to learn to use a clunky "word processor." Ensuing digital-age decades brought personal computers, the internet, social media, smartphones, digital apps, and AI. Yet I continued to think of *my* diary as something strictly on paper. It was physical, not virtual; written in a notebook, not on my cellphone; stored in a drab-gray fireproof filing cabinet, not in some amorphous cyber-neverland. I never considered my travel blog to be a diary. My Facebook posts and tweets (when they were called *tweets*) weren't diary entries.

It didn't occur to me that *anyone's* social media, even blogs, could be a diary—until my adventures in Diary-land, where I couldn't ignore the many people who accept or welcome the "born-digital" diary. Created by a digital device in a digital format, this category most recognizably includes private entries written in a computer file or journaling app. Arguably, it also includes public social media posts created for others to read.

If social media posts *do* count as a diary, the consequences for Diary-land's population are huge. If *all* of the world's more than five billion social media users are deemed diarists, that's nearly 66 percent of the world's population.

Most American teens, ages thirteen to seventeen, use social media and a smartphone, with 46 percent reporting they're online almost constantly. Diving into roiling digital waters, I learned how the digital diary (and our thinking about it) has evolved, how AI assists journaling, how paper and digital diaries compare, and how that old-timer, the physical diary, might survive.

ooo

The diary's digital day dawned in the mid-1990s, with weblogs (later *blogs*) and online diaries. Blogs began as people's lists of favorite websites, discovered while surfing the burgeoning World Wide Web. The online diary, meanwhile, was for long-form personal narratives. Blogs and online diaries soon morphed in style and content, becoming more alike and the terms used interchangeably. "Blog posts became longer and more essayistic, often using a more personal voice, and online diaries came to include more essayistic material and commentary in addition to the autobiographical content," writes Jill Walker Rettberg, a digital culture professor at Norway's University of Bergen.

During the internet's early unfettered "Wild West" days, the authors of diary-like online media were self-taught website creators, including an anxious nineteen-year-old college student from Chicago named Justin Hall, the so-called "founding father of personal bloggers." Hall was one of the first to publish his life on the "fucking internet," as he recalls in his online self-documentary aptly titled *Overshare*. "I would pick apart my daily life in public on the web. My need for attention and my coming of age somehow coincided with the dawn of participatory media online." In 1994, as a student at Swarthmore College in Pennsylvania, Hall launched his homegrown webpage, later titled "Justin's Links from the Underground." "Howdy, this is twenty-first-century computing," he wrote. "(Is it worth our patience?) I'm publishing this, and I guess you're readin' this, in part to figure that out, huh?"

By 1995, Hall had 27,000 daily readers. Hall's "Cool Shit" and "Personal Shit" categories offered "the weird, the wild and the wonderful on the growing *Web*—and a lot about myself on the side," he recalls. His early shared finds: a bootleg recording of Jane's Addiction, a photo of actor Cary Grant taking acid, and a link to the then-new computer magazine *Wired*, where

Hall successfully "begged" for an internship. Hall's links on sex and drugs became especially popular with other college tech pioneers who found his site by word of mouth. Early personal posts from this newly minted "cyber-celebrity" included a photo of himself (later called a *selfie*) with Oliver North, a key player in the Reagan-era Iran-Contra political scandal. By 1996, Hall was writing dated diaristic entries on his homepage, using the web to share intimate details about his sex and drug experiments, romantic relationships, family secrets, and losses. (His alcoholic father died by suicide when Hall was eight.) Readers responded with emails sharing their stories of alcoholism and suicide. To help his readers create their own webpages, he posted free web tutorials. Lauded as a blogging pioneer, Hall also got pushback for his self-revealing posts including nude photos of himself. In 1999, a *Times* critic described Hall as "a bratty, motor-mouthed exhibitionist."

Canadian Carolyn L. Burke is credited with creating the first true online diary, now known as a personal blog. An early website-building entrepreneur, Burke started "Carolyn's Diary" on January 3, 1995, posting candid self-reports about her thirty-something life. "I needed an outlet to talk about myself privately, with someone listening," Burke later recalled for an online diary history project. "Turns out that I totally loved it. Suddenly I had an audience from the Internet. Nameless, faceless people—the Internet—spoke back to me." By 1998, people could blog without knowing how to code, thanks to new sites like Blogger, which offered templates.

During the early blogosphere boom, blogging was very social, with people writing for themselves and like-minded others, reading and commenting on each other's posts. To share their diaristic posts with a limited group, bloggers joined early online diary communities (such as OpenDiary.com and Myspace.com) and aggregator sites (such as LiveJournal.com and Diarist.net). These early online diaries were "both private and public, both inward and outward-looking," writes Lena Buford, a University of Pennsylvania administrator who was an early blogger.

By 2004, Merriam-Webster's Word of the Year was *blog*, defined as "a Web site that contains an online personal journal with reflections, comments and often hyperlinks." At the same time, blogs became commercial, used for corporate branding and marketing, luring visitors to websites for Nike, Sprint, and Boeing. Google's blog advertising service arrived in 2003. Blogs also became news sites: *Gawker* launched in 2002 as a celebrity and media gossip blog, while *Huffington Post* began in 2005 as a political reporting blog.

By 2005, there were 19.5 million blogs, with the number doubling every five months. But by the 2010s, diaristic personal blogging was fading. Online diaries began to vanish. Once-thriving online diary communities disappeared or adapted. What happened? Beginning around 2004, during the Web 2.0 phase, the internet became easier to use, more interactive, and flush with user-generated content. Web 1.0, with its "clubs of strangers free to reveal the most intimate details of their lives with anonymity and impunity," writes Buford, was replaced by a faster, more crowded and potentially dangerous internet, rife with spam, identity theft, and online stalking.

Diary-writing fatigue and the rise of often-jarring comments sections also contributed to the diaristic blog's decline. So did the rise of search engines like Google during the early 2000s, dramatically expanding access to online diary communities and making them *too* public for some, producing negative feedback. Search engines "blew the lid off these private/public spaces and caused the first mass extinction of online diaries, as bosses and family members started to find the diaries they were appearing in as characters and didn't always like it," writes Buford.

Online diaries/personal blogs were further eclipsed by stunning newcomers: social networking sites such as Facebook and, later, Twitter, which encouraged quick and short personal posts shared with a wide audience. By the mid-to-late 2010s, these sites ruled the social internet, consolidating voices in contrast to the blogosphere's scattered topography. And who needs words? Instagram, YouTube, Snapchat, and TikTok let us self-report day to day via photos, audio, and video.

The rise of the smartphone and mobile apps designed to use with them further pushed us to compose quick-and-brief entries. By 2010, the American Dialect Society's Word of the Year was *app*. The first apps for journaling arrived in about 2008, producing unshared private diaries with dated entries, written and read digitally. Today, many journaling apps compete for users. As with the non-digital diarist population, the number of digital diarists using apps is hard to gauge. In 2021, after ten years in business, the Day One journaling app boasted of more than 15 million downloads across 225 countries and territories. In 2023, Apple shook things up by offering its free "Journal" app, which automatically accompanies an iPhone update.

The digital journaling apps market is forecasted to grow to $13.81 billion by 2034, according to one global market analysis. It made some interesting distinctions, reporting that *note-taking* apps dominate; *diary* apps are for "personal journaling and daily reflections"; *journaling* apps, with templates and prompts, are for "self-exploration and habit-tracking"; and *mood-tracking* apps provide "insights into mental health and well-being." A growing awareness of mental health/well-being *and* the journal as a therapeutic tool is cited as a market driver. Cutting-edge market trends include AI-powered "journaling companions," mindfulness/meditation features, and journaling apps used for professional development and goal-setting.

ꝏꝏ

The digital diary has gradually gained a foothold in Diary-land. In 2019, Desirée Henderson reported that "while some remain uneasy with claiming social media and other digital writing as diaries, many have embraced this idea wholeheartedly." Born-digital options are evidence of the diary's ability to evolve, to shift its mode of production from, say, quill on parchment to tapping on a smartphone app. "Is the diary obsolete? It would be more accurate to say the diary adapts and endures," continued Henderson. "The diary should be recognized for its incredible ability to adapt to new cultures, historical periods, and technologies."

Recent scholarship on diaries now includes respectful discussion of "online diaries," including social media—although not without some concern. "The digital revolution has transformed the basic principles of diary-writing, skipping over the boundaries of privacy, intimacy, and individuality," write Batsheva Ben-Amos and the late Dan Ben-Amos, who were University of Pennsylvania professors when they edited the 2020 tome *The Diary*. They later ask: "What are the possible changes that would occur in a society in which the internet becomes the primary mode not only of personal communication but also of writing, either about the self in private or in the performance of privacy in public?"

Social media, which is not specifically for journal writing, was initially a harder sell as a diary than a journaling app. Some experts argued that digital "new media" has no relationship to the past's analog "old media"—so even diaristic blogs shouldn't be viewed as diaries. Some diarists (including me) initially thought social media's public stance disqualified it as a diary, and some in cyberspace have been openly hostile to diary-like Facebook posts. Witness the meme: *"IT'S A FB STATUS, NOT YOUR FUCKING DIARY!"* Or the 50,363 followers who once populated a Facebook group called "It's a Status. Not a Diary." Others in Diary-land have been more welcoming. Soon after launching his study of the diary/journal in the 1980s, Philippe Lejeune tried out journal writing on a computer and then became among the first literary scholars to study the blog. Starting in October 1999, Lejeune spent a year reading online diaries, surveying online diarists, and (of course) publishing a journal account. In his April 23, 2000, journal entry, he pronounced the blog a promising "new frontier," with both constraints and possibilities: "On the Internet, the diary can finally breathe, stretch out on a chaise lounge and relax."

Other scholars point to parallels between new and old diary-like modes. Cornell University communication professor Lee Humphreys likens a twenty-first-century American soldier's blog posts from Afghanistan to a Civil War soldier's diary entries, which he later turned into letters. Both were written to share news and stay in touch with folks back home. And then there are apps like Fitbit, used primarily to track health indicators—something diarists have long done.

Considering all this, I began to see links from the diary to the blog to Facebook. As with a diary, people can use social media to document themselves on the day, from their relationship status to their latest career move. They can use social media to craft personal, mundane, and intimate confessions, sometimes for therapeutic or creative reasons, sometimes to connect with others. When someone posts a photo of a pretty sunset or blogs about their child's first day of school, "it's not narcissistic," Humphreys argues. "They're saying, 'This is my life and I want to share it with people that I love'—and we've always kind of done that."

०००

Does this mean that *all* social media is a diary? I vote no. Individual intent matters, given social media's multipurpose nature. Whether someone's social media is a diary depends on whether the user considers it a diary. When it comes to my travel blog, despite the diaristic qualities that I now recognize in my posts, I've never intended it to be a diary. I started blogging in 2010 to learn about blogging. I decided to write a travel blog (*TakeBetsyWithYou*) to make sharing my travel tips easier. Rather than hunting-and-pecking in my diary for restaurants and lodging to share with friends and family, my blog offers a user-friendly resource complete with handy tags and categories so visitors can quickly find details about that great Arkansas art museum, Wisconsin bike trail, Savannah restaurant, or Dodge City Airbnb. Sometimes strangers visit my blog but it's not really for them. (My kids call me the anti-social blogger.) I blog mainly when I travel, and I offer primarily practical (rarely personal) information, making the project more journalism than journal.

I originally joined Facebook and Twitter to connect with other people, even strangers, and some of my early posts were diaristic. But like many users, I've grown weary and wary of social media, turned off by the nasty comments, toxic lies, distortions, commercialism, oversharing, and social media companies that refuse to fact-check posts while profiting from addictive algorithms. I stopped tweeting *before* Elon Musk bought Twitter and rebranded it as X. My Facebook posts have become less about myself; less self-reflective, revealing, and personal; in short, even less like my diary. I post primarily to share news stories or pass along information, again more like journalism.

But that's just me. While some social media users insist that they are *not* writing a diary, and are offended by the suggestion, others welcome it. "Facebook is totally my diary," says my friend Wendy Whitcomb, a sixty-something Chicago-area business executive, although it didn't start as one. She realized she was writing an online diary after her previous posts occasionally popped up on her Facebook feed. ("Wendy, we care about you and the memories you share here . . . ") Also falling into this borderline accidental digital diarist category are smartphone users who gradually came to view their private accumulations of texts, photos, and voice memos as a diary. My friend Myra Shapiro, a sixty-something creative director/copywriter in Connecticut, considers her cellphone photos diary-like because they produce a life record, even if that wasn't her intention. Betsy Edgerton, the professor who used to keep a handwritten journal, considers her texts to family and friends "more like a journal now."

Other social media users are more intentional diarists, judging from what they name their blogs or TikTok accounts. Search Facebook, and the catchy diary account names abound: *Happy Mommy Diary*, *Diary of a Broken Woman*, *Pete's Diary*, *A Day Dreamer Diary*, *Diary of a Wimpy Eventer*. . . . Helen Churko, a sixty-something prolific self-chronicler in New York City, told me that her Facebook posts became more akin to journal entries during the early pandemic, when she felt so isolated. "I've written myself into being. That only continues to be more true over time," she says. But there are limits to what she shares: because her posts are public, she's learned how to write "very personally" while not violating the privacy of people in her life. Still, her primary journal remains the pen-and-paper one that she's kept for over forty years. (And it's a *journal*, she emphasized—not a *diary*, which she associates with the precious lock-and-key model from her girlhood.)

Mark Koester, a forty-year-old tech product designer in Southern California, views his blog as an extension of his journal. Sometimes he expands journal entries into blog posts. "My blogging is a form of journaling out loud," he told me. Sarah Fitzgerald, an Irish disability activist with cerebral palsy, keeps a personal blog, sharing diary-like personal details to demystify disability for her nondisabled readers and to advocate for her community. "I don't know what I consider my blog to be," Fitzgerald told me in 2023. "To feel confident in using my authentic voice, I do treat it like a diary and approach the writing of posts with the mantra 'write as if no one will ever see it'"—even though she has many readers. Elizabeth Grubgeld, an Oklahoma State University professor and expert on disability blogs, told me that for people whose disabilities cause episodic pain and fatigue, blogging (whether intended as a diary or not) is a more accessible form than, say, a memoir, because blogging can be done whenever, however. Video blogging via, say, TikTok is even more accessible.

In March of 2023, Fitzgerald blogged about deciding to get her first wheelchair: "I was just tired. Tired of pretending that my pain didn't affect me. Tired of trying to keep myself mobile," she wrote. "Then I cried. Big, ugly, wailing tears. What had I done? Was I admitting defeat?" By the end of the post, she had worked through her feelings—and likely educated readers about her condition. "Cerebral palsy is not progressive. However, years of unsteady gait, falls, kneeling on the floor, and pushing ourselves to do things that our bodies were simply not made to do are bound to take a physical toll. . . . I've always been fiercely independent and deciding to use a wheelchair more often will only enhance that. Less falls will lead to less pain."

Soon after a catastrophic fall in December 2022, the British Pakistani writer Hanif Kureishi started "a blog" as "a kind of diary of distress" from his hospital bed, posting on Twitter and later Substack, attracting a large empathic audience that helped him "survive the horror." Paralyzed from the neck down, he was desperate to "record the story of what was happening to me." He dictated his entries to his partner, Isabella d'Amico. In 2024, while still paralyzed, he published a memoir, *Shattered*, based on his revised, expanded, and edited dispatches. "I am speaking these words through Isabella, who is slowly typing them," he wrote on June 1, 2023. "I am determined to keep writing. It has never meant more to me."

ooo

Journaling apps have more diary cred than social media, primarily because they're more intentional as diaries. They also promise privacy, which appeals to the diaries-are-private crowd. "Always private. Never social," promises the app Dabble Me. "Privacy is our #1 concern," assures Penzu, an app that claims "over 2 million users." Journaling apps also offer security features that lock sensitive information and/or hide it from view. "Even when carefully kept, paper journals can be read by anyone who happens upon them," Penzu points out. The "Penzu Vault" keeps "your journals safe with double password protection and military strength encryption."

"It's unsocial. Indeed, it's downright antisocial," Farhad Manjoo gushed in a 2019 *New York Times* piece titled "Why a Digital Diary Will Change Your Life." Manjoo writes that the digital diary offers "something so rare it feels almost sacred: A completely private digital space." Like an "oasis on your phone," a digital diary is "one of the few digital spaces that provides you mental space for contemplation and consideration—for thinking about the world more deeply than as raw material for clickbaity memes."

But when consumer tech writer David Pierce began using a journaling app, he soon felt nervous about pouring out his heart and soul. He was also uploading countless photos of his new child and giving the app access to his location history, calendar, and camera roll. "All of that information is beautifully organized, collated, and deeply problematic in the wrong hands," Pierce wrote in a 2023 article. "It's also synced to the cloud, which means it's stored on a bunch of mysterious machines other people control who knows where." He worried about longevity: "Services break; products pivot; companies get acquired or go out of business or kill their less-loved stuff. No app is forever." His advice to us about personal apps, including journaling apps: choose ones that clearly commit to privacy, offer protections like encryption, are preferably financed by subscriptions rather than venture capital, and provide export tools (so entries can outlast an app that is discontinued). Pierce did find a few apps he could largely trust (Day One for daily journaling, Obsidian for projects and notes): "Everything is encrypted, everything is exportable, everything is in a place no one can get to it but me. As long as I don't lose my passwords."

Journaling apps include a range of bells and whistles, many for a monthly fee, that a traditional paper diary can't match. Apps let us journal via dictation. We can add location details and tags (as with a blog) that make searches a breeze for that long-ago, half-remembered Oklahoma City restaurant or Albuquerque hiking trail. Some apps can be used across platforms and devices. Dabble Me operates via email. No need to download an app or remember to use it. Instead, write your entry as an email and send it to a secure site. Grid Diary is part diary/part planner, with digital grids labeled "Today's Wins" and "Personal Growth." Daylio—a "Self-Care Bullet Journal with Goals Mood Diary & Happiness Tracker"—invites users to select icons indicating their mood, sleeping quality, eating habits, and more.

In 2023, some journaling apps started offering AI assists. "Artificial Intelligence helps you process emotions and experiences, deepen self-awareness, and improve your mental well-being," one app promises. And AI "automatically identifies and categorizes people, places, events and more in text and detects objects in text and photos." By 2024, users of Apple's Journal app could receive writing prompts developed with AI assistance, using customized data culled from the user's iPhone (photos, locations, media reading). This got an early mixed reception—like many things AI, which offers peril as well as promise, critics warn. While some have found AI helpful or a well-intended offering, others view data culling as a creepy intrusion and a disconcerting reminder of how much our phones track us. (The culling does require the user's permission.)

While AI tools can be "a huge boon to your life" by helping synthesize information and even creating "new things," writes David Pierce, using them "requires uploading data to someone else's servers and letting large language models ingest and process all your most sensitive and personal information." Mark Koester, the California blogger, is comfortable occasionally "collaborating" with the AI chatbot ChatGPT on his journal entries. He still does all the writing and decides what he'll write about. But he asks the chatbot to provide questions to get him started. Koester views AI as a tool, a companion, and an opportunity for diarists. "You can journal in a completely different way," Koester said. "When it gives me back an idea that I was almost there with, but didn't quite see, that's super exciting."

If we use artificial intelligence as a tool to help write our diary, is the diary still ours, still self-expression? Yes, Koester argues: if we use a chatbot to inform our entries but not to compose them.

ooo

Will paper and digital diaries continue to coexist? Grinnell professor Paula Vene Smith has noticed a shift among students she's assigned over the years to keep diaries for her London study-abroad course on diaries. In 2002, students were fine with handwriting a diary. In 2018, however, they assumed they'd keep their diaries digitally. Smith still required most students to handwrite diaries, in part so they'd have a physical keepsake from London. Some students opted to also keep a blog version, to share with people back home. "Like many children of the 21st century, I love the idea of keeping everything journaled online," one student wrote in a class essay shared in an article by Smith. "I can make notes on my phone as I walk, have them automatically update on my computer, where I can expand with more time."

Julie Rak, the Canadian scholar, argues that analog and digital "technologies of the self" are informing each other. Is social media even stoking a handwriting revival? On YouTube and TikTok, it's easy to find mesmerizing videos of pen-on-paper journaling. They tend to feature a young woman's disembodied voice excitedly narrating as slender hands with painted fingernails slowly turn pages filled with distinctive handwriting and illustrations.

Digital fatigue is one reason diarists opt for paper in the digital age. "When I close the laptop at the end of the workday, I don't want to open it up to create these thoughts through that medium," says Robert Ryan, the journal-writing New York father, who works in tech. Given digital media's "ephemeral quality," writing with a pen on paper is a way of "creating something that feels like it sticks and is firmly planted," Ryan told me. Peter Tomka, a thirty-four-year-old visual artist in Los Angeles, likes "the physicality" of journaling with pen and paper, and the "remnant" it creates. Journaling at the start of the day offers a welcome delay of the "instant dopamine check" that comes when he looks at his phone each morning. Madison Ollila, a nineteen-year-old Des Moines–area college student, told me she prefers handwriting her journal because it feels like a "disconnect from everything else going on."

I dutifully tried several journaling apps for research purposes but quickly lost interest. While I get their appeal, I spend enough time with my digital devices. And I'm too set in my paper-and-pen ways: Opening a blank book at the end of each day. Writing whatever comes to mind in my unique, however imperfect, handwriting. The solid weight of the faux-leather book in one hand, lightweight pen in another. The movement of the pen across the page. The satisfaction of filling the blank space. I don't know if my paper diary is, in fact, less ephemeral (or more lasting) than a digital diary. It does feel more solid—and, thus, more real. David Sax aptly titled his 2016 book on resurgent enthusiasm (even back then) for vinyl, books, pens, and paper during the digital age: *The Revenge of Analog: Real Things and Why They Matter*.

Nostalgia (and a paper fetish) are perhaps why I'm drawn to the cute journals at carefully curated stationery shops in trendy neighborhoods. I've chanced upon these cozy, cluttered stores—a fraction of the size of a sleek and streamlined Apple Store but often as crowded—in Chicago's

Andersonville neighborhood, New York's Nolita, and the college town of Cambridge, Massachusetts. These stores have a welcoming retro vibe, although their goods *seem* pricier and fancier than what I remember at the more pedestrian stationery stores of my 1970s youth.

At a revamped "indie-style" Barnes & Noble in Chicago, I found dozens of journaling notebooks, several boasting of sustainability and tree-saving, of plant-and-animal-protecting materials: with covers made from "reclaimed" olives or "ocean waste," pages made from "recycled stones" or "citrus paper." Various "iconic" and "legendary" journal brands have near-cult followings, stoked by proffered origin stories. The Rhodia journal, we are told, is named after the Rhodanien people, who live in France's Rhône River region around Lyon, where the first Rhodia pad was made in 1934. The popular Moleskine, born in nineteenth-century Paris and updated in the 1990s with an Italian redesign, claims legendary users: Vincent Van Gogh, Ernest Hemingway, Pablo Picasso, Bruce Chatwin. "The reason Moleskine gets away with charging so much for such an indifferent artifact is that [it is] not so much selling a product as an ethos," grumbled a journalist in 2013. Japan's Hobonichi Techo is a "life book/diary page book" with an ardent Instagram following and a website loaded with handy Techo-use suggestions: Track your weight, utility costs, child's development. Draw your favorite food dishes or manga comics logos. Review just-read books. (An analog, unsocial version of Goodreads, perhaps?) Other boutique journal brands include Midori (Japanese), Season Paper (French), and Cambridge Imprint (English).

My latest love is the Leuchtturm1917, from a German stationery company founded in, yes, 1917. I like that Leuchtturm is German for *lighthouse*. I also like the company's evocative motto: *Denken mit der Hand* ("Think with the hand"). For my money ($24.50), I can't do better than the Leuchtturm1917. Specifically, the A5 Medium Stone Blue hardcover plain notebook with blank, unruled pages, which is sized just right, about 8¼ x 5¾ inches, and about ¾-inch thick. Not too heavy or too light. A softish hard cover with rounded edges and 251 white pages, not too thick or thin. (Okay, I'll stop now.)

No dummies, journaling apps also offer features and products catering to analog nostalgia. Miss holding a diary in your hand? Convert your digital journal into a bound book! Want to co-write a journal, like the nineteenth-century Goncourt brothers in France? Check out Day One's "Shared Journal" feature! The Goncourts used "dual dictation" to compose their often-cutting entries. One brother dictated to the other, then they revised each other's entry. Describing the novelist Emile Zola, the brothers wrote on December 14, 1868: "A waxy, anemic complexion, a strapping young fellow with something of the delicate modeling of fine porcelain in his features, in the line of his eyes, in the angry planes of his nose, and in his hands."

ooo

"So, I'm actually totally blind. Handwritten journaling isn't an option," twenty-five-year-old Maycie Vorreiter, of California, told me via Facebook. "Keeping a journal digitally is really important to me . . . partly to document my life, and also to help me process things that happen."

Although Vorreiter could write her journal in braille using a typewriter-like machine, the process and storage are cumbersome. She far prefers Day One, which she reports is easy for users who are blind or visually impaired. Although fans rave about the digital diary's convenience, portability, searchability, and security, Vorreiter told me her entries once disappeared forever while she was using another journaling app (not Day One). (Talk about ephemeral!)

Vorreiter was among digital diarists who responded to a question I posted on Day One's Facebook community page asking, in essence: *Why digital?* They offered hearty food for thought for other diarists weighing a switch from print to digital. Some never looked back after switching, citing a variety of reasons, from their "atrocious" handwriting to e-journaling's built-in GPS for location tagging. One of my favorite replies: "My life is a giant Wikipedia article being built." Other digital diarists were conflicted—remaining fond of paper journals or still writing them. Here's what some shared:

- *Reid McClain, 53, South Korea:* "I think of Day One as my replacement for posting on Social Media and my paper journal is where I unplug."
- *Kate Mankowski, 32, Maryland:* "I like the security of having my journals online now and knowing it is less likely someone will read

my thoughts. I back up all of my entries and keep them on a hard drive. . . . I do miss how handwriting forces you to slow down and really think . . . but with typing I can get out my thoughts so much faster; my entries became longer when I switched to a digital format."

- *Michele Kendzie, 52, Virginia:* "I started keeping a diary in 1980 at the age of 8. I journaled (mostly) in spiral bound notebooks. . . . From the early 2000s, when having children encouraged me to record my life more, I started journaling in more digital ways, such as using computer text files . . . but didn't get into the daily habit of digital journaling until 2018. . . . I've always been compelled to record my life . . . and have tried just about every way possible. . . . There are good things about handwriting and a slight worry about a digital journal being obliterated. But it's the easiest way because we have our phones with us all the time nowadays."
- *Robert J. P. Oberg, 36, Mexico:* "For me nothing beats the experience of handwriting on a journal . . . But nothing beats the convenience of digital. So I journal both on paper (long form) and digital (I do little snippets throughout the day). Once a week I scan (photograph) my handwritten entries and bring them into Day One. . . . The reasons for enjoying handwritten journals have been different in different seasons of my life. The medium itself of pen, ink, and different kinds of paper allow for so much experimentation. . . . My thinking and writing flows without trying to go back and edit. . . . It slows me down. My life is so busy so slowing allows me to practice being present."

And here's my takeaway: as digital tech has pushed Diary-land into cyberspace, it has upended how we produce and understand diaries, and how we define diaries and diarists—driving that possible Diary-land population boom. Given the never-ending rush of digital innovation, what will arrive next that counts as a diary? The digital age may offer not only new ways to keep a diary but also a new reason: to counter technology's grip on our lives. One way to reassert our control and our sense of self is by keeping a diary—whichever way we choose.

3

About a Girl

Are Diaries Really *a Woman's Thing?*

As a diarist who began writing as a young girl, I've had mixed feelings about the common gendered assumptions about diaries. Among them: *More girls than boys and more women than men write diaries. Women's diaries differ from men's. Women write about the home and family, from the heart and the gut. Diaries are a feminine form, written by overwrought schoolgirls and menopausal women.*

While I've been happy for women to claim diary-writing, the women-diary link can quickly descend into dismissive stereotypes and snideness; for example, that the diaries of girls and women are whiney. This has contributed to the dismissal of diaries, often by men, as irrelevant, amateurish, and, yes, girlish. French diary expert Philippe Lejeune reported back in 1997 that detractors castigated diaries as *feminine*, among other "faults." Then there's J. D. Vance's off-putting 2010 description of his five-year blog from the 2000s as "like a diary, only far more masculine." (It was reported in a magazine article titled "J. D. Vance Can't Stop Saying the Dumbest Things Imaginable.")

Are most diaries today really written by women? Maybe. Between 2020 and 2022, women leaned into a pandemic journaling effort, created by a Cornell University research scientist. Women made up 89 percent of the seven-hundred-plus people who contributed entries to *Telling Our Stories in the Age of COVID-19*. Women also accounted for 80 percent of the more than 1,800 contributors to the Pandemic Journaling Project, run by professors from the University of Connecticut and Brown University. One of those professors, Sarah S. Willen, had hoped "men wouldn't balk as much" if the project referred to *journaling*. "The word *diary* felt a little more gendered female in US American English," Willen, a UConn anthropology professor, told me. Another hint: Alexander Mimran, cofounder of the journaling app Penzu, told me that the app has consistently had "higher female usage" since its 2008 debut, although the female/male split is not "extreme."

To learn more, I traveled back into diary history and scholarship, accumulating more questions along the way: Why and how do girls and women keep diaries? Does this matter in our gender-self-defining day?

ooo

The most famous early diarist in the United Kingdom is a man. Mention the word *diary* to a group of bookish Brits, and conversation quickly lands on Samuel Pepys (pronounced *Peeps*). I learned this during a small dinner party at my friend Jemima's cottage in England's West Midlands. An extroverted seventeenth-century London naval administrator, Pepys is called the Shakespeare of diarists. He is credited with penning the most famous English-language diary and with pioneering the modern autobiographical diary that shifts from "Eye to I," combining the *public* and *private*: eyewitness reports of historic events *and* candid details about his daily personal life, including extramarital affairs. Written from 1660 to 1669, Pepys's diary was published in 1825, long after his death in 1703. Although his diary was written over 365 years ago, Pepys remains a Diary-land rock star, with a private London club and website dedicated to his legacy. Pepysdiary.com has posted a daily Pepys entry since January 1, 2002, starting with the diarist's January 1, 1660, entry and continuing for almost a decade, as Pepys did. When the site reaches the end of Pepys's diary, it starts over again.

Pepys's entries ranged from personal to worldly. "Waking this morning out of my sleep on a sudden, I did with my elbow hit my wife a great blow over her face and nose, which waked her with pain, at which I was sorry, and to sleep again," Pepys wrote on January 1, 1662. Four years later, on September 2,

1666, he documented London's Great Fire: "Poor people staying in their houses as long as till the very fire touched them, and then running into boats, or clambering from one pair of stairs by the water-side to another."

In the entertaining 2020 coffee table book *Remarkable Diaries*, Pepys earns a rare four pages, followed by other big-name diarists—most men—writing between 1500 and 1800, when diary writing blossomed in Europe. Among them is the eighteenth-century Scottish biographer James Boswell and his nine-month London journal, started in 1762. Women don't appear in noticeable number until *Remarkable Diaries* nears the 1800s, joining prominent male diarists including the American Henry David Thoreau (writing for about twenty-four years, starting in 1837) and France's Goncourt brothers, writing together for about two decades, starting in 1851. Such is the "gender paradox" of diary literary history, reports diary scholar Desirée Henderson: "The most celebrated and canonical diaries are those written by men but the genre as a whole is characterized as feminine." Male diarists are credited with establishing the diary's conventions and perfecting its aesthetics, even though diaries are thought to appeal more to women. Feminist critics also note that Englishwomen wrote diaries *before* Pepys's 1660s diary. Lady Margaret Hoby's diary dates from 1599 to 1605, and Lady Anne Clifford's diary, started when she was a child in 1603 and kept until shortly before her death in 1676, produced a historical record of her family and the world beyond. (Neither woman makes it into *Remarkable Diaries*.)

One prominent early female diarist is Elizabeth Sandwith Drinker, a Philadelphia Quaker whose forty-nine-year diary (from 1758 to her death, in 1807) is said to offer the longest firsthand account of an eighteenth-century North American middle-class woman's life. Published in 1889, Drinker's diary gets a respectable two-page spread in *Remarkable Diaries*. Among the UK's best-known early diarists is Frances "Fanny" Burney, who edited entries from her seventy-two-year diary (spanning 1768 to 1840) with publication in mind. They were published starting in 1842, two years after her death. Celebrated today for her journal, letters, novels, and plays, Burney was part of an illustrious artistic family that inspired two literary "Burney" societies, one in the UK and one in Canada.

Fifteen-year-old Burney wrote in her first entry on March 27, 1768: "To Nobody, then, will I write my Journal! since To Nobody can I reveal every thought, every wish of my Heart, with the most unlimited confidence, the most unremitting sincerity to the end of my Life!" Burney ignored the social etiquette of her day—that proper women should write only private letters (considered an extension of conversation) or household notes (an extension of homemaking). Burney became known during her lifetime as an accomplished satirical novelist and playwright, but her fame as a diarist came posthumously, after her niece oversaw the publication of her journal and letters.

For the first ten years, Burney wrote journal entries often addressed to herself (or her alter ego, "Miss Nobody"), followed increasingly by "journal letters"—entries fashioned as a letter written over several days and addressed to a correspondent. Although a potential near-diary, the journal letters include two of Burney's most well-known entries. One chronicles her stint as a handmaid to Queen Charlotte, when Burney dealt with the erratic behavior of "mad" King George III, who had a mental illness. "Heavens how I ran!" Burney wrote in a February 3, 1789, journal/letter addressed to her sister Susanna, recounting how the king chased her through London's Kew Gardens. "I do not think I should have felt the hot Lava from Vesuvius,—at least not the hot Cinders, had I so ran during its Eruption." Twenty-three years later, Burney graphically described her mastectomy, performed without anesthesia, in a retrospective journal/letter from 1812 addressed to her sister Esther: "I began a scream that lasted unintermittingly during the whole time of the incision—and I almost marvel that it rings not in my Ears still! so excruciating was the agony."

Hot on Fanny Burney's heels came the English diarists Dorothy Wordsworth (sister of the poet William) and *Frankenstein* author Mary Shelley. They each started diaries in the early 1800s. Queen Victoria wrote for almost sixty-nine years, starting in 1832 at age thirteen. "I hate to be idle," she wrote as a sixteen-year-old on January 27, 1835. Beatrix Potter, creator of the children's classic *The Tale of Peter Rabbit*, wrote with scientific detail in her diary about the English countryside, developing a passion for mushrooms or ""fairy fungi," as she described them in an 1896 diary entry. (Potter later published scientific articles on mushrooms.) The British socialist reformer and sociologist Beatrice Webb kept a diary too. In 1900, when sociology was becoming an established field, Webb wrote: "The next ten years will prove whether we are right in devoting our energies to the establishment of a science of society."

Other prominent early American women diarists include First Lady Abigail Adams, who kept a journal in the 1780s before the start of her husband John's presidency in 1797, and author Louisa May Alcott, who wrote from 1832 to 1888. Alcott's beloved novel *Little Women* was published in 1868. A year after her death, her diary was edited by a family friend and published in 1889. Parts of Adams's diary, meanwhile, appeared in the 1961 publication of her husband's diary/autobiography.

Another Abigail Adams also wrote a journal: Abigail and John's daughter, who chronicled her glittering social life from 1784 to 1787 while living in Europe. Extracts were edited by *her* daughter and published in 1841. I learned about the daughter's diary from a little-known resource: a 434-page descriptive catalogue of New England diaries from 1602 to 1800. The catalogue was published privately (only three hundred copies!) in 1923 by Harriette Merrifield Forbes of Worcester, Massachusetts. Also known for her photographs of early New England gravestones (the focus of her 1927 book), Forbes spent ten years unearthing often-unpublished diaries, plus "orderly books" (a military officer's log of their orders) and "sea journals." Although she diligently wrote descriptions of the diaries' contents, locations, and (often private) ownership, Forbes noted in her book's preface that many of the diaries seemed to have "little value." But, she added, "however insignificant[,] they may contain facts saved by no one else and of great interest to a few."

Count me among the few! I read with great interest about "sea journals," written not only by ship's captains or mates but by passengers to break up the voyage's "daily monotony." Their entries offered "a vivid picture of the loneliness and danger of sea travel," writes Forbes. The sea-journal writers included First Lady Abigail Adams, who wrote while voyaging from Boston to England with her daughter Abigail. "Our ship dirty, ourselves sick," reads her June 23, 1784, entry (day four of a thirty-one-day voyage). I was also greatly interested (and pleased) to see that not all, albeit most, of the catalogue's diarists are men. Among the women is Martha Ballard, the Maine midwife whose diary (covering 1785 to 1812) famously inspired a book that won the 1991 Pulitzer Prize for history. Sixty-eight years earlier, Forbes didn't foresee the future value of Ballard's diary. Her assessment: "Some matters of local interest but most of the entries relate to family affairs, domestic employment and professional calls."

Published posthumously in 1905, Mary Chesnut's *A Diary from Dixie* offers a Confederate's personal account of the Civil War. Initially thought a masterpiece, it was later called a hoax by some because Chesnut (who died in 1886) reworked her original 1860s diary after the war. Twentieth-century big-name female diarists are aplenty, from Virginia Woolf and Anaïs Nin to Anne Frank and Sylvia Plath. By the twenty-first century, women diarists' entries were being published in print and online. "Right after I found that my fragmented and foolish writings were fit for public viewing (as my mother would put it if I talked to her anymore), I invited everyone I knew into publishing their works too!" recalled the pioneering digital diarist Caroyln L. Burke about her 1995 online diary.

∞∞

Did *more* men than women write diaries before the late 1800s? Yes, suggests diary scholar Margo Culley in her anthology of "ordinary" American women's "diary literature" since 1764, noting: "As all the standard bibliographical sources show, American men kept journals in numbers far exceeding those kept by women until well past the middle of the nineteenth century." Before the 1700s, "very few white women" in Britain or America "had the education, the economic means, or the social approbation to write," note English professors Suzanne L. Bunkers and Cynthia A. Huff in their 1996 collection of "critical essays on women's diaries." Even less writing by women of color exists because most "did not share the entitlement experienced by many white women," write Bunkers and Huff. Class also influenced who became diarists. "Working-class diaries in early periods are rare partly because literacy rates were lower than they would be when universal education became mandatory," writes Kathryn Carter, an English professor specializing in life writing at Wilfrid Laurier University in Ontario.

More women may have kept diaries long ago than the relative dearth of surviving women's diaries (compared to men's) suggests. "Historically, women's diaries have been consigned—literally or figuratively—to the dustbin of history," writes Carter. Women's diaries were less valued than men's because women tended to focus on their domestic or interior lives, not worldly matters, so they were less likely to be saved for posterity, preserved in archives, or published. Instead they were destroyed, neglected, censored, lost, or overlooked. Samuel Pepys's wife, Elizabeth Pepys, kept a diary. Sadly, we can't read it. We know about it because Samuel wrote in *his* diary about how he destroyed Elizabeth's "bundle of papers." Why? They revealed her "unpleasant" life, "most of it true," he wrote on January 9, 1663. "So in danger of being met with and read by others, I was vexed at it." So he "tore them all before her face, though it went against my heart to do it, she crying and desiring me not to do it."

"Evidence from around the world . . . shows that since the Middle Ages, women kept records of their lives," including diaries, letters, and scrapbooks, writes Carter. She introduced "unknown voices" in her 2002 anthology of twenty Canadian women's diaries from 1830 to 1996. Among them is the 1840s diary of Sarah Welch Hill, an English immigrant to Canada, living with two children under age two and an abusive husband. The diary is a rare example of a first-person account of domestic abuse in the nineteenth century. On November 2, 1844, Hill wrote: "He became outrageous threw the clothes off me & became extremely violent I kept up my spirits, but the agitation caused me to loose a good deal of blood."

Margo Culley points out that "from well before the American Revolution to the present, large numbers of women have kept regular written records of their lives." A notable exception: Black enslaved women. "Women we have never heard of, who were explorers, naturalists, miners, homesteaders, physicians, factory workers, political activists, preachers, farmers, and prisoners of war, have all kept diaries," Culley writes. Together, these diaries "document vividly, the strength, resilience, and resourcefulness of American women," as well as "the constraints" they lived under and "their pain."

Culley also notes that while some women's diaries have been edited and published, far more are unpublished manuscripts, tucked away in attics or archives. The odds of American women's diaries surviving improved if the diarist had prominent relatives, especially male relatives. "Whether a diary was saved and deemed worthy of inclusion in historical society archives, I found, often depended not on who the diarist was but on whose mother, wife, daughter or sister she was," Suzanne L. Bunkers writes in her 2001 anthology of forty-six largely unpublished Midwestern diaries by girls and women from the mid-1800s to 1999. Several of the diaries Bunkers studied weren't catalogued under the diarist's name but instead under her family's name. Bunkers also found that from the 1850s onward, "Euro-American" women from well-established families with "adequate resources" and some access to education were the most likely Midwestern female diarists. Her anthology includes diaries by women who had the "time and resources accorded by family wealth and white privilege" to be diarists but also diaries by immigrants, middle-class African Americans, and "poor and wealthy farm girls and women."

Bunkers also points out that male diarists dominated a large 1957 anthology showcasing the "world's great diaries," including entries written by famous historical and literary figures. The anthology's eighty-five diarists include twenty-one women, Bunkers reports. Women-only diary anthologies followed, including the 1974 collection *Revelations: Diaries of Women*, with entries by thirty-two women from around the globe, including well-known writers Katherine Mansfield (New Zealand), Carolina Maria de Jesus (Brazil), and Russian Sophia Tolstoy (wife of Leo). Margo Culley's 1985 anthology of twenty-nine American women's diaries (published by the Feminist Press) was focused on presenting "women writers in as wide a range of situations as possible." By 1996, Bunkers and Huff noted, "The second wave of feminism and the emergence of women's studies and feminist theory . . . renewed interest in and recovery of women's writing, including diaries."

In the twentieth century, the diary became a writing form "practiced predominately by women," writes Culley. An important reason for the gender shift, she argues, goes back to the 1800s with "the emergence of the self" as the diary's subject. Before this, writes Culley, secular American diaries as of the late eighteenth century were written as semi-public documents intended for an audience. (This was a shift, beyond the American diary's spiritual autobiography roots.) Women recorded births, marriages, illnesses, and deaths as the family/community historian. Men's lives differed—and so did men's diaries, which were a record of public life, imbued with a public purpose or audience. But the diary's function and substance changed, writes Culley, due to changing ideas about the self that arose during the nineteenth century influenced by the psychoanalytic "discovery" of the unconscious and individual consciousness, the split between the private and public spheres wrought by the Industrial Revolution, and the "romantic discovery of the secular self."

Women were all in when diary writing became all about creating a "secret" record of the inner life, a life "of personal reflection and emotion," writes Culley. Men dropped out. "It is only relatively recently . . . that the content of the diary has been a record of private thoughts and feelings to be kept hidden from others' eyes," Culley writes. The private sphere was deemed women's territory. The diary became women's vehicle for documenting the private. "American men, unused to probing and expressing this inner life in any but religious terms," argues Culley, didn't take to diary writing about the "secular self."

During the nineteenth century, American women turned "to the diary as one place where they were permitted, indeed encouraged, to indulge full 'self-centeredness,'" writes Culley. The self was "no longer witness and chronicler but the subject." Some women became diary writers in the wake of the wildly successful published journal of Russian French painter Marie Bashkirtseff, published in French in 1887 and two years later in English. "Oh! but there arises at the bottom of my heart such a storm, that it is better to cut all this short by telling myself that I shall always have the resource of blowing my brains out before they begin to pity me," Bashkirtseff wrote on July 23, 1880. She died four years later, at age twenty-five, from tuberculosis.

ooo

Why do women write diaries? American diary scholar Rebecca Hogan offered one reason that summed up what I heard often: "Many women have found in diaries, a tangible form for saving their lives," Hogan, now a retired English professor, wrote in 1991. Diary writing has long offered women a space to rebel against negative or limiting stereotypes. After digesting four hundred years of women's diaries for her 2024 anthology *Secret Voices*, British writer Sarah Gristwood pinpointed the single strongest emotion expressed: "anger—frustration." This, she added, was "something our cultural norms have allowed women to voice only secretly." In 1663, Elizabeth Pepys's diary was likely a vital confidant, offering self-validation and representing "her independent and secret identity," surmises British scholar Judy Simons. That Samuel Pepys felt threatened enough by Elizabeth's "secret text" to destroy it "amply illustrates the subversive potential of a woman's diary in a patriarchal world."

While diary writing might look like a retreat inward, nineteenth-century women could defy gender boundaries in their diaries, writes the American popular-culture scholar Marilyn Ferris Motz. White middle-class women in Midwestern small towns used their diaries to voice their views on current events and the books they read, writes Motz, now a retired professor. "Far from being isolated and provincial, these women used that most private form, the diary, to establish themselves as citizens of the world." Meanwhile, in Victorian England, women could write in their diaries about their bodies (if not their sexuality). In particular, writing about motherhood-related topics (pregnancy, birth, postpartum illness, nursing) was considered "perfectly acceptable," notes Cynthia A. Huff. In the twentieth century, women diarists used their private writing to rail against persistent sexism, condemn racism, defy convention or expectation, and transgress or even subvert. The late feminist author and activist bell hooks described her diary as "subversive autobiography" and "a narrative of resistance." "I could "talk back," hooks wrote in 1999. "Nothing had to be concealed. I could hold onto myself there."

As for diarists being *overwrought schoolgirls*, certainly my youthful diary occasionally supports this stereotype (with the periodic melodramatic entry about hating my mother or loving a boy). But schoolgirls also have kept diaries in active war zones, from Anne Frank in the Nazi-occupied Netherlands to Lena Mukhina during the 1941 siege of Leningrad. In 1993, twelve-year-old Zlata Filipović wrote in war-torn Bosnia: "It's as if Sarajevo is slowly dying, disappearing. Life is disappearing. So how can I feel spring, when spring is something that awakens life, and here there is no life, here everything seems to have died."

Bunkers's study of diaries by Midwestern girls and women pinpoints six themes. Diaries offer their writers a place to (1) record *and* justify their activities; (2) document and validate meaningful relationships; (3) release intense emotion considered inappropriate to express in public, such as grief and anger; (4) comment on world events, religion, and politics; (5) create a plan to leave home or otherwise venture into the larger world; and (6) send messages to an outside audience—*if* they anticipated other readers. Bunkers also points to psychologist Mary Pipher's observation, in her sobering 1994 book *Reviving Ophelia: Saving the Selves of Adolescent Girls*: "In their journals, their point of view on the universe matters. Girls this age love to write. Their journals are places where they can be honest and whole. In their writing, they can clarify, conceptualize, and evaluate their experiences. Writing their thoughts and feelings strengthens their sense of self."

Women's diaries have changed with the times. In the eighteenth and nineteenth centuries, American women *did* write about home and family, reflecting their then-domestic role, which solidified during the latter half of the 1800s with the Industrial Revolution. Margo Culley illustrates the changing content and function of women's diaries by contrasting the entries of Mary Vial Holyoke (who lived from 1737 to 1802) and Mary MacLane (1881 to 1929). The unofficial historian of her family in Salem, Massachusetts, Holyoke wrote in 1770: "April 7. Mr. Fisk Buried. / [April] 23. Went with Mr. Eppes to Mrs. Thomas. Took Down Beds . . . / . . . Made mead . . . "

More than 130 years later, "modern diarist" MacLane was inspired by Marie Bashkirtseff's diary. (A diary of "utter self-absorption" and "enthusiastic self-regard," as Culley puts it.) Accordingly, MacLane's diary "chronicles pure 'Ego,'" writes Culley, highlighting a 1901 entry from Butte, Montana, that begins: "And at this point, I meet Me face to face. / I am Mary MacLane: of no importance to the wide bright world and dearly and damnably important to Me."

Changes in the broader world, culture, and society—and in women's opportunities, education, and lives—also have provided new material to write about. In the wake of twentieth-century social movements advancing women, sexual freedom, gay rights, civil rights, and more, women diarists could write more freely about our bodies and ourselves, about careers, gender, race, and anything else we want or need to write about. Consider the 1979 diary of Barbara Smith, a Black feminist and lesbian activist in Boston, also excerpted in Culley's anthology. After twelve Black women were murdered within four months, Smith worked to educate women about self-defense and to pressure law enforcement officials. At the same time,

Smith aired her concern and frustration in her diary: "Random Thoughts: Violence against us is overwhelming," she wrote on March 19, 1979. "Racism from white women overwhelming and homophobia from Black people is a vice that will choke the Black feminist movement."

∞∞

Since Charlotte Forten's nineteenth-century diary was published in 1953 with the subtitle *A Free Negro in the Slave Era*, Forten has been variously heralded as the first Black woman diarist and the first whose diary was published as a book. Almost one hundred years earlier, on September 1, 1856, Forten was a Philadelphia-raised teenager attending a Boston-area college when she wrote in her now-famous journal: "We are a poor, oppressed people, with very many trials, and very few friends." The first African American graduate of what is today Salem State University, Forten chronicled her life from 1856 to 1892, including her abolitionist activism in the North. Twenty-seven years after the Forten diary's publication came what some have considered the next published Black woman's diary: *The Cancer Journals*, by the American lesbian feminist poet Audre Lorde. Published in 1980, it blends journal entries, memoir, and essays about her experience with breast cancer and mastectomy. "I must let this pain flow through me and pass on. If I resist or try to stop it, it will detonate inside me, shatter me, splatter my pieces against every wall and person that I touch," Lorde wrote on April 22, 1979.

Published diaries by Black women have been few and far between, especially diaries from the 1800s—although the late historian Dorothy Sterling found four of them to excerpt in her groundbreaking 1984 anthology of nineteenth-century Black American women's voices. "To be a BLACK WOMAN in nineteenth-century America was to live in double jeopardy of belonging to the 'inferior sex' of an 'inferior race,'" Sterling writes. Published to refute common stereotypes of Black women as "mammy or matriarch, sex object or mindless drudge," the anthology primarily features letters, oral histories, and autobiographies. But Sterling offers a shout-out to the diary: "Nowhere is the richness of their humanity better exemplified than in four diaries written by young women during the two decades after emancipation."

At least a dozen African American women's diaries have been published in book form, thanks to several scholars' efforts to unearth and highlight them. Most were published after 1992, and selected entries written by other diarists have appeared in anthologies like Sterling's. The net result is the critical mass necessary to establish Black women's diaries as a "distinct literary tradition," argues Grinnell College professor Paula Vene Smith in a 2022 journal article. No diaries written by Black American women *while* enslaved have been found, although some of these women were literate. In an arresting 1974 essay, author Alice Walker pointed to Black Southern US women's efforts to overcome the stifling of their creativity, during and after slavery. "For these grandmothers and mothers of ours were not Saints but Artists; driven to numb and bleeding madness by the springs of creativity in them for which there was no release," writes Walker. "How was the creativity of the Black woman kept alive, year after year and century after century, when for most of the years Black people have been in America, it was a punishable crime for a Black person to read or write?"

In 1984, the early-twentieth-century diary of American Black writer and activist Alice Dunbar-Nelson was published, with an introduction from its editor, American Black feminist writer Gloria T. Hull, who points out that "diary-keeping has not been compatible with the conditions of the vast majority of Black women." Although prominent African American women were well-positioned to write a diary, many of them were still disinclined, due to structural racism or because they were too busy fighting for social reforms. Some women preferred to share their stories via autobiographical "slave narratives" during the antebellum era—or the oral tradition "that suffuses all of Black culture," writes Hull.

The diary excerpts in Sterling's 1984 anthology were written by four women in their twenties during the mid-to-late 1800s in the US: one from the North, three from the South. Mary Virginia Montgomery (1850–1902) and Ida B. Wells (1862–1931) were both born in Mississippi during the last years of slavery, which ended in 1865. Each received an early education that helped make diary writing possible. Wells's "Memphis Diary" describes her life in 1886 as a young teacher and budding journalist in Tennessee, before she became a renowned journalist, civil rights activist, and anti-lynching crusader, eventually living in Chicago. Wells chronicled her struggles and responsibilities, her frustrations, worries, anger, self-doubt, and loneliness in her diary. After a federal court overturned a lawsuit that Wells had won in a local court against a railroad company, for forcibly removing her from a first-class "ladies" car, she took to her diary. "O God is there no redress, no peace, no justice in this land for us?" she wrote on April 11, 1887. "Thou hast always fought the battles of the weak & oppressed. Come to my aid at this moment and teach me what to do, for I am sorely, bitterly disappointed."

Montgomery wrote her diary in 1872 while living with her emancipated and entrepreneurial family on their Mississippi land (purchased post–Civil War by her father), helping at her family's general store, and preparing to attend Oberlin College. She wrote about everyday life, her bookkeeping work, and reading. "After supper I took up Darwin on the Origin of the Species," she wrote on April 16, 1872. "It bids to be interesting & will entertain me many nights."

Born in Ohio, Laura Hamilton (1864–1898) began her 1885 diary when she was six months pregnant and living with her husband in Virginia. Frances Anne Rollin (1845–1901), the daughter of free parents of color in South Carolina—who became an abolitionist, a suffragist, and a biographer—wrote one of the earliest-known diaries by a Southern Black woman. Rollin's 1868 diary documents Reconstruction-era life in South Carolina (including anti-Black violence), her first year of marriage, and the publication of her biography of the highest-ranking Black person in the military—the first full-length biography written by an African American.

Two of the diaries in Sterling's anthology have since been published in book-length form: Wells's in 1995 and Rollin's in 2025. In the foreword to Wells's published diary, African American literary scholar Mary Helen Washington wrote that the diary has been "a place where, physically and psychologically, black people felt free to speak . . . where one's truer self is affirmed and authorized."

Rollin's diary also was featured in a 1991 memoir by her great-granddaughter Carole Ione, highlighting an entry Rollin wrote while working in Boston on her book. "From the moment I read the words Frances Anne Rollin wrote in Boston on January 1, 1868—'The year renews its birth today, with all its hopes and sorrows'—she became my beacon, the foremother who would finally share with me our collective past," Ione writes in *Pride of*

Family: Four Generations of American Women of Color. In 2025, Rollin's diary was published after being edited by Jennifer Putzi, a professor of English and of gender, sexuality, and women's studies at the College of William & Mary in Virginia. Putzi is also working on a broader book about nineteenth-century African American women's diaries and told me she knew of roughly fourteen diaries, as of 2024, eight already published in full or in part. She was searching for more.

ooo

Like other women, Black women use their diaries to record intimate personal details about themselves and their families, relationships, home, work, life transitions, politics, and the world. They have even more reason to use their diaries, as other women do, to resist negative stereotypes and to recreate themselves. US Black women's diaries "invariably document unremitting racialized violence," "disease and resistance," and "white supremacy," which restrict them as US citizens, writes Joycelyn K. Moody, a scholar of African American literature, life writing, and Black feminism at the University of Texas at San Antonio. Even when writing for their own eyes only, Black women reveal a commitment in their diaries to ending "national myths" and replacing "devastating stories" with narratives promoting "equity and peace," Moody observes.

Paula Vene Smith detects a "surprisingly forward-looking vision" in diaries by several African American women, even those predating the Civil War. They document their personal experiences with injustice and how their actions make history, producing stories offering "evidence that apparently new developments like the Black Lives Matter movement . . . have long roots in the past," writes Smith, in a *Ms.* article. Ultimately, the diaries "challenge conventional assumptions about American history and offer lessons . . . only a diary can teach."

Smith points to Charlotte Forten, who started her diary in 1854 at age sixteen, initially vowing to use it to chronicle personal growth and document events that she thought would be pleasant to recall. But Forten soon begins documenting her times by writing outward facing entries about witnessing injustices. Forten realizes that American courts and law enforcement are "structurally unjust," writes Smith, and she grapples with this "just like modern justice seekers who encounter setbacks both enormous and state-sanctioned." When Forten opted to teach formerly enslaved people in the South Carolina Sea Islands for eighteen months during the Civil War, she "sees herself as having a place in history," Smith argues, combatting what Forten describes in her diary on December 21, 1856, as "the terrible curse of our country and of the age." Aware of her diary's value, Forten shared excerpts in letters to friends. They also were printed in abolitionist publications and in *The Atlantic Monthly*.

Alice Dunbar-Nelson's early-1900s diary also "signals an intent to record," argues Smith, which later benefited future generations when published. Dunbar-Nelson's "private glimpses of public figures and inside reports of major events . . . provide even more information for Black studies students and scholars," writes Hull, the diary's editor. For me, Dunbar-Nelson's September 6, 1921, entry was particularly striking. She describes taking her darker-skinned relatives to a movie theater in Atlantic City. "Suppose the ticket seller had sold the seats to me thinking I was white, and seeing Elizabeth and Ethel should make a scene," Dunbar-Nelson writes. "I choked with apprehension, realized that I was invoking trouble and must not think destructive things, and went on in. Nothing happened. How splendid it must be never to have any apprehension about one's treatment [anywhere.]"

In her journal article, Smith introduced me to contemporary Black American writer and diarist Morgan Jerkins. For Black women living in an "often-unwelcoming world," a diary is the only place to "simply be" and "hold onto safety for a little," Jerkins wrote in a 2016 *New Yorker* essay while in her early twenties. The "conversation with the self" that a diary provides is crucial, she writes: "When that world insists on racist and narrow paradigms, the diary gives these women a chance to scratch out and rewrite such definitions. That is what my own diary offers me."

ooo

The first book of the popular kids' series *Diary of a Wimpy Kid*, from 2007, begins memorably, with twelve-year-old Greg declaring: "This is a JOURNAL, not a diary. . . . All I need is for some jerk to catch me carrying this book around and get the wrong idea." A cartoon shows a beefy bully shouting "SISSY!" as he punches a smaller boy, sending his diary—err, journal—airborne.

Desirée Henderson presents this *Wimpy Kid* snippet in her book, illustrating how *the diary* is associated with *the feminine*—and not in a good way for any gender. To me, the snippet suggests (without condoning the bullying) that when a *diary* is deemed for girls, and girls are deemed to be, say, weak, boys who keep a diary are bound to be bullied (and considered a wimpy kid). The "feminization" of the diary has had other negative consequences—both cementing gender stereotypes and the diary's low standing in literary circles. This inspired Henderson's defiant embrace of the word *diary*. "In using *diary*, I seek to make an intervention, recovering the word and genre it describes from its status as a feminized, minimized, and even shameful form of writing," Henderson declares early in her book. Soon after, she observes: "Given the male-centered record of the diary's origins, it is ironic that over the course of the nineteenth century, the genre became increasingly perceived as a feminized genre, so that today it is a form of writing strongly associated with women and often stigmatized for this very reason."

Philippe Lejeune points to something similar in a 1997 piece about the diary being "on trial." He zeroes in on observations by a French literary critic (a woman no less) who wrote in 1976: "There is a certain 'femininity' to diary writing . . . this passivity, this casualness, this rather soft fluidity." The critic then mentions diarists with "homosexual tendencies"; diarists with an "unconscious, repressed drive" that may explain their "indecisiveness about marrying"; and diarists who are "fixated on the mother and refuse to confront the oedipal conflict."

Growing up during the 1960s, I was likely influenced by what historian Jane Kamensky calls "the Great American Diary Project." Girls were encouraged to write diaries by our mothers, teachers, therapists, clergy, *Seventeen* magazine, and businesses selling soap, lipstick, and feminine sanitary products. I joined legions of girls devouring Anne Frank's diary and Louise Fitzhugh's 1964 novel *Harriet the Spy*. (I still remember the fury of eleven-year-old Harriet's classmates after they read her diary-like secret notebook.) Boys weren't invited to the diary club. "We are still not likely to give boys diaries at Christmas," Thomas Mallon wrote in his 1984 book about diarists.

All this helps explain why calling the diary an inherently *feminine* genre has fallen out of favor. Instead, scholars tend to argue that the diary was *feminized*—that it became viewed as *feminine*, starting in the 1800s as girls and women were socialized to write diaries. Nineteenth-century etiquette guides for well-bred American women promoted diary writing as a genteel practice for recording "a lady's accomplishments." Etiquette lessons for well-bred girls promoted diary writing to show their industriousness, count their blessings, and uphold their moral virtue. Among the more sinister theories about diary writing: children's magazines promoted it so girls would develop a "submissive and self-effacing identity." So, too, in nineteenth-century France, girls were "systematically pushed to keep a diary, often supervised," writes Lejeune, arguing that "historical conditioning" explains why diary writing today remains "a group culture and rite of passage for French girls, while most boys are indifferent or even hostile to the idea ('a girl's thing')." In Britain, in 1819, a manufactured diary for an emerging market of fashionable urban women diarists was introduced as the "most elegant and convenient pocketbook" for "the ladies." This came seven years after the first commercial dated diary (nongendered) was launched by Letts, the enduring British stationer.

Labeling the diary *feminine* also has become complicated at a time when traditional notions of gender and sexuality are being dismantled. Critics of the "gender binary" concept—that only two gender categories exist, female and male—argue that gender is not bound to a person's assigned sex at birth but exists along a broader spectrum. Suzanne L. Bunkers told me she no longer views diaries in feminine or masculine terms, adding, "The old dichotomy does not work in these multigendered times." Ironically, *feminine* is among the descriptors that first lured feminist scholars to study the diary, notes Canadian scholar Kathryn Carter, but, in 2020, she asked: "How can diaries be feminine if the term itself is so unstable?" Carter argues that "well-intentioned feminist critics went astray in early scholarship" by relying "on stereotypes about women and their lives to make generic arguments" that strengthened rather than challenged the stereotypes. Newer feminist literary approaches may advance "more nuanced arguments" about the diary, Carter suggests. The scholar Rebecca Hogan told me she views gender as a valuable framework when studying diaries, adding: "I would stick to my guns about the diary being a form of writing particularly congenial to women writers" and offering "a formal place to express thought, emotions, and description directly."

Contemporary diary scholars also are quick to note that diary writing appeals to people regardless of gender identity (male, female, nonbinary, etc.) or sexual orientation (heterosexual, homosexual, pansexual, etc.). "The diary accommodates the life narratives of cisgender, transgender, and gender non-conforming individuals—as well as those by people across the sexuality spectrum," writes Henderson. This, in turn, has influenced diary scholarship. Canadian scholar Julie Rak notes another scholar's "queer archival reading" of cartoonist Alison Bechdel's childhood diary, as prominently featured in her 2006 graphic memoir, *Fun Home*. Bechdel came out as a lesbian "at a time when it was not publicly 'safe' to do so," writes Rak. (Bechdel was nineteen. The year was 1980.) Before this, Bechdel had her diary, started at age ten. "Bechdel is someone who would not have been able to be public about her identity or who would not have been taken seriously because of her age and her sexuality," Rak writes. "The diary form allowed her to explore events without external censure."

Has reductive thinking about *the diary* and *the feminine* faded over time? Scholars, especially feminist scholars, are working to speed this up. Their efforts to reassess and rewrite the diary's history and to champion women's diaries have naturally involved also working to "restore value to the feminine" and to women's self-expression, via their diaries, writes Henderson. "Resisting the idea that accounts of women's lives are trivial or self-indulgent, scholars instead assert that women's life writing testifies to the multifaceted, beautiful, and vital nature of the female and feminine."

Where does all this leave us—or me? I have come to question the traditional notion of gender and sexuality. I recognize that associating a diary with one gender limits our thinking about diaries—and can pigeonhole women. And I welcome diary scholars' attempts to challenge the dismissive view of women's self writing and "the pejorative characterization of femininity," as Henderson puts it. That said, I'd argue that "women's diaries" can still be categorized as women's diaries. Yet I am left hoping that "women's diaries"—and *all* diaries—will be studied in a more nuanced way, with a broader understanding of gender, sexuality, and "the diary." And as a self-identified female, feminist, and diarist, I remain proud that diaries are associated with women or the *feminine*, if *feminine* is rightly associated with, say, strength, not weakness, with caring, warmth, and intelligence. Then, here's hoping, diary writing by anyone will earn respect instead of a bully's punch.

FROM MY DIARY

Some of what I kept

1975, age 16: Sealed envelope labeled "Why I lied." Inside is a letter to my parents.

1979, age 20: List of traveler's check numbers.

1982, age 22: Sticker from Ali's Pension Restaurant in Pamukkale, Turkey: "Cheap End [*sic*] Clean Friendly Atmosphere."

1995, age 35: Lyrics on notepaper to "Do Do," an Italian lullaby I sang to my young children.

2004, age 45: Note from my 11-year-old daughter, decorated with lipstick kiss imprint: "Mom, I love you."

2012, age 53: Program from my father-in-law's funeral at Saint Andrew Parish, Wright, Kansas.

2021, age 62: "I received my COVID-19 vaccine" sticker.

Some of what I read

1988–89: *Leaving Brooklyn*, Lynn Sharon Schwartz; *The Mysteries of Pittsburgh*, Michael Chabon.

1991: *The Joy Luck Club*, Amy Tan; *What to Expect the First Year*, Heidi Murkoff.

1993–94: *What's Eating Gilbert Grape*, Peter Hedges; *Feather Crowns*, Bobbie Ann Mason.

2004: *Runaway*, Alice Munro; *The Lucky Ones*, Rachel Cusk.

2008: *American Wife*, Curtis Sittenfeld; *The House at Sugar Beach*, Helene Cooper.

2011: *Blood, Bones & Butter: The Inadvertent Education of a Reluctant Chef*, Gabrielle Hamilton; *The Art of Fielding*, Chad Harbach.

2014: *My Brilliant Friend*, Elena Ferrante; *The Goldfinch*, Donna Tartt.

2021: *Caste*, Isabel Wilkerson; *Shuggie Bain*, Douglas Stuart.

PART 2

Why We Write

4

Self-Help

Are Diaries Really Good for Us?

How to explain the astonishing success of *The Shadow Work Journal*, a guide on journaling for emotional healing, self-published in 2021 by Keila Shaheen, a first-time, twenty-five-year-old Texas author? TikTok deserves considerable credit, reports the *New York Times*. After excited TikTok influencers spread the word about the guide, it sold more than one million copies. Many were purchased through TikTok's then-new online shop, which offers commissions to its sales-driving influencers. Soon Shaheen was anointed the "self-help queen of TikTok."

Another factor in the journaling guide's success, I'm guessing, was its arrival during the COVID-19 pandemic, which sparked introspection and interest in self-help activities at a time when many millions became isolated and frightened. The guide's marketing promise to help journal writers "face your shadows" and "heal the deepest parts of your subconscious" stoked our desire to journal to a better place.

Journaling/diary writing has long been promoted by popular media, self-help product marketers, and lifestyle gurus as a way to boost our psychological and physical welfare, offering "free therapy," personal growth, and health/wellness benefits. Across Diary-land, the power of journaling is proclaimed as if journaling's self-help efficacy is a given. The journaling app Dabble Me invites users to "Increase your happiness with daily journaling." *The Five Minute Journal* pledges to "transform your life . . . spend only five minutes practicing gratitude to boost positivity, reduce anxiety, and improve well-being. It's the simplest, science-backed way to a happier you." Launched by Toronto entrepreneurs in 2013 to tap into the self-improvement space, the journal has sold more than two million copies and been embraced by actors, health spas, and aspiring influencers.

So many types of journals and ways of journaling cater to our endless appetite for self-care and self-improvement: *guided*, *wellness*, *therapy*, *gratitude*, *core values*, *mood*, *dream*, *mindfulness*, *meditation*. So many claims that journal list-keeping and self-logging (everything from our food intake to time use) will make us more efficient, productive, mindful, healthy, happy. So many journals with snappy titles (among my favorites, the 2020 self-care journal *I Am F*cking Radiant*). So many pages urging us to: *Punch today in the face. Banish the bullshit. Reconnect with yourself. Build your brightest damn future. Embrace your truth.* So many devotees of journaling for self-growth. The thirty-year-old British actor James Phoon, from the Netflix series *Bridgerton*, put "My Journal" atop his "My Ten" list, a *New York Times* feature. "Every year I buy a blank scrapbook and turn it into this wellness journal," Phoon explained in 2024. "At the beginning of the month, I write my goals, and at the end of the month I write a list of happy moments. And then I have This Month's Win . . . work-related or personal or just something that made you smile—that you want to hold onto." The next year, forty-three-year-old American actor Jay Ellis, from the film *Top Gun: Maverick*, put journals (black-leather Smythson journals) on his *Times* list. "I write what I'm grateful for from the previous day, then my hit list of things I want to get done," Ellis explained. "I burn through a lot of journals."

Can journaling really help us grow, improve, and be well? Can it make us unwell? What about more casual journaling that *doesn't* follow a structured therapeutic method? What does science say—and what do therapists and diarists think?

ooo

"Perfection of character requires this, that you should live each day as though it were your last, and be neither agitated, nor lethargic, nor act a part."

No, this isn't an inspirational quote on the cover of a self-help journal, although it has potential. It hails from Marcus Aurelius's *Meditations*, written around the year 167 CE. The Roman emperor took seriously the Delphic Oracle's edict to "know thyself"—and thought that writing regularly toward this end would be beneficial psychologically, philosophically, and ethically, a notion some diary experts say is echoed in contemporary self-help methods.

Christian theologian St. Augustine's *Confessions*, from the year 400, is another oft-cited precursor of today's self-reflective diary. (Potential wellness journal cover quote from *Confessions*: "There is, therefore, something in humility which, strangely enough, exalts the heart and something in pride which debases it.") In 1656, English Puritan John Beadle published perhaps the earliest instruction manual for diary keeping. Among the advice in Beadle's best-selling *Journall or Diary of a Thankfull Christian*: read old diary entries to "increase in us that self-abasement & abhorrency of spirit that is most acceptable in the sight of God."

Modern-day health and wellness journaling gained traction in the 1970s when New York psychotherapist Ira Progoff marketed his Intensive Journal method, promising personal growth and emotional wellness through his structured process of writing a journal *and* reading old entries. During the 1960s, Progroff was among many therapists using self-reflective journaling as a therapy tool. He went on to spread journaling to a wider audience beyond the therapist's office, teaching his method at workshops and later via his best-selling 1975 manual, *At a Journal Workshop*. The journal's workbook format (with prompts and exercises!) was a key development during the rise of the mass-market "how-to instructional diary," which became popular despite being badmouthed as a "'lowbrow' self-help genre," writes Kylie Cardell, a humanities and social sciences professor at Flinders University in Australia.

Traction became major momentum in 1986 when Texas social psychologist James W. Pennebaker published pioneering research showing that "expressive writing"—intentional writing about traumatic, stressful, or emotional experiences—produces potentially long-lasting physical and mental health improvements. In his study, forty-six healthy college students were randomly assigned to write about one of four topics for fifteen minutes daily, on four consecutive days. Three groups wrote about a traumatic event—the first writing only the facts, the second writing only their emotions, the third writing facts and emotions. The control group wrote about less momentous topics (say, their shoes or bedroom). The trauma-facts-emotions group reported a better immune system, improved health, and fewer visits to the health center during the six months after the experiment.

Expressive writing works not because of a cathartic release of bottled-up feelings or inhibitions, Pennebaker told me. Instead, it reduces "intrusive and avoidant thinking about a stressful experience." This, in turn, frees up working memory resources and increases capacity, said Pennebaker, explaining the findings of a 2001 North Carolina State University study. If you're not talking or writing about a traumatic experience, he said, "you're probably not processing this experience and you're reliving it in your mind every single minute, and your body is reacting." Writing intentionally about the experience and evaluating it from a distance helps produce clarity, he went on, allowing "you to organize the experience, to tuck it away in an organized way in your brain and move on."

I thought about Pennebaker's work when I read that twenty-one-year-old Hua Hsu bought a journal in 1998, soon after a traumatic event: his close friend in college was murdered. "Everything is wrong," he wrote on the journal's first page. (Hsu recounts this in his award-winning 2022 memoir, *Stay True*.)

Research on "expressive writing in psychology" has exploded: a 2022 study analyzed 1,429 articles on the topic. Many studies show that expressive writing helps people address trauma and emotional upheaval in a healing way. It has been linked to long-term benefits for psychological and physical health (reduced anxiety, fewer depression symptoms, less post-traumatic stress, lower blood pressure, quicker healing, less sickness), and for educational performance and social behavior (better high school grades and reduced work absenteeism).

Other research using MRI imaging of women's brain activity found that "gratitude journaling" activates a type of brain activity associated with showing altruism. Gratitude also was determined to be a positive emotion linked to well-being and better health. Another study found that a twelve-week web-based "online positive affect journaling" program helped medical patients reduce their mental stress and improve their psychological, interpersonal, and physical well-being.

Progoff died in 1998, but his son has carried on his work. During the late 1980s and 1990s, other journaling proponents developed a following, including Kathleen (Kay) Adams, a Colorado psychotherapist specializing in "journal therapy," and Christina Baldwin, a Washington State self-help author promoting writing as self-therapy. Adams's books include *Journal to the Self* (1990); Baldwin's include *Life's Companion: Journal Writing as a Spiritual Quest* (1991). By 2019, the journaling space was filled with famous people and mental health journaling apps: Michelle Obama released *Becoming: A Guided Journal for Discovering Your Voice*, a follow-up to her best-selling memoir. An app called Stoic offers "100+ science-backed exercises prepared by professional therapists to make you feel better," plus "Artificial Intelligence-powered writing analysis, personalized guided journal prompts, and smart reminders." The "mood tracker & therapy journal app" Clarity offers a "scientific approach to journaling" and "mental health chatbots" to "harness the power" of cognitive behavioral therapy (CBT), a popular psychotherapy. (Although journaling isn't a CBT component, some CBT therapists suggest that patients keep a journal of their thoughts.) *The Anti-Anxiety Notebook* emphasizes using CBT skills to help "identify, challenge, and change unhelpful thought patterns so you can feel better."

Some journalers I spoke to reported finding one or more of these methods meaningful, even life-changing. *The Shadow Work Journal* proved so essential to a forty-three-year-old Baltimore TikTok influencer's "spiritual journey" that he posted a 2023 video endorsement that garnered fifty-eight million views. He started offering online classes on how to use the journal and sold more than forty thousand copies of it on TikTok, earning more than $150,000 in commissions.

Skeptics of Keila Shaheen's best-selling guide to shadow work, which draws on Carl Jung's psychoanalytic approach, say it oversimplifies Jung's ideas, and possibly worse. "It can be risky to go exploring in the dark without guidance, without expertise," a psychotherapist who has published several books on shadow work told the *Times* in June 2024. Shaheen countered, in the *Times* piece, that her book is an introduction, not a comprehensive guide or therapy replacement.

ooo

"The coronavirus pandemic—or whatever they're calling it—is starting to feel scary, as much as I have tried to remain calm," I wrote on March 7, 2020. Although I didn't set out to write a "plague diary," COVID soon seeped into my entries. At the same time, news outlets, college extension services, therapists, and health-care providers were urging us to chronicle our fear, stress, loneliness, isolation, and depression. We'd feel better, headlines told us: "Feeling Anxious? Journaling Might Help" . . . "Journaling to Reduce COVID-19 Stress" . . . "Pandemic Diaries: Why Journaling Now Is the Best Time to Start or Restart."

As the virus grabbed hold of our world and wouldn't let go, I began writing about the health crisis more, although not overtly for therapeutic benefits. Instead, I was doing what I suspect other veteran diarists did: I wrote about the pandemic because it was inescapable. Did my writing help? Can diary writing, especially during our most stressful moments, provide therapeutic benefits?

I found no compelling science to support this. Too often, instead, I found popular media and marketers touting (explicitly or obliquely) Pennebaker's tested expressive-writing research as proof of the benefits of diary writing—which I found even more dubious when I learned that both Pennebaker and Progoff distinguished their structured methods from unstructured journaling. "Expressive writing is not simply a form of journaling or diary-writing," Pennebaker wrote in a coauthored 2016 book. Instead, it is "a self-help therapy method without outlandish claims" and it is backed "by scientific evidence."

Progoff bluntly stated in his 1975 manual that the "mere act of writing in a journal" would *not* produce his method's "particular dynamic effect." People often use an "unstructured" journal to pursue a goal, which is "helpful up to a point," by stimulating reflection, Progoff wrote. But this journaling, done without guidance or discipline, can be inadequate, misused, and even have "a negative effect," he warned. Furthermore, it "leads to subjectivity and solipsism," Progoff argued in a 1981 news story. "It's the side of the culture that becomes narcissistic and subjectively self-concerned that goes in for diary keeping."

It's easy to chalk up Progoff's views to his own self-interest, that he slammed casual journaling to promote what he calls in his book "new techniques" for using a journal "more fruitfully" to produce personal growth. But he's not alone in warning about potential ill effects. While diary writing is commonly viewed as beneficial, some therapists and diarists argue that it can deepen problems, intensify mental health struggles, and spur self-destructive behavior, noting (fairly or not) the suicides of the famous diarists Virginia Woolf and Sylvia Plath. Among the most common journaling bad habits: Thinking in circles, stirring a toxic stew of worry, anxiety, and stress. Over-accenting the negative or minor problems. Overlooking the positive. Fixating on one goal to the exclusion of others. Generating self-justification, denial, or guilt rather than growth or problem-solving.

The amiable Pennebaker, now a retired professor, welcomed my effort to distinguish between journaling and expressive writing. But he also told me, "Diary writing, at its best, does what expressive writing does: helps people come to terms with issues." Given the absence of scientific research on journaling's effect on mental health, he said, "you have to be your own inner scientist. You have to look at this calmly, objectively, truthfully. Is this being beneficial?" As for diary-writing pitfalls, Pennebaker was less concerned about diarists who write to process the everyday than diarists intentionally trying to work through major personal issues, especially trauma. If this writing helps you feel better or sleep better, fine, he says. If not, the writing may be stress inducing rather than healing. It may be best to stop. If you are writing the same story over and over without soon arriving at an answer, he warns, you may be "getting into the cardinal definition of depression, which is rumination."

The absence of scientific proof does *not* rule out the possibility that diary writing *is* beneficial, argues Ellen K. Baker, a Washington, DC–based clinical psychologist, veteran diarist, and admirer of Progoff and Pennebaker. If anything, she told me, this absence reflects the "tremendous undertaking" such research would require, given the diversity of diarists. As evidence that personal reflective writing is beneficial, she points to the many people who invest time and effort doing it. "People typically pursue an activity that they get something out of," she told me. What is that something? "There's a conversation with self, a dialogue with self, a mirroring of self,'" she answered.

In the early 1990s, when war disrupted Zlata Filipović's "happy and carefree" life in Bosnia, her teenage diary became more than a place to record daily events. "It became a type of therapy for dealing with everything," she recalled. Her diary became "a friend . . . willing to accept anything and everything I had to say; it could handle my fear, my questions, my sadness." Pandemic journaling projects also added to anecdotal evidence of journaling's mental health benefits. "I found journaling to be a coping method," wrote a student at Guttman Community College in New York City. This comment is quoted in a 2022 article in the social science and medicine journal *SSM-Mental Health* by the student's professor, Kristina Baines, a medical anthropologist.

Baines assigned her "clearly overwhelmed" students to participate in the Pandemic Journaling Project, run by professors at the University of Connecticut and Brown, which invited the general public to submit entries by email. Some entries were shared on the project's website, with the authors' permission. By submitting entries and reading what others wrote, her students became more self-aware, resilient, and empathetic, Baines reported. With its variety of responders, the project also "opened a space" where a nineteen-year-old Latina, first-generation college student from the Bronx can be in conversation with a fifty-year-old white woman from the suburban Midwest. Baines called in her article for more spaces "where we can share our common humanity and find wellness writing our shared history together." The mental health community has also shown interest in the pandemic journaling experience. The project's leaders have spoken to psychiatry, psychology, and gerontology groups, and in 2022 gave a keynote address at the annual meeting of the Society for the Study of Psychiatry and Culture.

ooo

During my research for this book, everyday diarists, especially women in their twenties and thirties, occasionally confided to me that, although they don't follow a specific journaling method, diary writing has helped them process difficult emotions and work through trauma. In her 1994 anthology of contemporary Black women's personal writing, American editor Patricia Bell-Scott notes that most women started writing at an early age to ease loneliness and anxiety. Some used the writing to bridge life transitions or as a reality check, and women often kept writing as a "form of therapy, self-healing, and emotional release." An unnamed young college student who found life "unbearable" at the predominantly white college she attended, reported that her journal "validated" her experiences, adding: "I could express how I felt . . . without censorship."

Another unnamed contributor wrote: "The journal gives me a place to whine in peace; to spot my internal contradictions before they get too out of hand; to praise myself for purely personal victories over fear and conventional wisdom." R. H. Douglas, who was sexually abused as a child, credited diary writing with saving her from madness and stagnation. "During my years in therapy, I came to realize the importance of the Diary," writes Douglas, a Trinidad-born New York City author. "My therapist did say 'the Diary kept you sane.'" The diary became "like an extra arm or a second heart in which I absorbed all of life's pain, disappointment, and emotional scrambling."

Diarists have long written about the mental health benefits of diary writing—*in* their diaries. "I owe a good deal to this journal," wrote thirty-year-old Anne Lister, on June 22, 1821, an English woman later known as "the first modern lesbian." "By unburdening my mind on paper I feel, as it were, in some degree to get rid of it; it seems made over to a friend that hears it patiently, keeps it faithfully, and by never forgetting anything, is always ready to compare the past & present & thus to cheer & edify the future."

In the late 1800s, Alice James turned to diary writing for an emotional release while living with debilitating physical and psychological pain caused by neurological issues and, later, breast cancer. "If I get into the habit of writing a bit about what happens, or rather doesn't happen, I may lose a little sense of the loneliness and desolation which abides with me," James wrote on May 31, 1889, the first entry in a journal kept during what became her life's last four years. "It may bring relief as an outlet to that geyser of emotions, sensations, speculations, and reflections which ferments perpetually within my poor old carcass for its sins; so here goes, my first journal!"

Although illness-focused diaries were uncommon before the twentieth century, because serious medical conditions often impeded diary writing, James produced the rare exception, noted the late American diary scholar Steven E. Kagle. In 2020, he credited James with writing "the most important diary of illness," focused more on her emotional distress than her physical ailments. When she lost the strength to physically write her diary, she dictated it. Before her death, at age forty-three in 1892, she gave her diary to a friend, and copies were printed for members of her prominent American family, including her famous brothers, the writer Henry James and the psychologist-philosopher William James. Diary versions published in 1943 and 1964 established James's reputation as a talented diarist and, to some, a feminist hero whose self-expression transcended stifling Victorian views of gender and femininity.

Eager to return to a "self-supporting" life, American poet and novelist May Sarton resumed journal writing after a debilitating stroke at age seventy-three. "It may prove impossible because my head feels so queer and the smallest effort, mental or physical exhausts, but I feel so deprived of my *self* being unable to write. . . . I must try to write a few lines every day," she wrote on April 9, 1986. Sarton candidly documented her challenges with treatment, solitude, and modern medicine's shortcomings but also nature's healing power and her friends' support. Her entries were published in 1988 as *After the Stroke*.

During the AIDS crisis in the 1980s, people affected by the disease deliberately wrote diaries to bear witness, raise awareness, counter homophobia, and push for government and medical action. The activist group ACT UP's iconic poster featured the powerful slogan "Silence = Death." Sharing stories via diaries and other methods was not only an activist strategy but also an example of the diary's political use, reframing the diary's function from "individualistic and introspective to the collective and public," writes Desirée Henderson.

Writer Suleika Jaouad is a contemporary example of diary keeping during illness. When she was diagnosed with leukemia in 2011 at age twenty-two, she returned to journaling, which, she writes, "saved my life." She wrote about the experience in her best-selling 2021 memoir, *Between Two Kingdoms*. In an interview that year, Jaouad recalled using her journal "to interrogate my predicament and to try to excavate some meaning from it." Journal writing helped her gain "narrative control" at a time when she was under medical care and "had to cede so much control to others." Early in the COVID pandemic, Jaouad created "The Isolation Journals," a collective online effort with journaling prompts to help others "convert that isolation into creative solitude and possibility and maybe even community."

Some life writers with disabilities avoid the words *health* and *wellness* because using them suggests, incorrectly, that their goal is to be *free* of disability or illness. Instead, disability rights activists emphasize their ability to lead fulfilling lives, countering the conventional perception of disability as interrupting life, write G. Thomas Couser and Susannah B. Mintz, editors of a 2019 anthology of personal narratives about "disability experiences." Through personal writing, people with disability or illness can "talk back" and "tell stories in which illness, injury, and impairment are but one part of rich, satisfying lives," the editors write. This writing offers the "radical potential" to "correct the stigmatizing of disability as helplessness or lack."

∞∞

And yet, some diarists warn that journaling is not therapeutic or otherwise beneficial for all—that diary writing can harm rather than improve, feed anxieties rather than allay them, and fuel self-centeredness, self-aggrandizement, and more. The English author C. S. Lewis wondered whether recording his sorrow over the death of his wife in his "terrible little notebook" was counterproductive. "I not only live each endless day in grief, but live each day thinking about living each day in grief. Do these notes merely aggravate that side of it?" he writes about entries that informed his 1961 book *A Grief Observed*. This recording proved "a defense against total collapse," but, he added, "if I don't stop writing that history . . . there's no reason why I should ever stop." In American writer Sarah Manguso's probing 2015 memoir, *Ongoingness: The End of a Diary*, she recalls trying to capture all of life's experiences in her diary and inevitably failing. She raises the specter of hypergraphia or graphomania, both terms for an obsessive need to write. (Lewis Carroll and Fyodor Dostoevsky are oft-cited possible hypergraphia sufferers.)

American memoirist Tara Westover's gratitude journal writing backfired. "I wanted to live a grateful life," she wrote in a 2025 magazine article. Attempting to rekindle her love for her estranged parents "without bitterness" and to "purge" her anger toward her eccentric, domineering father, Westover tried writing entries thanking him for his contributions to her life. "It was a disaster," she recalled. "When I reread what I had written, I did not feel grateful; I felt enraged." The writing brought up memories of bad experiences that she says her parents denied. Ultimately, she failed in her effort to "be grateful for the good and bury the bad." Nor did journaling help her find the will to become a "different person" with a different past and to "eradicate her rage." (Perhaps she asked too much from a gratitude journal—or, at least, gained clarity about her limited ability to rekindle love, especially through journaling?)

"Is it good? Is it bad?" Philippe Lejeune and Catherine Bogaert ask about diary writing. Although diary writing is widely practiced in France, and the country has produced famous diarists (Marie Bashkirtseff, the Goncourt brothers), paradoxically, the diary has been "under attack" as a "dubious practice" and "needs to be defended," they wrote in 2020. "In France there is a debate about diaries and, in general, a feeling of uneasiness with autobiographical writing." Critics view diary keeping as a sign of introversion, weak character, or dubious personality. They worry that diary writing for young people is dangerous, a waste of time, and a gateway to narcissism. Lejeune and Bogaert counter: "A diary, with its strengths and weaknesses, is simply human."

Meanwhile, in German- and English-speaking countries, "journaling comes as naturally as breathing" and isn't controversial, they note. One possible, albeit "simplistic," explanation they offer: Protestantism encourages journal writing, and Northern Europeans, early on, embraced self-care. But in Southern Europe and specifically around the Mediterranean basin, a "preoccupation with self is viewed with suspicion." Lejeune and Bogaert point to a comment from Pascal, the seventeenth-century French philosopher (and a devout Catholic): "The self is hateful." However, the diary enthusiasts I met during a 2023 visit to France told me the diary has gained more acceptance. Perhaps another sign: a young French TikToker (Cassandre) has become a viral star by reading her 2015 teenage diary to 180,000 followers (in a very irritating voice).

Is diary writing good or bad for digital diarists who use social media as a public diary? Certainly, the broader debate about whether social media use (as a diary or not) is a healthy activity or, instead, spurs "digital narcissism" can't be ignored. An overabundance of social media and our modern-day "culture of self-disclosure" are blamed for bad behavior: oversharing, exhibitionism, bullying, a lack of empathy. In June 2024, the US surgeon general, Dr. Vivek Murthy, called for Congress to require labels on social media platforms, pointing to research showing that teens who spent more than three hours a day on social media faced a significantly higher risk of mental health problems than teens who didn't. Other experts argue that there is no evidence that social media causes these problems, pointing instead to economic hard times, the opioid crisis, and social isolation.

For the early "mommy blogger" Heather Armstrong and pioneering online diarist Carolyn L. Burke, extreme online candor about their personal lives took a toll on their health. Armstrong's blog *Dooce*, launched in 2001 from her Salt Lake City home, was one of the first popular blog moneymakers, attracting 8.5 million readers a month, generating income from on-site ads, sponsored posts, book deals, public speaking, and corporate promotion. Armstrong was a lapsed member of the Mormon Church, which has long encouraged Mormon women to write diaries. (Many became early bloggers.) Armstrong blogged about parenting and marital ups-and-downs, about battling depression and alcoholism. Of motherhood, she recalled in her 2009 memoir, "I don't think I would have survived it had I not offered up my story and reached out to bridge the loneliness." But, starting in 2012, Armstrong's personal life and blogging career changed—her marriage broke up, infuriating some fans, and her severe depression returned. On the "mommy internet," Instagram influencers began replacing confessional bloggers. Other moms attacked Armstrong. "The hate was very, very scary and very, very hard to live through," she told an interviewer in 2019. "It gets inside your head and eats away at your brain. It became untenable." In 2023, Armstrong died by suicide at age forty-seven, a sad and sobering end.

For Burke, blogging was emotionally and socially uplifting, at first. "After I had written whatever it was I needed to write, I was happier, always made me feel better," she said in a 2022 podcast. Her blog's huge following—a hundred thousand regular readers after year one—also eased her struggles to connect with other people. "It changed me because I learned how to be a social person again. I learned how to interact," she explained. (The podcast mentions that Burke was eventually diagnosed with Asperger's syndrome, which is characterized in part by difficulty with social interactions.)

However, because Burke publicly exposed her private life in her blog—naming names and sharing personal emails—friends stopped talking to her. Public scrutiny and criticism got intense. She pulled the plug on the blog in 2002, after seven years. Two years later, she made her old posts available again on a fresh website—"including items which may offend," she warned online. "This site will remain public, come what may, even if and when it may harm me," she wrote. "When I started writing here, it was to make a point—that we have nothing to hide from each other. I still feel this strongly."

ooo

Wandering through an outdoor market in Las Cruces, New Mexico, I stop abruptly at a stall selling a decorative red potholder with an image of a book and the words *Dear Diary, Everything Sucks.* I laugh and buy it.

Does my diary writing dwell too much on what sucks, when I'm in one of my sour, anxious, sad, or bad moods? Probably. Do I sometimes ruminate in it? Yes. My husband reports that he can tell when I'm anxious (or excited) by the amount of time I spend scribbling away in my diary at night. (Fortunately, he's a deep sleeper.) While venting on paper can clarify issues, I've learned it can't guarantee a solution. And I've found some truth in the claim that too much self-reflective writing—especially the negative kind—can lead to unhealthy patterns: overanalyzing, self-pitying, obsessing, with thoughts spinning around and around, seemingly without end or enlightenment.

Yet, I found myself agreeing with Desirée Henderson's view. "Do [diaries] promote mental health, assist with self-improvement or learning, and contribute to happiness or well-being? Or do diaries promote self-destructive rumination, reinforce obsessive or narcissistic behaviors, and cut diarists off from the reality of their own experiences? The reality is likely somewhere in the middle," she writes. For me-me-me, diary writing has been positive for my mental health overall. I can write what I can't say to others (or wouldn't want them to hear)—a welcome release. It has helped me appreciate my life and, yes, be grateful. It has helped me get through occasional tough times, from deaths to back pain, broken arms, surgeries, miscarriage, challenging relationships, and career upheaval. I use diary writing to dislodge painful emotions, to self-analyze and self-correct (or try to). Which has helped me gain perspective and make sense. Many a time in my diary I've sorted out predicaments at home, school, or work. Diary writing has helped me make tough decisions or find the will and way to make a big change. Sometimes, after chronicling a bitter argument, blow by blow, I've landed on the perfect riposte, sadly too late. Other times, if I'm lucky, I land on a timely solution to a conflict.

In some old entries, I was surprised to find signs that I'd deliberately used my diary for psychological benefits. "There are certain things I feel I must say in ordinance with the purpose of this diary, which is to diagnose my emotions honestly and openly," I wrote on August 25, 1974, at age fifteen. (Today, I smile at my misuse of the word "ordinance." I offer an edit: "accordance.") The entry continues: "On the other hand, the things I should say I can't because 1) I'll be embarrassed should anyone read this and they will be too. 2) It will seem as if I'm ungrateful. . . . I really don't feel it's right to go into it." In a similar vein, fifteen-year-old me wrote on January 20, 1975: "I feel like I'm letting you—or should I say myself—down for not reporting accurately my true thoughts but it's all just too painful."

Perhaps the biggest mental health benefit from my diary writing is the self-understanding I've gained, for better and worse. My diary offers a way to reveal my strengths and shortcomings to myself. I can draw on this knowledge when I face a fresh dilemma. And since I am always changing, as is everything else, the diary keeps helping me discover myself. There are other ways to gain self-awareness, of course, but diary writing comes most naturally to me. Write long enough, particularly about your struggles, fears, or disappointments, and you recognize a cycle—the fall, the climb back up, the determination to soldier on. My diary offers a comforting reminder: The next day is usually better. So far.

5

Memorable

Do Diaries Really *Help Us Remember?*

Diarists have long used diaries to make and store memories. The eighteenth-century English author Fanny Burney kept a journal to have an account of her "thoughts, manners, acquaintance and actions" to consult when time became "more nimble than memory," she wrote on March 27, 1768. Centuries later, the American author Alice Walker explained in 2022 that she kept a journal "partly because my memory is notorious, among my friends, for not remembering much of what we've shared. The journal gives me back some of what I have lost." Eighteen-year-old Iowa diarist Aubrie Kiesling told me, "I'm documenting my everyday life so I can look back and recollect what I did."

I, too, have kept a diary, in part, to safeguard and revisit my past, especially as I entered my sixties—the stage of life when my mother's memory declined due to dementia caused by Alzheimer's disease. She died in 2004 at age sixty-seven. I suspect I am not the only person who has hoped diary writing will help me hold onto my memories if I develop dementia, which impairs remembering and other cognitive functioning. I'd been encouraged by hints, here and there, that diary writing is possible in early-stage Alzheimer's *and* helpful for remembering. In the UK, the Alzheimer's Society describes a journal as a "common memory aid" and a Dementia Diaries project organizes audio and video diary keeping (and sharing), which "gives a voice to people with dementia." A New York chapter of the Alzheimer's Association suggested a pocket-size diary as a holiday gift for people in the disease's early stage, "to help remember things." "Dementia gratitude journals" are pitched online.

Are we kidding ourselves? Is there scientific evidence that diary writing can help us remember, even during early-stage dementia? To start exploring, I used my unusual resource—over fifty years of diary entries—to compare my diary accounts of significant personal events with my memories of them. What would my diary give back? My diary keeper's discoveries raised other questions I tried answering with help from cognitive psychologists and neurologists who study memory: Why do today's story and yesterday's diary entry sometimes differ? Why do we remember some experiences from our diary, not others? Do we really need to remember?

ooo

We all tell stories about our experiences: funny, sad, bittersweet, sometimes self-serving stories about people who saved or hurt us, about amazing adventures, crazy coincidences, big breaks, bad mistakes. Like me, you may have long regaled people with your stories, embellishing just a wee bit. We learn to pause for effect, to see which lines win a laugh, an astonished look, or a sympathetic nod. Over time, we grind away boring bits and buff the audience-pleasers, polishing the story like a stone so it slowly changes, becoming a little too smooth and shiny.

One benefit of having a diary: we can use our entries to fact-check an oft-told story and see if it has changed over time. Without a diary, you might be able to check old photo albums or Facebook posts, but those won't offer much detail. You might be able to compare notes with friends or family who shared the experience, but chances are their story isn't your story—with you at the center.

And, so, at age sixty, I searched my diary for three A-list experiences from my formative college years: a Scottish hitchhiking adventure, riding for several days in a stranger's sports car, a chance encounter with a legendary foreign correspondent, and an embarrassing college mishap. I easily found the first two—the happy ones, often told as stories. To my shock, I never found the embarrassing college mishap (which I rarely share). Hence my first discovery: I did not always record significant experiences. No worries. I still remember waking up alone, early in the morning, half-dressed (or mostly dressed, I'm not sure) in an unfamiliar bed, after drinking too much beer with a freckled red-haired frat boy at a party the night before. I still remember shutting the obnoxious purple frat-house door behind me and running down the grassy slope to my apartment, embarrassed and angry with myself.

In my mind, this experience from 1978 (or was it 1979?) registered *not* as sexual assault—I remember no violence or coercion—but as a stupid mistake that, fortunately, ended there. I never put myself in that kind of peril again. I moved on, with no enduring trauma, never wanting to revisit the experience—until after 2017 when the #MeToo movement took off, promoting awareness of sexual harassment and assault. As "gray zone sex" (a murky incident somewhere between assault and a very bad date) became a hot topic, I, like many women, began to review past dalliances, landing on that freckled red-haired frat boy. Did I consent to whatever happened? Was I capable of consenting? I looked through several diary volumes for my embarrassing college mishap, with mounting frustration. I found no mention. My diary was silent.

My two happy experiences were from a golden 1980 junior semester abroad in London. Before reading my full diary accounts, I wrote down what I remembered about each experience. Then I compared the two versions. Second discovery: with each experience, the gist of the two versions matched, with some jarring discrepancies. Reading my diary versions, I saw that I'd known something remarkable, even historic (for me), had happened. About the hitchhiking adventure: "Soon after came the ride that may just go down in history as THE RIDE TO BEAT ALL RIDES!" I wrote on April 5, 1980, in messy microscopic script that practically vibrated with excitement. And from another entry two days later: "Tom drove 65 to 70 miles an hour on the steep road. I felt no fear. I figured if I was to die in a car crash it was fine. I had lived a full life." (I was twenty. Cue older Betsy eyeroll.)

Nine days later, after the legendary foreign correspondent offered me an internship (my first big journalism break), I wrote: "Today another incredible stroke of luck." Only after I read both diary entries, decades after writing them, did I realize that the two experiences were *both* about a stranger giving me a lift—and that they'd had a lasting impact, providing enduring lessons about risk, trust, generosity, and kindness.

The entries *did* reveal factual errors in my spoken-story versions. My diary told me that my "ride to beat all rides" began when my hitchhiking buddy and I were picked up outside Edinburgh. For years, I told people we were picked up outside Newcastle. More surprisingly, my dense diary account failed to mention that the sports-car driver had told us why he'd picked us up—because decades earlier, when he was a young hitchhiker, drivers picked him up. His comment was the reason I later told the story. How did I fail to mention what later inspired my story's kicker? I never saw that driver again, but the correspondent became a cherished mentor and friend. And their generosity inspired me to pay it forward later in life. I didn't pick up hitchhikers. Too risky. But I befriended young journalists and hosted foreign visitors and political campaign volunteers in Iowa—with the driver and the correspondent in mind.

While searching for other remembered experiences in my diary, I stumbled upon some B-listers I had forgotten. Third discovery: the memories jogged by my diary reading came in a variety pack, with my remembering varying in velocity, intensity, and familiarity. Some memories rushed out; others trickled. Some were hazy; others, clearer. Most unsettling were the experiences I *should* remember but still don't. Did I really see Richard Nixon in 1980 at a small gathering of British politicians when I was a college intern in the House of Commons? My diary says I did. I am shocked. Again.

Hunting for diary mentions of my girlhood crush, Caroline Kennedy—the slightly older sister I didn't have—was an odyssey of remembering, or forgetting. Over the decades, I found scattered "Kennedy entries," as expected. Yet some were surprising, in various ways. I remembered that Jacqueline Kennedy Onassis's death, at age sixty-four, hit thirty-five-year-old Betsy hard, but I didn't entirely recall *why* until I read my May 19, 1994, entry: "What I realized tonight is that her death scares me because she is six years older than my mother." While looking for something else, I stumbled upon perhaps my earliest Kennedy mention, about Caroline's then twelve-year-old cousin Edward Kennedy Jr.: "His leg is going to be amputated," fourteen-year-old Betsy wrote on November 6, 1973. "I hope he'll have the courage to live through such a terrible experience." I forgot that I'd noticed Teddy's bone cancer until this reading, which sparked my memory that I had. (Unlike the Nixon mention, which sparked nothing.)

Other Kennedy entries were unsurprising—and my reaction *was* as remembered: a thrilled twenty-something Betsy, passing "Jackie" on Madison Avenue one time in the 1980s; a shocked and saddened forty-year-old Betsy, learning of thirty-eight-year-old JFK Jr.'s death in a plane crash in July 1999 (John-John was born the same year *and month* as *my* younger brother, who I adore, as Caroline seemed to adore her brother); and finally, star-struck fifty-seven-year-old Betsy, standing "mere feet away from Caroline" at the American embassy in Tokyo in 2016. Caroline, then the US ambassador to Japan, was meeting with Iowa farmers—and I was there with my husband, who worked for a farm group. "She was charming, low-key, funny . . . also more frail looking than I expected," I wrote on July 8, 2016. "I looked up to her as a kid . . . when she did something, I'd think, I should do that too (get married, have kids, etc.). . . . But all we did this time is exchange the briefest of smiles."

ooo

"When I have a profound experience, I write it down in my journal and that way I am working through it," wrote the late American author Madeleine L'Engle. "I am also setting it in my memory." Many diarists think this—and I found some scientific thinking (albeit not diary-specific) to support the assumption that diary writing strengthens memory. I also found possible explanations for some, not all, of my diary keeper's discoveries, with invaluable guidance from two very patient cognitive psychologists at Washington University in St. Louis, Andrew Butler and Henry Roediger. They pointed me to pertinent research—much appreciated given that empirical research on memory dates to the 1880s and the scientific literature is vast.

Science has determined that remembering an experience involves three interdependent processes in the brain: encoding (learning the experience by perceiving and relating it to past knowledge), storing (maintaining it over time), and retrieving (accessing it on demand). Science also has classified varieties of memory (although psychologists still debate them). At the heart of my questions is episodic memory—the ability to remember past experiences, events, and episodes. When people say someone is "losing their memory" due to Alzheimer's, they're usually talking about episodic memory and often short-term memory loss: forgetting recent events or conversations, a common early symptom of the disease.

You don't have to be a brain scientist (phew!) to know that diary writing preserves memories for the simple reason that by writing them down, the diarist creates an external record, beyond their own internal memory, to revisit. "That's the beauty of having a written diary," Roediger, who retired as a professor in 2025, told me. Also, the act of recalling (or retrieving) the memory in order to chronicle it in a diary helps it become more established and, therefore, remembered. Some note-taking particulars may be relevant to diary keeping. When we take notes to summarize material in a textbook, for example, we may forget or skip many details, but we remember and record "big picture takeaways," explained Butler. "To me, that's diary writing in a nutshell." Seasoned diarists can become highly trained observers who view a day's experiences as potential diary fodder, deciding which experiences warrant recording *and* working through in words. This process, in turn, adds meaning, making the chosen experiences more likely to be remembered, Butler told me.

Does the act of handwriting a diary also help us remember? In school, I crammed for tests by repeatedly writing down information I might need. Some research suggests that handwritten notetaking improves our recall of a random series of words and helps with rote learning of, say, spelling because "the motor and sensory memory of putting words on paper reinforces that material," *The Economist* reported in 2023. Our visual memory of our notes on paper may also contribute.

Is typing entries into a computer better for strengthening our memories than handwriting? I wondered if a much-reported 2014 study might be relevant. With the pithy title "The Pen Is Mightier Than the Keyboard: Advantages of Longhand over Laptop Note Taking," the study found that students who take notes by hand during a lecture may gain and retain information better than those keyboarding notes. This is because speedy keyboarders tend to type what's said verbatim—a shallower processing of information that hampers encoding and learning, compared to slower-going hand writers, who must synthesize and summarize, reframing what's said in their own words—a deeper processing that's conducive to learning. Alas, the study was *not* relevant to diary writing, my WashU brain trust ruled, because it focuses on a very particular situation. "Taking lecture notes from a lecturer speaking rapidly is different from recalling my daily or weekly experiences and ideas from memory," Roediger explained. It "probably makes little difference whether a diarist writes or types." Butler knew of no evidence suggesting "something special about handwritten versus typing or other methods of recording a diary that improve memory for an experience." Also worth noting: the 2014 study was countered by a 2021 study with an equally pithy title: "Don't Ditch the Laptop Just Yet: Replication Finds No Immediate Advantage to Writing Notes by Hand."

ooo

Why do our memories change over time? Because memory retrieval is a reconstructive process. Retrieving a memory is not like pulling a book from a shelf, reading it, and then putting it back. "The memory is constantly changing. In fact, every time we retrieve a memory, it is altered," write Roediger and Kathleen B. McDermott. We mix the basic concrete details of an experience (example: hitchhiking in Scotland) with our own assumed, or preferred, details to construct a cohesive and compelling story. Errors creep in (example: where we were picked up) and stay in, "especially if they're a good part of the story," Butler told me. After multiple retellings, the errors become basic facts in our mind. Repeated retrieval of the memory strengthens both the accurate and the inaccurate bits.

"Memories are continuously sculpted and after long passages of time, the creative mind abstracts, contorts, and even distorts the past," writes neurologist Scott A. Small, director of the Alzheimer's Disease Research Center at Columbia University in New York. As the daughter of art dealers, I appreciated Small's metaphor—that our "minds store the past less like a museum of personal history than a gallery of memory art." Then there's the pioneering 1932 study by British psychologist Sir Frederic Bartlett, which focused on *how* we remember something, especially how errors creep in as elaboration or simplification—and stay. British students read a Native American folktale and then recalled it at various times. In their retellings, they changed the story here and there, creating an "imaginative reconstruction." They swapped unfamiliar Native American elements for more familiar ones: *seal hunting* became *fishing*; *canoe* became *boat*.

Decades later, a research team led by Elizabeth J. Marsh at Duke University showed how memories change when shared as stories, supporting "the claim that everyday conversational retellings often have goals other than accuracy." (I plead guilty.) In a 2004 study, thirty-three undergraduates kept a diary-like account of their own retellings of personal memory–laden stories over the course of one month. Later, the students reported that 42 percent of their retellings could be labeled "inaccurate" and that one-third of the "accurate" retellings still contained "distortions." Regarding the purpose of the retellings, almost 60 percent were done to share facts, 40 percent to entertain, and 25 percent to seek sympathy or express pride. The students were more likely to exaggerate their stories' entertaining bits, and they often streamlined the factual bits to cut out irrelevant information. "Because memories are frequently retrieved in social contexts, retellings of events are often incomplete or distorted, with consequences for later memory. . . . Retellings can be linked to memory errors," writes Marsh. What people remember about an experience may be the last story they told about it, which has potentially big implications for court testimony, eyewitness accounts of historical events, and "not least of all psychologists who study remembering."

As for the social aspect of memory construction, 40 percent of our casual conversation involves storytelling, according to one analysis. "Stories are the way we express memories," says Robyn Fivush, a developmental psychology professor at Emory University in Atlanta. "But as we tell stories, the memories are going to change because stories allow them to become more organized, coherent, more historic." Our understanding of our stories also changes as we change. "Now, days later, weeks later, years later, we're not a completely different person but we've had different life experiences, challenges, stressors, joyous moments, and that all plays into how we now bring that previous experience to mind in a new light, a new perspective," Fivush told me.

So what I tell people today about my Scottish hitchhiking adventure is not the static version from my long-ago diary entry. I'm not traveling down memory lane back to that adventure. I'm an older person traveling a shorter distance—back to the last time I thought about or shared the adventure. And research suggests that a story may change depending on our audience. I recall regaling friends about my "ride to beat all rides" soon after it happened. But the version I told my parents likely skipped my hitchhiking. (Why alarm them?) The version I'd tell my own kids, much later, might tone down the hitchhiking and add a Jewish mother's plea: Please don't hitchhike.

I also learned from research studies that diaries have long been used to study memory accuracy (*how much* we remember vs. *how* we remember), in experiments far more scientific than my diary-keeper experiments. Between 1952 and 2020, six memory researchers each conducted investigations of their autobiographical memory (akin to episodic memory) using their personal diaries or other life writing. One was Marigold Linton, a cognitive psychologist who, in 1964, became the first Native American to receive a doctorate in psychology and, in 1974, the first woman hired as a full professor at the University of Utah. Linton tested her autobiographical memory by daily writing a short description of two or more personal events (producing 5,500!), followed by monthly self-administered memory tests (11,000!). Linton discovered that her forgetting occurred slowly. Only 32 percent of the recorded items were forgotten after six years. She also remembered far more positive events than negative ones.

Inspired by Linton's 1975 study, a Kansas State University psychologist and colleagues elsewhere used college students' diaries to study memory accuracy. Over the course of fifteen years, they collected more than four hundred commissioned diaries. The students typically described one personal event daily, for ten to fifteen weeks, and rated it in terms of memorability, pleasantness, and other qualities. Later, they rated the entries to assess what and when they remembered. Published in 1996, the research showed that memory recall declined over time. People best remembered events that they experienced first-hand (versus a second-hand account) and events that were atypical, emotional, and/or positive (the so-called "Pollyanna effect"). More surprising, or odd, was the discovery that students tended to remember the good things that happened to them and the bad things that happened to their roommates—suggesting the "self-enhancing properties of memory," as one scholar put it.

ooo

Why do we recall some experiences and not others? In brain-science speak, the question becomes: Which experiences can be retrieved through memory—and why? While we can hold and store many memories, there is a difference between availability (Is the memory in my brain somewhere?) and accessibility (Can I get to it right now?), Butler explained. Some experiences may not be forgotten but are also not immediately accessible. There's debate over whether experiences can be forgotten forever.

As we acquire more experiences and prioritize remembering them, we may lose access to memories from further in our past. But this doesn't mean we can't regain access, according to research by the now-retired American memory scholar Harry P. Bahrick. Accessibility is affected by how recently the experience happened, how often we've thought about or shared it, and the strength of the potential retrieval cue that jogs a memory (or doesn't). Some cues work better than others, and different cues can lead people to retrieve different aspects of a memory, research suggests. Reading my diary entry about seeing Nixon in London didn't jog my memory. Would a photo of the gathering have done the trick?

Diaries don't always cough up memories on the page (such as my college mishap) because diary writing is a selective process. We choose what to record and remember, and our choice is shaped by our psychological state on the day, as well as by what we want to or can bear to share. Those were my takeaways from two memoirists who revisited their childhood diaries. In Martha Hodes's absorbing 2023 memoir, *My Hijacking: A Personal History of Forgetting and Remembering*, the New York University history professor hopes her girlhood diary will help her better remember an extraordinary ordeal from long ago. In 1970, twelve-year-old Martha and her thirteen-year-old sister were among the passengers held hostage for six days in a hijacked plane parked in the hot Jordanian desert. The girls were traveling as unaccompanied minors between the homes of their divorced parents, their mother in Tel Aviv and their father in New York City. Reading her diary entries from that week, Hodes discovered that some of her scarier memories were unrecorded, including one of a hijacker holding a gun to the copilot's neck. Historian Martha confirmed with other sources that this had happened but concluded that, for hijacked Martha, the "image had been too frightening to include" in her diary.

Young Martha didn't want her ordeal's worst moments "to be a part of the story I'd tell when I got home. It was all too much," writes older Martha. Young Martha opted *not* to tell the full or honest story in her diary but, instead, told a tolerable one. "The diary that I, the historian, approached as my prized then-and-there document had turned out instead to be a record and a relic of erasure," Hodes writes. "In the desert, I worked so hard to remember so little because I didn't want to have to tell my father about the bad parts."

During a radio interview about her 2024 memoir *The Exvangelicals: Loving, Living, and Leaving the White Evangelical Church*, National Public Radio journalist Sarah McCammon found that journal entries written during her evangelical youth didn't match her adulthood memory of being a teen who questioned her faith. McCammon suspects her younger self feared "writing down a doubt" about her faith. "What you write down with a pen and paper feels so serious and . . . permanent," she told an interviewer. "I think I would have been afraid to sort of say it out loud."

Such disconnects between diary and memory offer more reasons to reject *truth* as a diary descriptor. Despite the diary's immediacy, it may be an imperfect vehicle for discerning the truth of the moment—or the truth in retrospect. Then again, maybe concealing a truth in a diary reveals another truth about the diarist's mindset. Maybe these diary questions would be best pondered with help from philosophers or poets, not memory researchers. When I first began comparing my diary writing with my latest memories, I wondered where "the truth" lay. Later, I ended up wondering: *What is truth anyway?*

ooo

I dreaded asking about dementia, having clung to the hope that my diary might somehow be a buffer against lost memories (or even memory impairment). I hoped, in my unscientific way, that my personal diary archive could serve as an external hard drive of sorts—a backup file of memories that I could consult if my internal system failed. If this was a false hope, did

I even want to know? Again, my search for diary-specific research came up dry, and I was left with experts' well-informed hunches.

Can diary writing help people with dementia remember? "Unfortunately, research in this area is somewhat limited," an Alzheimer's Association spokesperson responded. "Anecdotally, writing can be one activity to keep people cognitively engaged in the early stage of Alzheimer's but we know that as the disease progresses, reading and writing becomes more difficult even for avid readers and writers."

Dementia caused by Alzheimer's or other diseases can take years to fully emerge, and progression varies by individual. Regardless of what disease causes the dementia, symptoms such as memory loss are common. People may experience dementia symptoms or move through the stages (early/mild, middle/moderate, late/severe) differently. During the early stage, a person may be able to function independently and live well but also experience memory lapses—such as forgetting recent conversations. A person with dementia may forget recent events but still recall long-ago events. One explanation: older memories that have been more frequently recalled or spoken become more firmly established than newer ones. Also, dementia is caused by damage to the brain, which can affect areas of the brain involved in creating and retrieving memories.

Surely it is wise to keep our brains healthy by staying mentally active. But the suggestion that cognitive exercise in general can delay the onset of Alzheimer's is controversial, according to David Balota, a Washington University professor of psychological and brain sciences and neurology. He has long researched dementia-related memory issues but knew of no related research specifically on diary writing. I was pleased to learn that people in the early stage generally *can* write, read, and comprehend what they read, and that reading a diary filled with rich personal memories to revisit may be particularly beneficial. (Again, actively retrieving episodic memory is a brain-healthy activity that also strengthens the particular memory at hand.) "In general, this is a good strategy for keeping the personal past alive," Balota told me. However, diary writing involves memory *and* language—and during the classic Alzheimer's progression, memory breaks down earlier than language. "What is written in the diary may not be totally accurate," he said, but "producing a structured language description of some events could be a positive experience." And, in the disease's early stage, diary writing may add narrative structure to a day and across the days. No small thing, perhaps, for people living with a disease that can hamper time perception.

Veteran journalist Greg O'Brien has found some comfort in writing while living with Alzheimer's—he was diagnosed during his late fifties, in 2008. His parents and grandfather also had dementia. (People with a parent or sibling with Alzheimer's have a higher risk of developing it than others.) O'Brien is the author of the illuminating 2014 memoir *On Pluto: Inside the Mind of Alzheimer's*. I was encouraged and impressed that he wrote a memoir, given his cognitive challenges. Yet as I read his self-described "horror story," some sentences hit me hard as a fellow writer: "Words are the core of my life, and they are now lost on me, at times. . . . I have a formidable enemy—my mind. It used to be my best friend. I don't see any chance now for reconciliation. . . . It is vital for those with Alzheimer's to connect with the past, the long-term memories and relationships. The short term is a flash."

O'Brien's candor, clarity, and even humor kept me reading. "On doctors' orders, I try vigorously to exercise my body and mind every night. After the gym, I usually write for two hours. Medical experts encourage those with Alzheimer's and other dementia to pursue the creative arts, particularly writers, musicians, and artists with the disease. The writing makes me feel whole again—until the confusion takes over." This made me hope that if I do develop dementia, maybe diary writing can help me, as a writer, at least initially, the way that painting seemed to help my mother, as an artist. Mom spent decades selling art and raising four kids with my father, moving away from making much art herself. During her illness, which surfaced in middle age, she returned to her artwork. Painting kept Mom busy. Whether she found this satisfying or self-affirming, I couldn't tell—she largely lost her ability to speak. And, at the best of times, who knows what someone else is thinking? At the worst of times, this was even harder to know. Still, I like to think that painting provided a critical connection for her to who she is or once was.

The famous "Nun Study" on aging and Alzheimer's disease made me wonder if I should look more closely at the complexity of my writing in the entries I wrote in my early twenties. Begun in 1986, the multifaceted longitudinal study of 678 elderly Catholic sisters included a language analysis of the autobiographical essays the nuns were required to write, at roughly age twenty-two, before joining the order. The sisters who produced writing, some fifty years earlier, that was less grammatically complex and idea-dense were more likely to develop Alzheimer's. But this finding shows only an *association* between early simple writing and later dementia, not a causal connection or a proven early warning sign, the study's director cautioned during a 2010 interview.

I also welcomed experts' reminders that not all forgetting is a sign of dementia. Typical age-related memory change involves sometimes forgetting names or appointments but remembering them later. The memory loss related to Alzheimer's is more lasting. With typical aging, we'll experience a lot of *forgetting* (struggling to recall "that slippery word on the tip of your tongue," which is a memory-retrieval issue: the memory is there but not currently available) and a little *Forgetting* (when a memory is lost), writes neuropsychologist Charan Ranganath, at the University of California, Davis. Due to age-related brain changes, we become more easily distracted, and remembering takes longer, requiring more exertion. Can a brain-stimulating activity like, say, diary writing stave off age-related cognitive functioning, including memory decline? What little research has been done is hard to interpret, others report. Some studies suggest that people who regularly engage in cognitively stimulating activities such as writing (not diary writing specifically) are less likely to experience memory loss compared to those who don't, but this, again, shows only an association.

Typical forgetting may, in fact, be "a cognitive gift," argues Scott Small, in his 2021 book *Forgetting: The Benefits of Not Remembering*. "As our brains intrinsically know, not everything we store is worth remembering, and there is a real advantage—for the sake of our own sanity . . . to forgetting details of the world we temporarily encode." Small's observation jogged my memory, so to speak, of Sarah Manguso and her extreme effort to use her diary to prevent forgetting: "I wrote down everything that happened and everything I remembered thinking while it happened and everything I thought while recording what I remembered had happened," she writes. Though Manguso "failed to record so much," she gradually came to accept this. "Now I consider the diary a compilation of moments I'll forget, their record finished in language as well as I could finish it—which is to say imperfectly. . . .

Someday I might read about some of the moments I've forgotten, moments I've allowed myself to forget, that my brain was designed to forget, that I'll be glad to have forgotten and be glad to rediscover as writing."

Overall, I found the results of my memory exploration encouraging, although less so on the dementia front. One epiphany: I am glad to have my diary. Even if it doesn't cough up all the memories I'd hoped, my diary's external record offers the chance to remember some of what I forgot—and to refresh what I remember (while my brain is reasonably healthy, at least). By reading a particular diary entry from my youth, do I return lost exuberance, optimism, and nuance (or truth) to my memory of an experience—and to the too-smooth story I tell? (Perhaps it's good to scruff up that polished stone.) While I welcome the idea that diary writing adds meaning to my experiences, this makes me wonder if I should be more thoughtful about my daily diary writing. Has it become too slapdash? Given the value of my diary's external record, perhaps I need to become a choosier curator of my experiences and prioritize writing about what I value most.

6

Creatives

Do Diaries Really *Help Us Create?*

For Anaïs Nin, diary writing counted—literary snobs be damned. "Someday I want to write about this, as a tribute to a much despised form of literature, as an answer to those who have shrugged their shoulders when they saw me bending over a mere diary," reads a 1923 diary entry by Nin, whose literary reputation rests on her diary, not her fiction. "I shall demonstrate the uses, the purpose, the visibly beneficial effects of the much deplored habit."

Virginia Woolf, among the twentieth century's most famous literary authors, thought differently. "[This] diary writing does not count as writing," she wrote on January 20, 1919. "I have just re-read my year's diary and am much struck by the rapid haphazard gallop at which it swings along, sometimes indeed jerking almost intolerably over the cobbles." Still, Woolf wrote that diary writing was useful for her art: it had accidentally swept up "several stray matters" that were actually "diamonds of the dustheap."

The list of other literary lights who have kept a diary (or diary-like notebook) is a name-dropper's dream, among them William S. Burroughs, Annie Dillard, F. Scott Fitzgerald, Allen Ginsberg, Franz Kafka, Anne Lamott, John Steinbeck, and E. B. White. A partial list of visual artists (who often sketched alongside their writing) is impressive too: Eugene Delacroix, Paul Klee, Frida Kahlo, Keith Haring, and Andy Warhol. The list of actors, musicians, and media personalities who are diarists is *People* magazine–worthy: Julie Andrews, Louis Armstrong, Beyoncé, Kurt Cobain, Lena Dunham, Courtney

Love, Matthew McConaughey, Issa Rae, Emma Thompson, Emma Watson, and Oprah Winfrey.

I had many questions for creatives: Is there a relationship between their diary writing and professional work? How do they use their diary—does it serve or become art? Do they differentiate between the two? Can diary writing help aspiring artists find their way? For answers, I looked to novelists, poets, actors, painters, and pop stars who have discussed the interplay between their diary writing and other creative efforts; to scholars and critics who read artists' diaries for insights; and to professors and self-help authors who recommend diary keeping to fledgling writers.

ooo

Yes, many authors' diaries have been linked to their famous published work, in one way or another. Nathaniel Hawthorne's idea for his 1850 novel *The Scarlet Letter* first appears in a journal entry: "The life of a woman, who, by the old colony law, was condemned always to wear the letter A, sewed on her garment, in token of her having committed adultery." Albert Camus's journal includes material found in the beginning of his 1942 novel, *The Stranger*. Beyond raw material, diaries can be confidantes, used by writers to air their anxiety and grapple with writer's block, isolation, loneliness, and frustration. Playwright Tennessee Williams voiced self-doubt in his diary. Novelist Louisa May Alcott vented about *Little Women* readers. "Girls write to ask who the little women marry, as if that was the only end and aim of a woman's life. I won't marry Jo to Laurie to please any one," Alcott wrote on November 1, 1868. Writer and activist Alice Dunbar-Nelson despaired in a May 13, 1931, entry: "Oh hell, what's the use. No good. Nobody wants my stuff."

Among the many authors who have used their diaries to develop their craft or stockpile ideas, limber up, kickstart projects, and untangle creative knots (or try to), Virginia Woolf stands out because she expounded on much of this *in* her diary, which she kept for twenty-seven years until four days before her death in 1941. Credit also goes to Woolf's husband, Leonard, who selected entries from Virginia's twenty-six diary volumes that address her writing life to include in *A Writer's Diary*, first published in 1953. In his introduction to the abridged diary, Leonard wrote that, as a diarist, Virginia "communed with herself about the books she was writing, or about future books" and "discusses the day-to-day problems of plot or form, of character or exposition." She also charted her writing schedule for her novel *Mrs. Dalloway*. Of diary writing itself, she wrote in an entry on April 20, 1919: "The habit of writing thus for my own eye only is good practice. It loosens the ligaments."

Woolf distinguished her "diary writing" from "writing." Yet she "explicitly approached the diary itself as literature," maintains Canadian scholar Elizabeth Podnieks. Woolf edited her entries and worked to create a steady narrative, partly by rereading old entries before writing new ones. She often imagined her diary in "fictional terms," writes Podnieks, a Toronto Metropolitan University English professor, pointing to Woolf's March 20, 1926, entry that seems to envision an external audience for her entries: "I daresay there is a little book in them; if the scraps and scratching were straightened out a little."

Leonard Woolf caught flak for withholding Virginia's entries about her personal life. Virginia's English audience wanted everything related to "her existence as an entirety," writes novelist Elizabeth Bowen in her 1954 review of *A Writer's Diary*. Leonard had his reasons, notes Bowen: he didn't want to publish too-personal entries about people still alive, and he thought that a diary provided a distorted portrait, because diarists, he said, so often write only when they're miserable. Leonard's editing corrected "the unbalance there might have been," writes Bowen. Plus, Bowen added, he knew Virginia best.

Over two decades after the publication of Woolf's abridged diary, an unabridged version was published in five volumes between 1977 and 1984. The full-bodied version shows how Woolf used her diary not just to explore writing ideas but also to record travel, ponder illness, detail nature, and describe the soul. This version also shows that Woolf's writing was influenced by reading the published diaries of Samuel Pepys, Fanny Burney, Dorothy Wordsworth and the like, notes a review of Barbara Lounsberry's acclaimed three-volume critical study. To Woolf's nephew and biographer, Quentin Bell, the diary proved to be her true masterpiece.

ooo

Contemporary authors' diaries also intersect with their art. When American poet Adrienne Su was a child, she channeled her writerly aspirations into journaling, she told me. "Writers write journals because they're writers," she recalled at age fifty-six. "It felt very much like I was a writer, and it seemed like the thing to do." Su told me that her journal is for herself, to process her life, while her poems are for other readers *and* for herself, "to understand something."

Su's occasional ambivalence about her journal writing surfaced in her poem "The Days," published in the *New Yorker* in 2022. The poem questions whether chronicling her life detracts from experiencing it in the moment and describes her attempt to destroy journal volumes by putting them out "with the trash." (Her mother rescues them.) "The Days" raises many questions about journal keeping: Maybe our thoughts should remain in our head, not put on paper. Maybe we are gazing not examining, writing just to write, our constant reflection producing "simply an image." Maybe nightly writing to detail "what happened," like a kid trying to make "her small life exciting," mistakes the plot for the story. While the written page promises permanence ("sanctifying time"), readers may misinterpret it. The page may be vulnerable, the poem declares, to "accidental download by enemy."

Brooklyn writer Tyler Wetherall used her 1990s teenage diary to tap into "the inner workings of a young girl's mind" for *Amphibian*, her 2024 debut novel about girlhood. Although her adolescent entries are "a litany of boy crushes and girl cruelties, they do offer my adult self material," Wetherall explained in an essay at age forty. "It's hard to recall our childhood selves without superimposing an adult narrative." The diary allowed Wetherall to "feel what it is to be in a 12-year-old body again. To have 12-year-old thoughts." As a novelist, she is "not reflecting back any longer; I am reexperiencing."

For British-born novelist and diarist Pico Iyer, "the lines between what I write for myself and what I will ultimately write for publication are pretty blurred." The overlap between journal and fiction is mysterious when described by Alice Walker. In 2022, Walker published a book of selected journal entries, *Gathering Blossoms Under Fire*, that address her personal life, art, and activism from 1965 to 2000. "While I was writing the journals, I was also writing, in another realm, worlds that I discovered in my imagination. Novels, poems, short stories, etc.," Walker writes in the 2021 postscript. In a journal entry dated January 8, 2000, she suggests this overlap was common: "I picked a line from this very journal & soon it expanded into—the beginning of something. I was amazed. As usual."

For journalists who keep a personal diary while reporting on, say, a war or a political race (that may feel like a war), publishing entries later in an article or book is a way to share material that didn't make an editor's cut or to voice personal opinions deemed inappropriate for "unbiased" old-school media. "The Barnsley public baths are very bad. Old-fashioned bathtubs, none too clean, and not nearly enough of them," George Orwell wrote in a March 18, 1936, journal entry during a fact-finding trip to England's depressed industrial North. The trip provided raw material for his 1937 book *The Road to Wigan Pier*, which documents hard times for the working class.

ooo

Singer-songwriters also report harvesting material from their diaries to write aching personal songs. Most of Alanis Morrissette's intensely introspective lyrics on her blockbuster 1996 album, *Jagged Little Pill*, came from her diary's interior monologue. Stevie Nicks, of the band Fleetwood Mac, leafed through the tear-stained pages of her velvet-covered journal during a 1997 interview and said: "As I'm writing prose, I'm also writing songs." Taylor Swift offered a special CD version of her *Lover* album in 2019 that came with a booklet of her diary entries written between ages thirteen and twenty-seven. "I frequently and drastically changed my opinions on love, friends, confidence, and trust," Swift, then twenty-nine, explained in an introduction.

The diary entries recall the pop superstar's shaky early days. "Oh, I tried to practice my songs for Nashville, but I completely psyched myself out and broke down crying. I don't know if I can do this," thirteen-year-old Taylor wrote on May 19, 2003. A photo of this handwritten entry appeared in the *New York Times*, along with a spirited conversation between two music writers dissecting her entries. Noting Swift's "seven varyingly diaristic albums," reporter

Joe Coscarelli declared, "These carefully selected and expertly pruned diary pages might somehow be the single most revealing cumulative [Swift] artifact. . . . I'm not sure she'll ever need a memoir if she has hundreds more of these pages lying around." He describes Swift's entries as the "skeleton key to an Established Persona," revealing her acute self-awareness. Critic Jon Caramanica was stunned by the "prescience" of Swift's early entries: "Here was a teenager with uncommon drive, fully formed ambition and the wherewithal to write it all down as if anticipating the needs of fans, scholars and The New York Times."

Singer-songwriter Lucy Dacus's childhood journal informed the songs on her third album, but she focused on what was *missing* in the entries. "Almost reliably the perspective is true and the entry is not and I'm pissed about that because I would really like to know what I thought in the moment," Dacus, then twenty-six, said in 2021. "I really was just hovering around the fact that I was not straight. A lot of the songs . . . are about that." Comedy writer Merrill Markoe struggled to connect with her teenage self, as found in her diary. She illustrates this in her 2020 graphic memoir by drawing her adult self and her adolescent self sitting on a park bench. The elder Merrill asks: "Just curious. In what way did you think this stuff you were writing could help people?" Young Merrill responds: "WHO ARE YOU? WHY do you care? Leave me alone."

Not every successful creative finds diary keeping useful for their art. English writer Zadie Smith gave up trying to keep a diary. "I have some mental block when it comes to diaries and journals," Smith wrote in a 2015 essay. She couldn't block out a possible audience—which ruined diary writing for her. Diary writing feels like homework; the writing, dishonest. First-person entries make her self-conscious and even a bit ill. "I realize I don't want any record of my days," Smith recalls. Instead, she suspects that her selective "non-memory" is "obliquely connected to the way I write my fiction." She wonders if her inability to remember dates or major events "clears a path" to remember salient details such as the exact "warp and weft" of the doormat in her former apartment.

ooo

Among the diarists who intend their diary *as* their art—and written to be published—Claude Fredericks proves a colorful, if extreme, example. As a classics professor at Vermont's Bennington College, a poet, printer, and playwright, Fredericks was an epic self-chronicler, writing a journal for eight decades, from age eight until shortly before his death in 2013 at age eighty-nine—some 65,000 pages. He was producing "one of the longest books about a single hero ever written," Fredericks wrote, adding, "This journal is a work of permanent importance." Because a journal writer doesn't know what comes next, a journal "captures how complex experience actually is," better than a novel can, Fredericks argues.

Unable to get a publishing deal, Fredericks started transcribing his journal late in life and self-published six volumes up to 1943. The Getty Research Institute in Los Angeles later bought the journal, as well as other papers, which is where writer Benjamin Anastas found them. The journal "may well prove to be the longest continuous record of an American life on paper," wrote Anastas in a 2021 *New Yorker* profile titled "The Most Ambitious Diary in History." When Anastas joined the Bennington faculty in 2012, he learned about Fredericks, who taught at the college from 1961 to 1992. After two years of reading as much of the journal as he could "manageably digest," Anastas declared that what he'd read was "addictively engrossing and fatally tedious . . . the strange chronicle of a 'great' man whose genius is recognized almost exclusively by the chronicler himself."

One opportunity for Fredericks to publish his diary came and went in 1954 when Anaïs Nin—who knew Fredericks from Greenwich Village literary life—proposed that they team up on a publication with entries from their two journals, using pseudonyms because some would be considered scandalous. Fredericks—"not one to share the stage," observed Anastas—did not seize the day. In 1966, at age sixty-three, Nin began publishing her diary, becoming a renowned literary diarist. "Perhaps no one sought recognition through her diary more than Nin," writes Elizabeth Podnieks. And she got it.

"Anais Nin, Author Whose Diaries Depicted Intellectual Life, Dead," reads the headline of Nin's *New York Times* obituary on January 16, 1977, which notes: "Miss Nin began writing in the early 1930s and produced criticism, essays and fiction. But her literary reputation blossomed with the publication . . . of her diaries." Nin became determined to publish her diary after her stories and novels failed to earn more than "underground recognition," writes Rupert Pole, Nin's second husband and literary executor. Diary readers were initially drawn to Nin's introspective entries on topics such as the nature of self. After an "uncut" diary version was published posthumously, readers were drawn to Nin's descriptions of soon-to-be-famous friends and sexually explicit accounts of affairs with some, which she cut from the first version.

An early review hailed Nin's initially published diary as a "literary accomplishment," helping to establish her foothold in "a pantheon of literary authors as diarists," notes Podnieks. Tracing how it all began, Podnieks writes that Nin, as an aspiring writer, initially viewed her diary (begun at age eleven in 1914) as a practice space. Gradually, her diary also became a literary site, where she produced work blurring the boundary between diary and fiction. This was her ticket to commercial and critical success. On June 10, 1931, Nin notified her diary that she had begun her "life's real work, the transposition of my Journal into a printable form." She painstakingly prepared her entries for publication by creating typescripts of her journals that she rounded out with new entries. "In this way Nin was working like a novelist—inventing, controlling, editing, and revising her material," writes Podnieks. At the same time, Nin wrote novels, which she offered to publishers as a package deal, of sorts, with her diary. This is how her diary found a publisher.

Nin's novella *Djuna*, published in 1939, echoes the love triangle with writer Henry Miller and his wife, June, that she chronicled in her diary. But, in an October 27, 1933, diary entry, Nin distinguishes between the writing in her book ("the work of art," she writes) and in her diary: "In the book, restraint, indirectness, trickeries! But I need a place where I can shout and weep. . . . I record here the hysteria life causes me." Nin the novelist and Nin the diarist had "an uneasy relationship," notes Rupert Pole. He points to another 1933 entry in which Nin had written: "My book [the novella] and my journal step on each other's feet constantly. I can neither divorce nor reconcile them. I play the traitor to both. I am more loyal to my journal, however."

For some, Nin as diarist-artist became an inspirational feminist symbol: lauded for surviving in a male-dominated literary world, for her daring sexual freedom, and for bravely sharing a woman's take on sex. For others, she was self-centered, pretentious, a bigamist (she married Pole while already married), a pornographer (she published erotica), sexually perverse (as an adult, she had an affair with the father she didn't grow up with), deceptive, and too fixated on her relationships with men. Nin was criticized for "self-advertising," reported the *New York Times*, but she countered that "the 'self' in my work is merely an instrument of awareness" and serves as a springboard to studying relationships.

Predating Nin was that other ambitious diarist, Marie Bashkirtseff, the young Russian French painter in Paris who hoped her self-absorbed diary would be published and earn her immortality. (Her artwork had garnered little interest.) Bashkirtseff, whose lungs were badly damaged by tuberculosis, knew that she'd die young—as she did, at age twenty-five, in 1884. Her diary was published in 1887 (initial title: *I Am the Most Interesting Book of All*), thanks to the efforts of her grief-stricken mother. It quickly became a cultural phenomenon in France and, later, the US. "If I should not live long enough to become famous, this journal will be interesting to the psychologist," Bashkirtseff wrote in the preface. "The record of a woman's life, written down day by day, without any attempt at concealment, as if no one in the world were ever to read it, yet with the purpose of being read, is always interesting; for I am certain I will be found sympathetic, and I will write down everything, everything, everything."

The 1889 English translation of Bashkirtseff's diary won a following in the US, as well as consternation for its "immense egotism." More recently, Bashkirtseff has been likened to the modern-day self-curating/promoting celebrity Kim Kardashian. Bashkirtseff's diary was read by future diarists, including Anaïs Nin (at age eighteen) and Mary MacLane, of Montana, who at age twenty made a big splash (as the "American Bashkirtseff") with the 1902 publication of her teenage diary, titled *The Story of Mary MacLane, By Herself*. No slouch in the ego department, MacLane wrote in her opening entry on January 13, 1901: "I of womankind and of nineteen years, will now begin to set down as full and frank a Portrayal as I am able of myself, Mary MacLane, for whom the world contains not a parallel." Although MacLane earned notoriety and some financial success, she died "poor and obscure" in a Chicago hotel room in 1929.

ooo

Imagine uploading five hundred thousand words from ten years' worth of old journal volumes into a computer program to arrange the sentences alphabetically—and then trimming and shaping this into a new work. That's what Canadian-born novelist Sheila Heti did to write *Alphabetical Diaries*, published in 2024. Heti is among several writers who have used their diaries in weird and wonderful ways to produce hard-to-define texts that may resemble another literary form (say, memoir or fiction) or are a hybrid. An early version of Heti's project ran as a ten-part newspaper series, billed as "an intimate self-portrait that started as a diary and evolved into an experimental work of autofiction." (Autofiction combines autobiography and fiction.) Heti reports that, over the years, the project "grew into something more novelistic. . . . The self's report on itself is surely a great fiction."

American novelist Heidi Julavits—a friend of Heti's—challenged conventional notions of diaries and time with her clever 2015 nonfiction book, *The Folded Clock: A Diary*. Although written in diary form with dated entries, the dates are scrambled, so, for instance, a June entry is both preceded *and* followed by an August entry, with time folding into itself. (I soon gave up trying to figure out the timeframe and started ignoring the dates, which made me wonder if I do this when reading other diaries, taking for granted the forward march of time.) Each entry begins with "`Today I`"—an homage to Julavits's childhood diary—but often meanders away from chronicling the day's events into bracing, sometimes funny meditations on time, truth, relationships and beyond. (More conventional diaries often do this too.) Was each entry written on the date that accompanies it? In one entry, Julavits admits she's "pretending" that she wrote the diary over the course of a year.

Twentieth-century French writer Simone de Beauvoir produced a diary-memoir hybrid by inserting portions of her diary into her memoir. "It is now, in an agony of loneliness, that I began to keep a diary," she wrote. "Its entries strike me as more vivid and accurate than any narrative I could piece together out of them, so I give them here, omitting only certain boring or over-intimate details, and a mass of tedious repetition." Tina Brown's

2017 *The Vanity Fair Diaries* also reads as part diary and part memoir, for good reason. Brown read the 1980s diary she'd kept during her high-flying magazine-editing career as prep for a possible memoir about the "Crazy Eighties," but, as she recalls in her book: "I realized I had already written one." For the book, she cleaned up entries "written in the heat of the moment . . . inevitably rife with errors, names half remembered, dates scrambled, relationships confused, professions and titles bollixed up." Yet she made sure to leave "intact the immediacy of the original text."

Other diarists write "diary fiction," making creative use of their diary-writing *experience*, if not their diary's *content*. Although diary purists argue that *true* diaries are nonfiction or "antifiction," the fictional diary is a literary staple, ranging from a novel written in diary form to a diary used as a literary device to reveal a character's thoughts. You don't have to be a diarist to create a fictional diary. But I wasn't surprised when British writer Helen Fielding reported in 2024 that she'd discovered her college diary. Fielding hit pay dirt with her 1996 novel *Bridget Jones's Diary*. In her personal diary, Fielding self-tracked her calorie intake (Egg 75/Cottage cheese 100/Pickle 10), reminding me of the fictional Bridget, who wrote: "128 lbs. (v. bloody g. but what is point?), alcohol units 2 (excellent), cigarettes 7, calories 3100 (poor)."

Reader reactions to *Bridget Jones's Diary* also reveal views about diary writing and diaries. When I first read this fictional diary, I was a single thirty-something like Bridget (and like Helen Fielding, when her novel was published). Especially as a diarist, I found Bridget's diary writing about her struggle to lose weight and establish a career and relationship familiar and funny. (I'm not alone in relating to the novel, given its enduring popularity, sequels, and film adaptations.) But in Diary-land, I was surprised to learn that some view Bridget as a poster child for the diary's ineffectiveness as a self-help tool because her diary writing fails to change her. (All that self-monitoring and she's *still* obsessing about her body's shortcomings and about men.) The "idea of using [a] diary to take control of your life and access an authentic self . . . is what the novel both promises and parodies," writes Australian scholar Kylie Cardell. In a 2025 interview, Helen Fielding offered a revealing description of her "huge collection" of self-help books as "inspiring but sadly ineffective." All this clashed with my memory that

Bridget's life *did* improve; she found love with a good (if dull) guy, although I didn't give diary writing the credit.

For better or worse, Bridget Jones was among seven real-life women (including Margaret Thatcher, Germaine Greer, and Beyoncé) credited with having the biggest impact on women's lives in a 2016 "Power List" concocted by an English radio show. Bridget made the list for being relatable to many women and helping them accept themselves, flaws and all. With Bridget already damned as a navel-gazing, insufficiently feminist, diet-culture dupe, the character's appearance on this list was also criticized because she's fictional. Yet this tell-tale sign of the cultural impact of *Bridget Jones's Diary* made me wonder if some of that fairy dust has drifted onto the diary, making it a cultural icon too.

The late British writer Sue Townsend also created an unforgettable fictional diarist in her funny and poignant 1982 novel *The Secret Diary of Adrian Mole, Aged 13¾*, the first of a popular series. "Now I *know* I am an intellectual. . . . A bad home, poor diet, not liking punk. I think I will join the library and see what happens," Adrian writes in one entry. But when a journalist asked Townsend in 2009 whether she kept a diary of her own, she laughed and answered with a non-answer: "I prefer to keep my secrets to myself."

ooo

Is diary writing a useful practice for aspiring artists? Madeleine L'Engle, who started her journal at age eight, advises young writers to "keep an honest, unpublishable journal that nobody reads, nobody but you. Where you just put down what you think about life, what you think about things, what you think is fair and what you think is unfair."

Joyce Carol Oates devoted a section of her online course "The Art of the Short Story" to the "immensely helpful" practice of journal writing. She recommends writing longhand "because it's so intimate and so private." Write to develop a writer's essentials, she says: the ability to observe closely, to think deeply for sustained periods of time, to describe the world in language. Write quickly, impressionistically, she says, describing places, conversation snippets, and reactions to the world—all this sharpens the senses. "It's the self that you're expressing when you write a diary," Oates tells students. It "doesn't have to be elegant writing." And, yes, entries that appear "ordinary" today may provide material for future art.

Humorist David Sedaris encourages aspiring writers to kickstart their careers, as he did, by diary writing. "When you start writing, you're going to suck. So it's kind of good to keep the writing to yourself, until maybe you don't suck as much," Sedaris advises in a video. A diarist for over forty years, Sedaris initially kept his diary to himself. "I never handed my diary over to anyone. I would die," he says. "I mean I was sitting at the International House of Pancakes in Raleigh, North Carolina, with a beret screwed to my head. So it's the writing you would expect from that person."

But diary writing is the gift that keeps on giving, providing material for Sedaris's personal essays, stage performances, and books, including diary entry collections. "It's sort of how I became a writer, reading back through my diaries, and just choosing things and thinking 'Oh, this might be of interest.' Sometimes it would only be like three sentences in a four-page diary entry," Sedaris recalls. Suspecting, while diary writing, that an entry might later be read on stage does risk the writing becoming "overproduced," he admits in his 2021 published diary collection. Some entries that worked well on stage didn't make it into the collection "because they seemed too self-conscious, too eager to please."

Rick Steves credits his 1978 trip as a twenty-three-year-old on the "hippie trail" from Istanbul to Kathmandu—and the diary he kept documenting the trip's "vivid" moments—with inspiring his successful travel writing career, although his guidebook's audience and content differ from his diary's. "I was writing that for me," he said while promoting the 2025 publication of that long-ago diary, which was written "in the humid buggy reality with all the cacophony of culture all around."

Some professionals offer formal instruction in diary writing for creative purposes. In Copenhagen, in 2022, three diary-writing artists founded Dagbogsskolen (The Diary School), offering a semester-long course on creating and developing a personal diary practice. It has attracted primarily women ages thirty to sixty-five. "We wanted to build a community based on diary writing," the founders told me via email, adding, "The diary can be a room of sorrow, of finding your own voice, of inspiration to artistic practice." In

New York, journaling coach and entrepreneur Laura Rubin offers journaling workshops to corporate workers to help them "tap into their creative flow." In Washington, DC, psychologist Ellen K. Baker has taught journal writing workshops at the National Museum of Women in the Arts, presenting the diary as a creative assist to art making *and* to the art itself.

Grinnell College English professor Paula Vene Smith has assigned students to keep diaries as "an antidote" to our frenetic multitasking culture, offering a rare opportunity to focus, with sustained attention, on observing life. The novelist and creative writing professor Martha McPhee has assigned diary writing to students at New York's Hofstra University. She wrote in 2020, "I could see in this new social media world a need for my students to return to something elemental, something that would peel them away from clicking and posting, tapping out haikus with their overworked thumbs. Something that they create by hand and for themselves and no one else." American diary scholar Angela Hooks raises an interesting dilemma: when instructors assign diary writing, should they read and grade their students' diaries? "How can the self be graded, particularly for students who are discovering themselves?" writes Hooks. She devised a workaround, reading only her students' final entries, which were responses to an assigned reflective prompt on diary writing.

Sometimes a best-selling self-help book includes what resembles diary writing. Julia Cameron's *The Artist's Way* (offering, per the subtitle, *A Spiritual Path to Higher Creativity*) prescribes writing daily "Morning Pages." This stream-of-consciousness writing (three handwritten pages per day) is meant to clear the way for creative thinking and your inner artist. As the "bedrock tool of creative recovery," Morning Pages are "not high art. They are not even 'writing,'" explains Cameron. Instead, they "provoke, clarify, comfort, cajole, prioritize and synchronize the day at hand." *The Artist's Way* has sold more than four million copies since 1992 and boasts well-known practitioners like Elizabeth Gilbert, author of *Eat, Pray, Love*. Helen Churko, the New York–based multi-form self-chronicler, has written Morning Pages for over thirty years and says that what she writes doesn't matter. "I could write 'I eat peanut butter' repeatedly," Churko told me. If the pages produce something worth saving, she transcribes it into her "regular journal." Morning Pages have produced the occasional creative breakthrough, but she credits the practice more with fostering a creative approach to life.

In 2007 came the self-described "guerrilla artist" Keri Smith with *Wreck This Journal*, marketed as the "anarchist's *Artist's Way*." The bestseller reads as part spoof, part sincere nonfiction, with illustrated pages that invite mistake making and chaotic prompts to inspire creativity. Among my favorites: "Tie a string to the spine of this book. Swing wildly, let it hit the walls." Suleika Jaouad's 2025 guide to "the art of journaling" highlights "how this life-altering and even life-saving practice can help us transform life's interruptions and tap into that mystical trait that exists in every human: creativity." Jaouad's journaling evangelism has since included offering her personally designed "alchemy journal" and promoting "journaling clubs." A gathering in Jaouad's Brooklyn living room to journal and discuss journaling was featured in an August 2025 *Wall Street Journal* story headlined "How Journaling Went from a Solo Activity to a Social One."

Alexandra Johnson's 2001 book, *Leaving a Trace: The Art of Transforming a Life into Stories*, made me a tad defensive. Her well-intentioned offer to help me repurpose my diary entries into "a lasting piece of work" or "something permanent" (perhaps a "celebrated published memoir") suggested that my diary is a *mere* diary (as Anaïs would say). And the emphasis on being a productive diarist who churns out "the successful journal" felt to me like a killjoy way to turn diary writing into a chore and the diary into a commercial product.

ꝏꝏ

Sometimes I write in my diary about my professional work, chronicling impressions that may later surface in published pieces. Sometimes I scribble down my ideas or adventures because they might, as Alice Walker puts it, prove useful for writing in another realm. (Who knew that realm would produce a book *about* diaries?) I also occasionally use my diary as a commonplace book, jotting down inspiring bits and bobs that I've read or heard. And I am not afraid of the blank page (or screen), thanks to my diary, which compels me to face one every day. As a writer, what I most appreciate about my diary is that it offers a break from journalism. In my diary, I can be uncertain, unclear, sloppy, foul-mouthed, inaccurate, and, yes, biased. Diary writing offers a mental break from my day job and the freedom to write whatever the hell I want and to not care if my diary is *successful*. Diary writing is a creative act and an art, letting me explore ways of writing, thinking, and being. It feeds my soul.

I was taken by French writer Annie Ernaux's comparison of two of her published works, both about a tempestuous affair she had in the 1980s, while she was in her late forties, with a thirty-five-year-old married Russian diplomat. One is a fictionalized account of her affair, published in 1992 as *Simple Passion*. The other is her journal account, first published in French in 2001. An English translation, *Getting Lost*, followed. "I perceived there was a 'truth' in those [journal] pages that differed from the one to be found in *Simple Passion*—something raw and dark, without salvation, a kind of *oblation*. I thought that this, too, should be brought to light," Ernaux explained in her opener to *Getting Lost*.

When Ernaux won the 2022 Nobel Prize in Literature, she was cited for "the courage and clinical acuity with which she uncovers the roots, estrangements and collective restraints of personal memory." During her all-consuming affair, she only "truly wrote" in her journal, which she'd kept on and off since adolescence. Ernaux recalls: "It was a way of enduring the wait until we saw each other again, of heightening the pleasure by recording the words and acts of passion. Most of all, it was a way to save life, save from nothingness the thing that most resembles it." She wrote in her journal on October 16, 1989: "I wanted to make this passion a work of art in my life, or rather this affair became a passion because I wanted it to be a work of art."

Ernaux's journal is, by turns, fascinating, embarrassing, and horrifying to read, with unflinching descriptions of acrobatic sex and desperate longing. Publishing it was a stunning and appalling act of literary bravery, especially given the author's insistence on making no changes or deletions other than obscuring some people's names, including her lover's name. She explains in *Getting Lost*: "For me, words set down on paper to capture the thoughts and sensations of a given moment are as irreversible as time—are time itself."

7

Hindsight

Should We Read or Burn Our Diaries?

Standing onstage before a large audience, thirty-five-year-old Eileen Tull reads with gusto from the diary she wrote in August 1999, when she was eleven: "My favorite band is The Backstreet Boys. Brian Littrell is hotter than anyone alive . . . his caring blue eyes, his pouty mouth, his locks of brown curls, his buff body. His romantic side. Everything I want in a guy. I wish Brian were 12 and was going out with me. By the way, we got the Internet. It's cool."

A wave of laughter fills Chicago's funky Music Box Theatre during a performance twenty-four years after that 1999 entry. The live audience, including me, laughs again as Tull shares her diary's star-studded "Summer of 2000 Hotties" list: "Number one, Matt LeBlanc; number two, Josh, a boy from my youth group; number three, Ben Affleck; number four, Will Smith . . . " The diary reading shifts to young Eileen's embrace of Roman Catholicism in August 2000—and another crush: "The Pope is so cool. Today we had youth group. There was a teaching. . . . . It really applied to my life so much. It was about persecution," reads Tull, who then adds: "This from a white girl in Ohio."

More laughter.

Thus unfurled another rousing, relatable performance of *Mortified Live*, billed as "humorous storytelling from everyday people" who read aloud "their most embarrassing, pathetic, and private teenage diary entries" and other personal jottings "in front of total strangers." A self-described forum for "personal redemption through public humiliation," *Mortified* is arguably a sign of our over-sharing, over-self-documenting candor culture. But the show struck me as a healthy way to process the old diaries that so many of us have lying around, packed with youthful indiscretions, humiliations, and frustrations. Why not recast our geeky teen entries as humor for a crowd? Although, of course, diarists whose early decades (and diaries) offer little to laugh about, then or now, may prefer to burn their scribbled proof of pain.

Diary burning is a hot topic in Diary-land. Although I couldn't burn my diary, I questioned the value of *reading* it. Is there a feel-good (or feel-okay) way to read our diaries—and even learn from them? To investigate, I read more of my old entries, which proved, by turns, illuminating, disorienting, distressing, and amusing. And I turned to journaling gurus and mental health experts, as well as diarists who have also dived deep into their old entries.

ooo

Yanking and yanking the overstuffed drawer of my drab-gray fireproof filing cabinet, it finally opens, revealing a helter-skelter of diary volumes: my life boiled down to a mishmash of old, battered books. Stacked any which way they'd fit, the volumes have the makings of a museum exhibit: *Diary Design Across the Decades.* First: "Teen Classic," a worn preformatted chunky one from 1976, with a screaming Day-Glo yellow cover and "Diary" written in a flower power–ish font. Next: "Young Adult Aspirational," 1980s and 1990s journals with minimal formatting and tasteful covers clad in Scottish plaid, Italian marbled paper, or pressed wildflowers. Finally: "Middle/Older Age Sensible," from the early 2000s forward, mostly no-name hardcover notebooks (unlined pages preferred!) but also some fancy-pants imported notebooks.

I love and fear them all.

I generally view my old diary volumes with wistful affection, as tangible evidence of my life's various and sundry chapters. They are a record of my most enduring relationship—the one with myself—but sometimes they seem to lurk, their presence verging on the menacing. So many pages, so densely populated with my messy microscopic script; so much hidden that I'll never know (because I'd need another lifetime to read them all); so many questions they might raise or answer, or not; so many potential surprises.

I have expectations that my old entries can tell me (or help me understand) who I was and how I became who I am—kind or cruel, knowing or naïve, smart or oh so stupid. I'd like to think they include favorable, if not always glowing, accounts of the many people and places I've come to adore; that they confirm, not contradict, what I have labeled a mostly good, happy, and lucky life. Will I find the self I think I know? Should I disregard the moody, *everything sucks* entries as atypical? Will I want to destroy *my* diary?

How to even begin reading my old dears? After initially searching my diary for A-list experiences to investigate memory, I decided to explore the notion that diaries chronicle a diarist's *life* and document our *times* (and, yes, *world*). First, I'd look to see if entries revealed my so-called "arc of a life," a term that harkens back to Aristotle. Studying why Greek tragedies packed a punch, Aristotle identified their common dramatic features, including a narrative arc with a beginning-middle-end and an issue-change-resolution. To discern my life's arc to date, I set out to read entries from the same day of the month over fifty years. Call it my *Fifty-Year Journal*, an extreme version of those five-year journals with each page per date divided into five measly sections for "micro-entries." I chose May 12, a nod to the UK's 12th May Diary Day, a social research project that has inspired thousands of people to document their May 12 over the years.

Second, to see if I'd documented *our times*, I picked a handful of days from each decade that became historic—Nixon's 1974 resignation, the 1979–81 Iran hostage crisis, the September 11, 2001, terrorist attacks—to see what, if anything, I wrote. (Was I more preoccupied with chronicling *my life*?)

ooo

Need to burn your diary?

Some variation of this question pops up periodically in advice columns and online discussion sites like Reddit, where I found a lively back-and-forth in its well-populated r/Journaling community. Online and off, journal destroyers and journal keepers (who write *and* save a journal) debate. Some destroyers sound relieved: Do it! You'll feel lighter, happier! How healthy to purge your unpleasant thoughts and bad habits! Why keep a journal obsessed with life's dark matter or offering an outdated self-portrayal? God forbid family and friends discover your frivolous, poorly written self-reveals or caustic commentary about *them*! Don't dump them in the dumpster. Too risky—they might be found. Better to burn, baby, burn!

But other destroyers express regrets, sounding much like the journal keepers who argue: Don't do it! You'll wish you had it later! How healthy to read about your old life and selves, however dark or dissatisfying. A journal is a time capsule, therapeutic to write *and* read. You're reading your former self's mind! No one else wants to read it or if they do, they'll know it's not the entire, current, or true you. Share it with your struggling teenagers. Still worried? Redact what you don't want revealed.

Elsewhere on the internet, I found a mother-daughter battle over diary burning, recounted by the daughter in a 2019 essay for the online literary magazine *Cagibi*. Recalling the battle, Taymiya R. Zaman tells us that in 2015, her seventy-something mother, Riffat, wanted to burn the diary she kept during her teens in the 1960s—writing first in Pakistan and later in the United States, where she did doctoral training in clinical psychology. Burning would help Riffat declutter her life, but Taymiya wanted to save the diary volumes, for professional and personal reasons, as a historian "committed to preserving the past" and a loving daughter. "A mother is a first archive, the most primary of sources," writes Taymiya, a University of San Francisco history professor studying historical memory in South Asia. But her "mother is an archive that talks back, argues, and insists her words do not belong to me and are not mine to interpret."

Riffat's 1960s teenage diary, Taymiya argues, is a valuable historical source that documents a girl's adolescence during Pakistan's adolescence. (The country was founded in 1947.) "Your diary is the story of a feminist girlhood," she recalls telling her mother, showing an early "awareness that an all-female world is threatened by men and marriage." Riffat counters: "That's ridiculous. Why can't you think about anything other than gender?" Just because Taymiya has "mastered" the diary, counters Riffat, doesn't mean she can change Riffat's past. Furthermore, Riffat says of herself, she is "not important."

In the end, the daughter quotes her mother's diary in her essay. "I took my mother's diary away from her and began transcribing her words with the same frenzy with which she must have once written them," writes Taymiya. Whether quoting the diary is wise, or even ethical, and whether Riffat accepts it, Taymiya doesn't say, but, she writes, "I am tired of women's silences.

Riffat's mother couldn't be a writer because she was a wife and mother. And Riffat gave up writing because words seemed futile. Am I trying to prove her wrong?"

Why not wait until Riffat is no longer living to write about her mother and her diary? Because, writes Taymiya, historians "do enough violence to the dead by claiming their texts and inventing their lives. I want to have arguments with the living. . . . I want to hold my mother's hand as I write about her." Published excerpts from her mother's teenage diary show Riffat questioning why she sleeps in a warm bed while others with less sleep outside in the cold; Riffat lamenting the many lives lost during Pakistan's war with India; Riffat bristling at how women are treated in Pakistan. "When I was young I used to be enthusiastic to see brides but now I hate it," reads a September 17, 1962, entry. "I really pity them, they are treated like animals in a zoo, everyone coming and staring at them."

In the media, I also found diarists debating themselves. "I Don't Want Anyone to Read My Diaries, Yet I Can't Burn Them," reads a March 2025 headline of a *New York Times* opinion piece by American novelist and memoirist Dani Shapiro. Faced with a potentially life-threatening illness, Shapiro starts burning entries full of "obsessions, petty jealousies, fantasies, secret crushes, stinging rejection." But after a few sentences grab her, she stops. She realizes she is setting fire to "an entire world of lost relics," which feels akin to killing her younger self, who "was more eloquent and self-aware" than remembered. She recalls finding "wise counsel" from the published diaries of Virginia Woolf and sculptor Anne Truitt: "Reading about their inner lives helps me make sense of my own." Now unable to "let go" of her diary, Shapiro suggests that diarists own our "flawed, messy narrative, rather than burn it," concluding, "Whether we encounter our own long-ago words or our children do or our grandchildren or a world of rapt strangers, perhaps it is in this dialogue of one—unpolished, raw, without discipline—that we offer testimony into the void. That we say: This is me. I was human. And so are you."

"My journals nearly destroyed me, so I nearly destroyed them," reads the headline of a 2019 online essay by Ruth Estelle of Australia, who likens journal burning to *dostadning*, the Swedish "death cleanse" done to clean and declutter one's home, sparing others from having to do it after your death.

Estelle describes her desire to destroy her journal volumes (started at age eleven) as "part Marie Kondo, part sort-your-crap-out as if you are about to die." Eight years earlier, she recalls, she started reading years' worth of entries, searching for "maternal musings" to give her son on his eighteenth birthday. She stumbled upon entries confirming issues in her long-term relationship. "Those damn journals, with their damn record keeping, had been harboring a ticking emotional truth bomb," she writes. "It exploded and changed my life . . . *utterly*." Estelle ended the relationship.

"I'm much happier now," she writes. But the journal still reminds her of unhappier years: "The thought of burning each and every one of those books has become *very* appealing. All that angst could be turned to ash." Time for a "cathartic bonfire!" But before striking the match, she revisits some entries and finds something unexpected: "A heartfelt journey towards authenticity. A persistent struggle through the vagaries of a creative life. Signs of success. Happiness. . . . A record of a life well-lived by a woman overcoming obstacles and enjoying a blessed life." She nixes the angst-to-ash plan.

Another catchy headline in 2021: "My early diaries filled me with so much shame I burned them. I'm publishing the rest." Australian author Helen Garner writes that when she revisited her diary as she neared her eightieth birthday, she got "so bored with my younger self and her droning sentimental concerns . . . this shit had to go." Into the fire they went: "Flames from the barbecue licked the heavens. . . . I have never for a second regretted this conflagration." She spared later entries, written since her mid-thirties, because reading "what I'd written back then gradually ceased to embarrass me," perhaps because the writing's tone and content had shifted. The entries were "somehow less grinding and neurotic. And a lot funnier."

Why publish them? Garner fears some assume (incorrectly) that her diary is "a narcissistic spilling of the guts, the sort of ghastly self-glorifying mush that women like Anaïs Nin used to spew out." Instead, Garner deems her diary of interest to readers because it contains common and relatable human experiences. While reading old entries, she found that her "shame and embarrassment gradually shed their power." Memories of her wrongdoings "lost their punitive force, ceased to be weapons I could use to lacerate myself." It helped that her "take on the past" had already relaxed. With time (and psychotherapy), she had learned "to accept that pretty much everybody crashes through the world, hurting other people and hurting themselves—cheating, lying, sneaking, betraying, laying about them with the broad sword—and there grew in me a new camaraderie with the rest of the human race." And her diary is not her full story: it rarely mentions "untroubled times of happiness. . . . Its purpose was always—and still is—to help me get a grip, to keep me on the rails." Her diary writing helps her "understand the things that hurt me, and the hurtful things I can't believe I did to other people," Garner writes. It helps her recognize patterns in her behavior and deal with them.

British journalist Helen Coffey can't stomach her teenage diary's accounts of "searing insecurities and heartaches," let alone that they "were so appallingly written: poorly constructed, desperately self-conscious," she writes in a 2025 article titled "If Someone Published My Diary After I Die, I'd Die Again—of Shame." True, diary writing "allows you to explore and express without the need to impress anyone or edit your thoughts." But Coffey laments how differently she writes "when there is no intended audience." Noting the controversial 2025 publication of Joan Didion's "deeply private" therapy notes/journal, Coffey concludes: "Until there's better legal protection for the dead, perhaps we're all better off doing a Henry James or Charles Dickens and burning our personal papers . . . to ensure they never get into the wrong hands. Excuse me while I find a lighter."

But bell hooks regreted destroying her early entries. Writing them while growing up in rural Kentucky offered solace. Reading them as an adult proved painful. "Growing up was not supposed to be hard and difficult, a time of anguish and torment. Somehow the diaries were another accusing voice declaring that I was not 'normal,'" she recalls in her 1999 memoir. "I destroyed that writing and that tormented and struggling self." Years later, during a "therapeutic process of retrospective self-examination," hooks changed her mind about her early diary, viewing it as "a place of reconciliation and reclamation." Too late. "They were all destroyed," hooks writes. "I really missed this writing and mourned the loss. Since I use journals now to engage in critical self-reflection, confrontation, and challenge, I know that I would be able to know myself differently were I able to read back, to remember with that writing."

"Don't Burn Your Diary!" pleads the title of a post on Desirée Henderson's website, *The Diary Index*. The Texas diary scholar rejects the standard arguments for destroying personal writing: that the writing is silly, shameful, ordinary, dull, or embarrassing, with no inherent literary or historic value. Instead, she argues, "it's possible that there are future uses of your diary that neither you nor I can imagine." She asks readers to consider saving their diaries for their family, descendants, posterity.

Joan Didion argued in favor of reading our writing about our former selves. "I think we are well advised to keep on nodding terms with the people we used to be whether we find them attractive company or not," she wrote in "On Keeping a Notebook," her 1960s essay oft-shared by diarists. "Otherwise they turn up unannounced and surprise us, come hammering on the mind's door at 4 a.m. of a bad night and demand to know who deserted them, who betrayed them, who is going to make amends. We forget all too soon the things we thought we could never forget." (Postscript: Soon after Didion's death, thirteen of her blank notebooks sold for $11,000 in an online estate sale.)

ooo

Mortified Live could be billed as a diarist's worst nightmare. Or at least mine. Yet the event is popular: since its 2002 launch, it has grown to many chapters in cities worldwide, producing live shows and podcasts. At the end of the *Mortified Live* I went to in 2023, the emcee asked the audience: "What did we learn tonight?" and then answered for us: "We are freaks. We are fragile. And we all survived." Hearty applause.

Maybe the secret to positive diary reading is to adopt the self-accepting attitude of *Mortified* performer Eileen Tull, who mined the most relatable humor in what she calls her "very cringey" adolescent diary to best connect with an empathetic crowd. Months after her *Mortified* gig, Tull told me: "We are not making fun of our childhood selves. We are using their words." A career solo performer of autobiographical work, Tull worked with a "story curator" to search her diary for suitable material. She bypassed entries with "big, sad, emotional feelings," choosing others that were more "ripe to make fun of" and would create compelling, cathartic theater. "Writing and performance is an empathy machine," she says. "It's reaching out and saying, 'Here's what I experienced,' so someone else can say, 'I did too.' And now you feel less alone."

Granted, some diaries may be too emotionally difficult or harmful for a diarist to read—and those who suspect they'll be revisiting a traumatic episode from their past should tread cautiously. But, in general, do psychologists and journaling gurus consider reading old diary entries good for our mental health? It depends, Ellen K. Baker, the Washington, DC–based clinical psychologist, told me. If you *do* read, she recommends approaching the diary "in a careful, thoughtful, gentle way." Be aware that you may need to stop. Consult a therapist, if need be, and if you can, summon the trust to share sensitive material.

James W. Pennebaker, the expressive-writing expert, told me that some diarists find it beneficial to read *and* edit old entries. Others find revisiting their diaries sad and depressing. "If you think it's good for you, do it. If you think it's not, don't," he advises. Rosalie Deer Heart and Alison Strickland, coauthors of *Harvesting Your Journal*, another how-to guide, write: "Expect an 'Oh No' experience" and "Be gentle with yourself." Honor the person you used to be, they say. Give your struggling younger self credit for asking hard questions and imagining a better life. The psychologist Ira Progoff declared that "the mere fact of continuously writing entries . . . is not sufficient in itself to bring about deep changes in a person's life." Journal reading (using his structured "feedback process") is a key part of Progoff's Intensive Journal method. Other therapists argue that people can benefit from journaling *without* reading old entries, but that occasional reading can be productive, especially if read with a not-too-critical eye, looking for exaggerations or "negative thought loops" or emerging themes.

An interesting twist: intensive-care or coma patients may benefit from reading a diary written *about* them by a nurse and/or relatives. Studies from Scandinavia, which pioneered the practice in the 1970s, found it can help a patient's psychological recovery. For a former COVID patient, reading a patient diary helped him understand the forty-eight "lost days" he spent in an induced coma and appreciate the compassionate care he received, notebook enthusiast Roland Allen reports.

Destroying a diary is a common choice, Progoff said in a 1981 interview, adding, "I remember saying to one young woman, 'Better your journal than you.'" Diary burning is variously described as a positive experience, a rite of passage, a ceremonial throwing away, a rebirth that was cathartic, moving, or transformative, Henderson reports. Baker, the clinical psychologist, is in the *don't destroy* camp, at least not right away—something she did during a difficult time in her twenties (to get "a fresh start") and now regrets because of the finality. She advises others to put "those journals, those tender feelings, in a safe place" for possible reading later.

As for those diary-like posts on social media, people often write them "to remember, relive, recount, reconcile, and reckon at future points," according to communications professor Lee Humphreys. Why does this later reckoning with our former selves, as found in our old posts or more traditional diary entries, inspire disdain for who we were and even lead to the destruction of what we wrote? One possible answer comes from Canadian psychologists Michael Ross and Anne E. Wilson, whose research explored a human tendency to judge our former selves harshly. "We propose that people are motivated to evaluate their past selves in a way that makes them feel good about themselves now," they write. Alas, they suggest that people's perception that they've improved over time "is sometimes illusory and motivated by the desire to enhance the current self."

ooo

Tears drip down my face as I read diary entries from my forties, when my mother had dementia. My diary's distant words hit me hard today. So do the sometimes-unchronicled memories and the insight, gained in hindsight, that those words prompt. My older self remembers my younger self's exasperation with Mom's odd, distracted behavior, before we knew the cause: *Why does she keep asking me the same question? Why doesn't she listen?* Especially after we knew something was very wrong, I could have—should have—done better, been more patient, giving, kind. Some entries seem more focused on how Mom's illness affected me than her. (Typical self-involved diarist, right?) Yes, I had a lot going on, beyond my mother's illness, and I tried to be supportive. But I see now, including from those twenty-year-old entries, that I distanced myself from Mom. My explanation (or excuse) is that I was psychologically bracing for a devastating loss. My lackluster behavior now seems a desperate, selfish attempt at self-preservation. I was trying to keep it together. I think. I try to forgive myself.

Reading now what I wrote then proved to be a trippy, time-traveling carnival ride. Receiving dispatches from various versions of Betsy, I found myself crashing into my past on a bumper car, disoriented in a funhouse of frenzied noise and light, gaping at sometimes unflattering reflections in a hall of mirrors. This inspired a strange dialogue between my current and former selves. My verb tenses and pronouns got messed up. One minute I am, or was, ashamed of her, or me: when teenage Betsy ditches a friend who agreed to be her date for a Sadie Hawkins high school dance, after a *popular* guy she asked first belatedly said yes. (His car caught on fire as he drove to pick me up.) The next minute I am proud: when adult Betsy has her "Norma Rae" moment, shouting at a boss during a staff meeting to stop bullying her colleague. Or I suddenly have a long view: when I read twenty-eight-year-old Betsy's chronicle of early adventures with her boyfriend's young daughter, a cutie who will become my cherished step-daughter—and today has two young children (my grandsons!). Or I see how relationships change with time: when I read about long-ago squabbles with siblings who today are among my best friends.

Reading, I smile, laugh, wince, scold. Younger Betsy's occasional pontificating and questionable behavior pushes Older Betsy's judge-y buttons. But she tries to be open-minded and tolerant, to find humor in, yes, some mortifying moments, to view her former self in the context of that former era, to protect and justify her former self. (Horrified by my mid-1970s teenage description of a family friend as a "fag," I decide that I lacked better vocabulary back then or didn't recognize the word as a slur.)

Although I tried to stay focused on my chosen "life-and-times" search, I inevitably veered off-course, easily distracted by discoveries—life souvenirs that sometimes dislodged a memory or triggered a struggle to remember. When I opened my 1980 college-semester-in-London diary, ticket stubs for a Chelsea Football Club match (£3.50) and the 12th Inverness Folk Festival (£1.50) fell out. Opening my 1982 roaming-around-the-world diary, I found a long list of the stops I'd made—"Sharm el Sheikh, Corfu, Istanbul, Yugoslavia . . ."—and a tally of my expenses: "Italy—4 weeks $400; Istanbul to London bus—$85." Between the pages of my 1990s diaries, I found a newspaper photo of the French early 1900s actress Sarah Bernhardt (I'm guessing I liked her hairstyle) and a handwritten note from my sweet, funny daughter in grade school—"Mom, here's $5 for the ostrich egg." I suddenly remembered her fascination with that huge egg. (Did we buy it at the Iowa State Fair?)

I began to ask questions about my diary's content, wondering about recurring subjects, emerging themes, shifting perspectives, hidden misdeeds, problematic statements. For convenience, and my sanity, I tried to impose order by creating categories for my entries—People, Places, Problems, Pain, Joy. That soon fell apart. The entries rarely fit neatly into only one category.

Some entries that weren't written to be funny read as funny now. Other entries are an emotional tripwire. When Anne, my plucky friend from Nebraska, occasionally surfaces on the diary page, I remember the pivotal newspaper reporter and mom years that we helped each other through. I miss her. She died of cancer shortly before her sixtieth birthday. Then there's this entry from November 30, 1991, written around two tiny footprints while I was in a Des Moines maternity-wing bed. "Dirck and I have a son. His name is Noah, he's about three hours old and these are his footprints. He was born looking up at the world, which I thought appropriate for the son of two journalists." And this September 4, 2004, entry, written from an assisted living home in Tucson: "Each day seems more grueling than the next. We sat and watched my mother die for 10 hours today. . . . At one point she appeared to [die]. Her breathing went from deep and difficult to shallow and then stopped. [M.] and I sat on her bed beside her painfully thin body and wept. Just wept."

Deep breath.

While I found no high crimes, my diary documents some misdemeanors—often teenage screwups. Although the vast majority of my entries are innocuous (and many bland), my diary is lightly sprinkled with harsh comments about myself and, worse, others. I found the occasional argument, spilled secret, awkward encounter, fractured friendship, blunder, botched effort. I'm relieved these entries are infrequent, that I did not spew venom primarily to be venomous, that instead I was venting, exorcising, trying to understand, get along, salvage a relationship. Or so I tell myself.

I am only human. Or a typical human. But I have regrets. Sometimes, a heated, angry entry is warranted or understandable—I was frustrated, worried; other times I was rash or unfair. I overreacted, messed up. Or my intention was good, my execution faulty. Reading these entries was, by turns, painful, shameful, illuminating, and, occasionally, gratifying because I know now that a once-strained relationship improved.

Reading my May 12th diary entries, I don't see a grand narrative arc worthy of a Greek tragedy. Instead I find a progression, a developing person, an evolving life—and, yes, growth. Even with all the changes, I sense a continuity that strings my thousands of diary entries together, giving my life story a squiggly throughline. My diary offers the long view of me, the process of becoming (as Michelle Obama might say), inviting me to balance self-examination with self-empathy. While I *do* tend to accent the negative, my diary pages recount the positive too: when I was excited, inspired, in love, enjoying family and friends. I found no need to remove that label testifying to a mostly good, happy, and lucky life—although I don't rule out the possibility that my chipper assessment is an attempt to force an upbeat story. Sure, I dislike some of what I wrote, and who I was, but nothing made me want to destroy my diary (or to read much more of it).

As for documenting our times and world, I *was* more interested in chronicling my life and self, at least early on. Any future historians rummaging through my diary may be pleased, disappointed, or puzzled, as I am today, to see which major moments I noted and which I didn't. On December 31, 1974, at age fifteen, I wrote: "I'm very aware that this year is a historic one because of Watergate and the downfall of Nixon. For the record it was a good test of the durability of this nation. It's remarkable that we endured and that things were never that far from normal." (Reading this in 2025 during a harsh new political reality, when we are being sorely tested and so much is *not* normal, I wonder if we'll endure.) Yet, I failed to mention many other major events, including the fall of the Berlin Wall (December 22, 1989) and Nelson Mandela's release from prison (February 11, 1990).

I more often documented big news as I got older (typical, perhaps): terror attacks, especially when close to home (the 1995 Oklahoma City bombing, the World Trade Center bombings in 1993 and 2001); wars (Iraq, Afghanistan, Ukraine, Gaza); Supreme Court decisions (2022's *Dobbs* abortion ruling!); natural disasters (especially severe floods in our Iowa neighborhood during the 1990s that I now connect to climate change); and school shootings, although sadly my reporting on them tapered off, as they became so common. Readers will get a clear idea from my diary entries about my views on various presidents, especially since the 1990s, and especially Donald Trump. Sometimes I was intentionally documenting the world, other times unintentionally. In some instances (Trump), I was writing more to vent than document. Even when I wasn't directly writing in my diary about political changes, cultural highlights, or technological upheavals, they feel present in the background as I read entries today: Vietnam, Watergate, COVID-19; Nixon, Carter, Reagan; the women's movement, *Roe v. Wade*, #MeToo; Carole King, The Pretenders, Billie Eilish; *The Graduate*, *A Chorus Line*, *Thelma & Louise*, *Hamilton*; landlines, faxes, ChatGPT.

Reading my diary, I never felt compelled to critique the quality of my writing, as other writers do. I was focused on the content and purpose. Reading helped me better understand why I write. Thomas Mallon proposed seven categories of diarists in his 1984 diary book: *Chroniclers* (Samuel Pepys, Virginia Woolf); *Travelers* (Lewis and Clark, Queen Victoria); *Pilgrims* (Henry David Thoreau, May Sarton); *Creators* (Mary Shelley, Sylvia Plath); *Apologists* (Richard Nixon, Lee Harvey Oswald); *Confessors* (Puritans, adolescent girls); and *Prisoners* (Alfred Dreyfus, Anne Frank). I probably have fit several categories (in a more modest way), at one time or another. Like many other diarists, I don't write for only one reason, and the reasons fluctuate. An aside: when Mallon describes a Midwestern girl in the early 1960s who ends each entry with "`Love`," I feel a shock of recognition. I signed my early entries: "`Love, Betsy`," later shortened to "`#LB`," used to this day.

Why did I begin and keep diary writing? My guess is that I started writing as an eight-year-old girl because someone gave me a diary (that quintessential 1960s gift for girls) and that I started habitually writing *every day* around age thirteen because a lifesaver of a teacher (thank you, Lolly) made me believe I could be a writer. A diary would get me started, I think I thought. I remember that by college, my diary writing had become a thing that I *do*, that I *must do* to understand and steady myself, to keep track and remember, to savor life. Writing a diary became fundamental to who I am, how I know myself (and how others know me). It's part of being me.

FROM MY DIARY

My life on May 12, as chronicled from ages 14 to 62

May 12, 1973, age 14: Dad's still the best tennis player in the world.

May 13, 1983, age 24: *(technically* not *May 12 but close enough) written while traveling in Greece:* A car passes and skids to a halt. I heard a man shout my name and thought, *Now who do I know in Crete with a car?* My Aunt and Uncle [from NYC] came running out of the car. . . . Damn good to see them.

May 12, 1984, age 25: *written while working the night shift at the UPI Boston wire service:* Drove straight to New York after a solo overnight shift. Probably was not very bright but I was anxious to get out.

May 12, 1988, age 29: I found myself in the middle of a drug bust in a suburban Kansas City restaurant.

May 12, 1991, age 32: I got my first Mother's Day gift today—a robe from an eager expectant dad.

May 12, 1992, age 33: *written while trying to balance my job with new motherhood:* I worry I'll be told my four-day week is no longer feasible. . . . Such is the modern workplace.

May 12, 2007, age 48: *written on the day of my stepdaughter's college graduation in Oklahoma*: Mission accomplished . . . The graduation ceremony was very long . . . but we wouldn't have missed.

May 12, 2009, age 50: *written about my 16-year-old daughter:* [She] went to a same-sex wedding today—an occasion worth missing a half day of school for, and my guess is she learned more.

May 12, 2016, age 57: *written about a book I didn't finish:* [It] did have a memorable line: "He was 57. Too old to start over. Too young to quit." That's how I feel right now.

May 12, 2021, age 62: *written during a trip taken after the COVID-19 pandemic weakened:* A highlight of this trip was being able to hug young and old—something we haven't been able to do for over a year during the pandemic.

PART 3

Why We Read Other People's Diaries

8

Other Eyes

What Do We Learn?

Across Diary-land, I found an astonishing array of people reading diaries that weren't theirs: a friend reading her late husband's diary; Midwesterners reading their ancestors' diaries; scholars, artists, and researchers reading little-known strangers' diaries; and archivists, volunteers, and entrepreneurs devoted to making "found" and donated diaries accessible to readers.

As readers, we're curious about the people we know, or sort of know. We read the published diaries of famous people, good and evil, looking for dirt or intel. We're tempted to peek into the unpublished diary of a parent, sibling, friend, roommate, spouse, child (especially a teenager) to find out who they are (or were), why they're so angry or sad, what's really going on, what they really think. Is this diary reading a good idea—or useful? And why read the unpublished diaries of people we *don't* know, people who aren't public figures or long-gone relatives? What do diary readers look for? How do they use diaries? What do they learn?

Fortunately, diary scholars have been exploring similar questions, so I tuned in to three of their events: A 2020 webinar streamed from the UK titled *What to Do with a Diary?* A 2021 online book launch for *The Diary: The Epic of Everyday Life* (my diary tome!). And in spring 2023, a session titled *Researchers Using Diaries: How, Why, When, and What For!* that was offered during a gathering of European diary archives staff. For that one, I traveled to Deutsches Tagebucharchiv (the German Diary Archive) in the city of Emmendingen, near the Black Forest. I was soon awash in answers to *how, why, when, and what for!*

∞∞

My friend Pam Patton was dusting the top of a bookshelf in her home office near Des Moines in 2023 when she spotted the long-missing diary that had belonged to her late husband, John, who died from cancer in 2014. "It was like [he was] . . . standing in front of me saying, 'You finally found it!'" Pam told me. "I stopped everything, put down the Swiffer, and started to read. There was no way I was going to leave it alone."

Pam knew that reading would not be easy, at times. John had long suffered from depression. His diary revealed his mindset around the time of a suicide attempt—"what was building and building," says Pam. "I had not really ever figured it out. . . . I wish I could go back with the knowledge that I have now."

She did find happier entries—John in 1993, thanking their baby daughter for "giving me the most wonderful year of my life," and thanking Pam "for coming this far with me." The diary also displayed his writing talent—John studied poetry writing in college: "April 9, 1992: The days are uncertain, my walk unsure. Not knowing–the crying of a child or sleep. We struggle quietly to establish places of peace or solitude. Struggle alone, or sometimes against one another. Meanwhile, spring comes." Ultimately, Pam said, "it is a gift that I have his writing, and no matter how hard it is to read, it helps me remember him and feel closer to him."

Darla Ewalt of Ames, Iowa, has a rare and amazing family history resource: the nineteenth-century diaries of her great-great-grandparents, Mary Caroline Coffin and Alexander Norton Coffin. In the mid-1800s, they moved west from New York to settle in Iowa. Darla is the latest generation of "family historians" to safekeep the diaries, which were found by Darla's mother and siblings in their mother's farmhouse in 1981, after her death. The diaries offer valuable "little details" not found in other material that Darla had consulted during her genealogical research, material including US Census records, birth certificates, newspapers, letters, and Ancestry.com. During the 1890s, Mary Caroline wrote about the weather, births, church-going, visiting relatives, planting apple orchards, and harvesting wheat. "Just the basic simple daily life of this family," Darla told me. "For me, it's fascinating."

The diaries hold detailed, matter-of-fact descriptions of historic events, including when Alexander was a Union soldier during the Civil War. In a thin diary, bound in black leather, he wrote about "Bill" (General William Tecumseh Sherman) and about a march in Washington, DC. Ewalt's research determined this was likely an 1865 military procession by 145,000 victorious Union soldiers. Other diary entries contain sentiments that Darla found surprisingly relevant to the present day. On Sunday, December 31, 1899, Mary Caroline wrote: "Soon to be another century & may the Good Lord Bless us & help us live nearer him next year." With Americans so divided, Darla remarked, in 2023, "It struck me because of what we're going through right now. We need to take that to heart. It's been a rough year for the country."

Amy Elbert, another Iowa friend, picked up fresh details about her grandmother Blanche Ford Hardin by reading Hardin's 1913 diary, written when she was a twenty-four-year-old schoolteacher living on her own in southern Idaho, far from her Missouri family. "It's so intimate, and she's so vulnerable," Amy told me. In a school composition book, on November 28, 1915, Blanche wrote: "Thanksgiving day has come and gone. I ate my turkey or chicken rather by myself. . . . It is sure cold now. I wonder if I will freeze sleeping alone." The entry's last line brought tears to Amy's eyes: "Good night everybody that happens to read this."

ooo

Picture chancing upon a diary written not by an ancestor but by a stranger, not handed down by relatives but found in the trash. Would you read it? Or use it? If so, what are your ethical obligations? During the UK webinar, filmmaker Becky Edmunds and writer Alexander Masters each used a "found" diary to usher an unknown diarist into public view in an ingenious and complicated way, with chutzpah *and* respect.

The journal volumes that Edmunds found in a rubbish pile near her home in the English seaside city of Brighton in 1998 revealed their author's name. Dick Perceval's journal—handwritten over the course of fifty-one years, from 1925 to 1976—documented his life from ages fifteen to sixty-six, including his teenage stay in 1920s Berlin; his work as a journalist in 1930s London; his world tour in 1937; his stint at Bletchley Park, the World War II codebreaking center; and his relationships: "[S.] has gone without a word to me, just gone," he penned on January 1, 1932, about an older, then married German woman who would eventually become his wife.

Perceval died in 1997, but Edmunds tracked down one of his relatives for permission to use the journal. After years of research, in 2020, Edmunds released a poignant video web series about "the extraordinary life of an ordinary man," using selected entries read by an actor and accompanied by period film footage. The result captures moments from the mundane to the historic. On September 3, 1939, at age thirty, the diarist is "filled with an immense sadness" while waiting for Prime Minister Neville Chamberlain's anticipated announcement that Britain has gone to war. On July 21, 1969, at age sixty, he watches television "with fascination and wonder" as two astronauts become the first people to walk on the moon. On December 31, 1972, he reports that Britain is "divided about joining the European Common Market. . . . It is going to be most interesting to see how it works out."

Prize-winning author Alexander Masters had a different challenge with the 148-volume diary, written from the 1950s to 1990s, that a friend found in a "skip" (dumpster) near Masters's Cambridge home in 2001. The diary didn't provide its author's name. One entry described a shocking event—the diarist seemingly stabbed and staggering through the family garden, bleeding. Or so Masters thought—until the entry mentions the unsympathetic reaction of the diarist's mother. Masters realized he was reading a young woman's account of her menstrual period.

With help from a detective and graphologist (handwriting expert), Masters determined the diarist's name, Laura Francis; that she had worked for many years as a live-in housekeeper for an elderly professor (although she couldn't really cook and was not especially tidy); and that she was seventy-eight and lived near him. Masters wanted to use her diary but not without her permission. "You can destroy a life. You have to get their approval," he told the webinar Zoom audience. After Francis answered Masters's knock on her door, he told her he'd read her "magnificent" diary. "You have an insight into a type of life I don't understand, that I found fascinating, and I think you have something to say to the world," he said. "Would you mind if we worked on a book together?" She agreed, and the two collaborated on a series of short stories, based on the diary entries, that were published in the *Paris Review* in 2017. Masters also shared royalties with Francis from his nonfiction book titled *A Life Discarded: 148 Diaries Found in a Skip*.

Rather than use a stranger's diary for a writing project, the late Nobel Prize–winning Canadian fiction author Alice Munro allegedly read, uninvited, her daughter Jenny's diary-like writing and then used it to influence a short story, Jenny told a magazine in 2024, months after Munro's death. The magazine piece was among several reports with disturbing posthumous revelations, disclosing that Munro stayed with her second husband after he pled guilty in 2005 to sexually abusing his stepdaughter, Andrea, in 1976, when she was a child. The youngest of Munro's three adult daughters, Andrea shared her story of abuse publicly after her mother's death; literary gumshoes saw connections between Munro's fraught personal life and her intimate short stories. Jenny alleged that her diary-like writing, critical of her stepfather, was used for a Munro short story about a middle-aged woman and her boyfriend being visited by the woman's daughters—one whose journal writing was critical of the boyfriend.

Then there's "bad boy" English novelist Will Self, who used his late mother's diaries to write his thirteenth novel. Titled after his mother, the novel *Elaine* is about a frustrated 1950s American wife and mother stuck at home, struggling with mental health issues, and unhappily married to a college professor. Despite the book's third-person narration, Elaine's raw inner voice dominates: by turns angry, acerbic, funny, and profane, as she candidly addresses her bad marriage, sex life, and her three sons. There is only one obvious diary quote—in the epigraph—dated February 1956: "A woman who cannot, or will not, accept the conditions of her servitude naturally and gracefully, deserves what has happened to me." The novel includes italicized snippets, but it's unclear whether they're from the real diary. The book jacket informs us that by using his mother's diary, the novelist produced "perhaps the first work of auto-oedipal fiction" in an effort to reach "the almost unimaginable realm: a parent's interior life prior to his own existence."

For the book, Self read about five hundred pages of his mother's diary—even teaching himself to write in Elaine's tidy cursive. A daring take on "diary fiction," *Elaine* uses the real diary's particulars (if not its actual words) to shape a long-form prose narrative about an Elaine who may or may not be fictional. I couldn't help noticing that Elaine the character burns her diary, while Elaine the novelist's mother did not. And look what happened!

ooo

When I was about thirteen, I began drawing tiny asterisks next to the dates of several consecutive diary entries each month. I continued for decades. I thought this was my clever invention. Incorrect. In Germany, I learned that I was not alone in self-tracking my menstrual periods with a discreet symbol. Women have long done this. And diarists of all genders have used other little symbols to self-track other highly personal bodily functions or sexual activities, from masturbation to intercourse. Once decoded, these symbols offer rare data for researchers in physiology, psychology, pedagogy, and history.

"Diaries can tell a lot about bodies. There are not many other historical sources for that," Leonieke Vermeer, a history professor at the University of Groningen, in the Netherlands, told diary archivists and scholars at the 2023 gathering held near Germany's Black Forest. Vermeer searched many archived diaries for self-tracking symbols that denote bodily activities. She found symbols indicating masturbation in six diaries written between 1660 and 1940 from the UK, the Netherlands, and Switzerland. Five were written by men, one by a woman. For another study, she scrutinized five Dutch diaries written between 1780 and 1940. Three are men's diaries with symbols for masturbation, and two are women's diaries with symbols for menstruation. Beyond the asterisk or star, diarists used symbols including #, X, †, ‡, ---, and my favorite: !!! Vermeer told me that she inferred the symbols' meaning from the surrounding text, other diaries with similar self-tracking, and other mentions from the period of tracking physical habits.

"Tiny symbols in diaries can tell big stories" about the diary as a genre and about private behavior, public norms, and how they've changed, Vermeer writes. Similar self-reports can be found in other historical records, from medieval Chinese people's "ledgers of merit and demerit" to Benjamin

Franklin's moral self-accounting. Like the modern-day Fitbit, the diary is a "technology of the self," Vermeer argues, that can be used to turn our "body, mind, and habits into data" and to gain "self-knowledge through self-tracking."

Secretly recording masturbation has been a way to "register and control this secret vice" and to "change or resist" society's view of it as immoral or unhealthy, Vermeer contends. Although far more men than women did this particular tracking, social pressure likely led many women to self-censor any aspect of their sexuality during the "long nineteenth century" (1789 to 1914), Vermeer told me. One woman who *did* track her masturbation was the bold nineteenth-century English diarist Anne Lister, who used two symbols (an X and a cross), plus the euphemism "incurred the cross."

While some women track their menstrual cycles for birth-control purposes, one nineteenth-century Dutch diarist noted when she *didn't* get her period—a possible sign of pregnancy. (She had eighteen pregnancies.) A nineteenth-century American woman chose three exclamation marks to denote sex with her husband. A Dutch woman denoted her *daughter's* menstrual cycle (with three dashes). Leonard Woolf kept a detailed account of his wife Virginia's menstrual cycles and menopause for ten years in his diary, as well as her weight and mood. One theory: Leonard's tracking was evidence that he was controlling or had a paternalistic view of female biology, linking an irregular menstrual cycle with a mental and emotional instability. (Or he was simply concerned about Virginia's frail mental and physical health.)

At the German gathering, we also heard from a French musicologist who read Nazi-era diaries from the German Diary Archive for evidence of the Nazi-propagandizing effect of German folk songs. A Dutch literary journalist spent five years reading diaries at the Nederlands Dagboekarchief (Dutch Diary Archive), which inspired several books, including one whose Dutch title when translated into English means "People will still hear from me." Li Gerhalter, a senior scientist in the University of Vienna's history department who also oversees its women's personal papers collection, explained how everyday people's diaries have long been used for "citizen science" (research that involves the public) in German-speaking Europe. In 1771, researchers asked parents to write diaries tracking their young children's development. "They were looking for so-called regularities in human development," said Gerhalter, such as when a small child typically sits, talks, or walks—and for ways to combat the high child-mortality rate.

In the nineteenth century, diaries were used for other early childhood research and then, in the 1920s, to study adolescents, Gerhalter shared. Linguistic researchers in Germany and Austria used their own diaristic notes about their young children. In 1830s England, Charles Darwin wrote a "parent's diary" about his young son. Forty years later, in 1877, he published his findings—based partly on observations of his son—that human physiological expression of emotion does not differ from that of other animals. In 1920s Vienna, the famous developmental psychologist Charlotte Bühler led a large team that collected teenagers' diaries to generalize about the "normal course" of adolescence, producing influential research. But after the Nazi occupation of Austria, Bühler and her also-famous husband and colleague Karl Bühler emigrated to the US. (Charlotte was raised Protestant, but her father was Jewish; Karl wasn't Jewish but was arrested for his connection to the political left-wingers.) The diaries, and some letters, were seized and disappeared. Gerhalter has found copies of four diaries!

∞∞

"The Jews are once again the scapegoats. Now they must walk around with a star on their clothing. A big yellow star with the word 'Jew' written in the middle," Ina Steur, a nineteen-year-old factory office clerk in Amsterdam, wrote in her diary on Tuesday, April 28, 1942. A few days later, Douwe Bakker, a fifty-one-year-old Dutch Nazi policeman in Amsterdam, wrote in his diary: "Now there are friends of the Jews who also want to walk around wearing the star. Today we caught one such joker." The day after that, Elisabeth van Lohuizen, a worried fifty-one-year-old shopkeeper in the town of Epe, wrote in her diary about her non-Jewish son's decision to wear the yellow star to church, a gesture of protest that risked arrest: "It's so hard to know what to do." She became a member of the resistance.

These three Dutch diarists are among several featured in American journalist Nina Siegal's thought-provoking 2023 book, *The Diary Keepers:*

World War II in The Netherlands, as Written by the People Who Lived Through It. Siegal uses entries written by a variety of Dutch wartime diarists to present compelling personal stories—*and* to explore questions about the use of diaries by prosecutors and historians. While diaries can be important sources, how do they stack up with other sources, from newspaper accounts and polls to oral histories? While diarists are direct and powerful witnesses, are they always reliable?

The Dutch Nazi policeman's diary entries proved the deciding factor in his later conviction for collaborating with the Nazi occupier, revealing that he did so in "his heart and soul," according to one newspaper account. In his defense, the policeman claimed his diary's words were more fanatical than his deeds, and he disavowed some of its sentiments during the trial (his second for collaboration). For Siegal, this raises the question of whether diaries document the truth. Not necessarily, she learns from Alexandra Garbarini, author of a 2006 book on diary writing by Jewish people during the Holocaust. A diarist may *not* be the same as their diary's "persona" or even alter ego, and the diary may not accurately reflect their activities, Garbarini, a professor at Williams College in Massachusetts, tells Siegal. For diarists who write regularly over a long period, "the diary becomes a world in which the diarist lives."

I recalled this discussion when I read in 2025 that a diary-keeping former French surgeon was convicted of sexually abusing 299 patients, most children and many sedated or recovering from operations so they were unaware of the abuse. His diary and computer spreadsheets detailing the abuse from 1989 to 2014 exposed his crimes. Police found the diary while investigating another charge. The focus of what is considered France's largest-ever pedophilia case, the diarist/surgeon was sentenced to twenty years in prison after pleading guilty. He initially denied some charges, claiming some of his writing had been fantasy. I found a chilling newspaper photograph of thick bundles of the pedophile's diary volumes stacked on a courtroom table.

Diary-based scholarship also has played a controversial role in the Netherlands' contentious "knowledge question," writes Siegal. Dutch Jews had the lowest rate of survival among Western European Nazi-occupied countries. About 75 percent of the Jewish population in the Netherlands was killed: 105,000 out of an estimated 140,000 people. Did Dutch "bystanders" *know* what the Nazis were doing to their Jewish neighbors during Germany's five-year wartime occupation? If so, did they do enough to stop it?

Siegal details two much-debated books that produced different answers: one based on studying diaries concluded that ordinary Dutch people didn't know; another based on studying news reports concluded some did know. After reading 164 Dutch wartime diaries, historian Bart van der Boom reports in his 2012 book *We Know Nothing of Their Fate* that people didn't have enough solid information to know. Yes, some diarists mentioned mass executions, gassing, lethal medical experiments, and the deportations of Jewish people. But they didn't know what to believe, given conflicting reports. So their failure was caused less by indifference than by doubt, confusion, underestimating the threat, and uncertainty about how best to help. Van der Boom's book refuted researcher Ies Vuijsje's 2006 book, which concluded that "We didn't know" was a national myth, reflecting postwar Dutch historians' self-deception and denial. Vuijsje estimated that up to one million Dutch people had heard about the mass murder of Jews from twenty-four national media mentions of it in 1942. They likely told others.

It was Van der Boom's diary-based study that won a major Dutch history prize, although some called him an apologist, notes Siegal. She also points out that in 2013 two diary experts questioned his use of diaries as source data. Unlike a scientific poll, diaries are not representative of the overall population, they argued, and diaries never offer clear, direct insight into their writer's thoughts. All this further bolsters *my* case for rejecting *Truth* as a broadbrush diary descriptor, although a diary may still contain truths and valuable information. All the more reason to use a diary with knowledge of its limitations and in conjunction with other sources.

In the 1950s, Dutch historian Jacques Presser used wartime diaries and other life writing such as letters (or *ego-documents*, a term he coined) as a source for his government-commissioned study of the persecution of Dutch Jews during the Nazi occupation. Presser was Jewish and survived the war in hiding. His wife was murdered. Presser's 1965 book *Ondergang* (*Destruction*) took fifteen years to complete and used diary accounts to continually confront readers so his book would "resonate in a highly personal way," writes Siegal, adding, "More than 1,000 pages, it was a stinging indictment not only of the Nazis' genocidal program, and the cruelty and violence committed by the occupying forces in the Netherlands, but also of Dutch complicity and indifference," then a taboo topic.

Presser once memorably referred to diaries and other ego-documents as historically meaningful sources produced by "people in their underwear." He promoted ego-documents in his college courses and articles. But how do diaries compare in accuracy to oral histories, including the powerful spoken testimony of Holocaust survivors? Because oral testimony comes from survivors, it "bends towards an uplifting ending" and may be influenced by the interviewer, writes Siegal. Diaries, in contrast, include stories from people like Anne Frank, who did *not* survive. Instead of oral testimony's retrospection, diaries offer "an immediate response" to events, when memories are "still vivid, detail oriented, and potent." From this, Siegal concludes that diaries should be read not as a form of history or eyewitness accounting, but rather "as a first draft of memory."

ooo

Historians have long used diaries that were deliberately written as testimony to document atrocity, war, and other conflict. Today, more than two thousand Dutch wartime diaries are housed in the NIOD Institute for War, Holocaust and Genocide Studies, in Amsterdam, where Nina Siegal and other researchers have read and used them. This diary collection didn't happen by chance. On March 28, 1944, a Dutch government official in exile urged Dutch citizens to keep and save diaries and other "simple, everyday material." During a radio broadcast from London, he told listeners: "History cannot be written on the basis of official decisions and documents alone. . . . What we really need are ordinary documents, a diary, letters." While some people were inspired to start diaries, others already writing diaries (including a young Anne Frank) found a new sense of purpose. As promised, when the war ended, the Dutch government established NIOD and collected this simple, everyday material for future use in documenting the war's human toll. Otto Frank donated his daughter Anne's diary to NIOD, although it is now on permanent display at the Anne Frank House in Amsterdam.

Researchers have also used an archive of diaries, essays, photos, and letters from Jews trapped in the Warsaw Ghetto during World War II, producing projects including a 2023 British radio series *about* the archive, *Warsaw Ghetto: History as Survival.* The "secret archive" was the brainchild of historian Emanuel Ringelblum, who recruited more than sixty ghetto residents to write, collect, and bury the material. After the war—and the murder of most of the ghetto's half-million residents, including Ringelblum—some (not all) of the archive was found. Now a major source of Jewish pre-war and wartime documentation, the Oneg Shabbat archive (also known as the Ringelblum Archive) is housed at the Jewish Historical Institute in Warsaw.

So, too, diaries produced or serving as evidence have been published, including the diary of the late Russian dissident Alexei Navalny. The goal was to "bring his voice to as many people as possible," said Navalny's wife, Yulia Navalnaya, to an interviewer in October 2024, shortly before Navalny's part-memoir/part-diary was published. "If they do finally whack me, the book will be my memorial," Navalny wrote in his diary on October 21, 2022, from a remote penal colony. His death, during his imprisonment, was announced by Russian officials on February 16, 2024.

In 2024, the unearthed diary-like manuscript of the late Volodymyr Vakulenko was published in Ukrainian as a "diary of occupation," detailing the brutality of life in Ukraine under Russian control. Sensing he would soon be arrested after Russian troops seized his village in 2022, Vakulenko buried the manuscript under a cherry tree. His body was found in a mass grave after his arrest in March 2022. In 2017, a twenty-four-year-old Syrian man's diary was published under a pseudonym as *The Raqqa Diaries: Escape from Islamic State*, shedding light on the harsh conditions in the eastern Syrian city controlled by ISIS terrorists. The author had been recruited to write the diary by a BBC journalist.

For scholars of modern China, the diary of Li Rui, a former Chinese Communist Party (CCP) member who later called for political reform, is a potential goldmine of political knowledge about the Chinese government, which tightly controls information. Written from the 1930s to 2018, the diary was donated to Stanford University by Li's daughter, who said she was acting on her father's wishes after his death in 2019 at age 101. Ownership of the diary has been disputed ever since, with lawsuits filed in Chinese and American courts between Stanford and Li's elderly widow, thought to be a CCP proxy. The latest trial began in August 2024 in California, with no verdict as of this writing. Among other things, Li's entries contain an eyewitness account of the Chinese army's infamous 1989 crackdown on student-led protests in Tiananmen Square. "June 4, 1989, Sunday—overcast, rain showers . . . Black weekend," reads the diary. "Around 12 o'clock, the sound of gunfire advanced gradually." Some entries describe interactions with China's current leader, Xi Jinping, whom Li reportedly thought favorably of, at least early on, before Xi came to power.

Since the 2023 start of the Israel-Hamas war in the Gaza Strip, at least two high-profile diaries have been published, offering differing vantage points. "Yesterday I saw death approaching," Palestinian novelist Atef Abu Saif wrote in his diary on October 16, 2023, which was published in 2024 as *Don't Look Left: A Diary of Genocide*. "I heard its steps growing louder and louder. I saw its jaws open, as it grew closer. Just be done with it, I thought." Saif is the culture minister of the Palestinian Authority, which partially controls the Israel-occupied West Bank (where Saif lives). He started the diary when he was unexpectedly caught in the Israeli invasion of his native Gaza, which was controlled by the militant Hamas group. What was supposed to be a four-day trip to Gaza lasted a harrowing eighty-four days. In gripping personal entries, Saif documents massive death and destruction during the Israeli invasion that followed the Hamas attack and hostage taking in Israel. Some entries began as WhatsApp and voicemail messages; some were first published in newspapers in 2023. They show Saif rushing for shelter with his teenage son after their hotel was bombed, helping and reporting on efforts to rescue relatives and colleagues, living in a makeshift refugee camp and in other shelters, searching for food, trying to maintain contact with the outside world, and deciding to leave his father in northern Gaza for his son's safety.

Israeli American historian Saul Friedländer's anguished 2023 entries about the turmoil unfolding in Israel, where he immigrated after surviving the Holocaust, were published as *Diary of a Crisis: Israel in Turmoil*. Friedländer, who moved to the US in 1988 to become a professor at UCLA, has supported a two-state solution to the Israeli-Palestinian conflict as a moral imperative and as critical for Israel's legitimacy. In January 2023, Friedländer starts diary writing at age ninety-one from his California home, prompted by a domestic political crisis that he believed threatened Israel's democracy—the Netanyahu government's controversial judicial overhaul plan, which inspired mass demonstrations. The diary begins as "a private chronicle of an ongoing drama" that he fears could spell the end of "the vibrant country I lived and worked in for decades." He stops writing in July but starts again in October, emotionally jolted by the Hamas attack.

Friedländer's diary account, written through December 2023, raises the question: How does an immediate diaristic account of an unfolding crisis differ from a retrospective historical account? Some reviewers faulted his diary for lacking the insights expected of an eminent historian—Friedländer is known for his definitive, Pulitzer Prize–winning history of the Holocaust, *The Years of Extermination: Nazi Germany and the Jews, 1939–1945*. "Too many issues raised by the specter of Oct. 7 and the war in Gaza remain underexamined," writes reviewer Ruth Margalit. Friedländer's near-daily entries register shock as Israel lurches from one crisis to another—and some entries prove eerily prophetic, notes Margalit. She points to a prescient entry Friedländer wrote seven months before the attack: "Israel's enemies are aware of the internal rift and are ready to exploit it." So, too, the diary's tone shifts "from straightforward synthesis of the news to something more anguished and raw," writes Margalit.

Yet Margalit laments that Friedländer doesn't accept a diary's liberating invitation to "grapple with demons" and that the "diary's astringent, fragmentary form seems only to box him in." She is bothered that the famed historian raises a question about rising antisemitism worldwide but doesn't attempt to answer it. She doesn't seem to buy his explanation, in a diary entry, that this "demands more than a few sentences, and a lot of thought."

I buy it. He's writing a *diary*, and writing during turmoil. When there's "ongoing drama," the diary's intrinsic immediacy appears to be a strength and a limitation. With its dailiness and self-focus, a diary is not a natural tool for deep, dispassionate analysis of developments during political upheaval and war. Why expect this of a diarist (even one as knowledgeable as Friedländer) who is writing during, not after, a crisis? Diarists can get caught up in their own reality, grappling with the present as it piles up. Not that a diary's dispatches can't have historical context or value. As a historian, Friedländer has used other people's diaries. A crisis diary's value to history, especially when written by a knowledgeable historian, may lie in its personal account of what it is like, day by day, to live within a historical event still in the making.

ꝏo

"It's important to go beyond the Western literary tradition to understand diary writing in different cultures," Kimberly Katz, a contributor to *The Diary*, stressed during the anthology's 2021 online book launch. A Middle East history professor at Towson University in Maryland, Katz shared scholar George Makdisi's argument that Islam developed the diary very early in its history, in striking contrast to the West, and that the Islamic world's tradition is separate and distinct from Europe's. Makdisi argued that the eleventh-century Islamic text by Ibn Banna is an early diary, contrasting it with what he views as Europe's earliest diaries, hailing from the mid-fifteenth century. Not that there's a straight line from that eleventh-century Islamic diary to twentieth-century Palestinian diaries, according to Katz. Many things changed over time—for example, the terms used to describe this writing, Katz notes, shifted from "self-biography" and "interpretations of the self" to "memoir."

In her essay for *The Diary*, Katz focuses on the twentieth-century diaries of two young Palestinian men writing during a tumultuous period, bookending the era of British imperial rule in Palestine (1920–1948) and including two world wars. Ihsan Turjman, from Jerusalem, wrote a diary for roughly two years, starting at age twenty-one, during his World War I service as an Ottoman army soldier. (In a strange turn of events, Turjman was murdered by an Ottoman officer in 1917 at age twenty-four.) Sami 'Amr, from Hebron, wrote his diary from age seventeen to twenty-one (1941–1945) during World War II, while first working as a clerk in Jerusalem for the British military and then as a welder aiding Britain's war effort. Both diarists "put pen to paper to help them process the events of their lives but also to document the trying periods of the world war," writes Katz. As such, she adds, they were writing both the *self* and *history*.

Both men's diaries provide rich material with "color and context" that broadens our understanding of life during a critical period in modern Palestinian history, notes Katz. Palestine was primarily Muslim and Arab, with a Christian minority and a gradually rising Jewish immigrant population.

The First World War ended four centuries of Ottoman Muslim rule in 1918, ushering in what was effectively British rule for thirty years, followed by Britain's withdrawal, a failed United Nations partition effort (to create separate Arab and Jewish states), civil war, the mass expulsion and flight of Palestinians, the 1948 founding of Israel, and a war between Israel and Arab neighbors. "With limitations on the availability and access to Arab archives," Western historians "benefit from rare family papers like diaries," Katz told the online audience.

The survival of these diaries is remarkable, given the circumstances, Katz notes. There is no official Palestinian state or Palestinian archive. Turjman's diary was likely transported after his death, unbeknownst by his family, during relocations and was studied by a scholar prior to Katz. 'Amr later moved to Amman with his family and died in 1998. His son helped Katz with her research on his father's diary. What both men wrote were clearly diaries: their self-focus and dated entries are proof, Katz argues. They also represent two kinds of diarists described by French scholar Philippe Lejeune: those who write daily (Turjman) and those who write when they need to ('Amr), she argues. They each wrote about political and personal matters. Turjman wrote disdainfully about Ottoman ministers: "It's hard to take seriously . . . [their] claim of devotion to Islam and of wanting to liberate Muslims from British yoke." While 'Amr's diary was not as overtly political as Turjman's, he wrote about resistance: Palestinian Arabs "would not leave our country . . . bearing the pain of exile and dispersion."

The Diary anthology's wide variety of contributors, hailing from many academic fields, illustrates the interdisciplinary nature of modern diary studies, which took flight in the 1970s. Beyond including scholars of literature, history, and the humanities, who have long studied or used diaries, the anthology also features scholars of popular culture, cultural theory, travel studies, African studies, digital culture, and digital history and archives. "How I detested the poor diary," Philippe Lejeune, one of the world's foremost diary scholars, wrote in 2005, admitting that he ignored the diary in his six books on autobiography, written between 1967 and 1986. The diary was often viewed as a "series of insults," he wrote in 1997. In addition to being derided as "feminine," the diary was badmouthed as "unwholesome, hypocritical, cowardly, worthless, artificial, sterile, shriveling."

Deeming his own "badly written" adolescent diary "rubbish," Lejeune initially thought autobiography "meant growing up." But in the 1980s, during his fifties, Lejeune resumed diary writing and began studying and writing about diaries, especially those that had been ignored—the unpublished, private, harder-to-find diaries. Lejeune became an "unabashed evangelist for the diary," drawn to its democratic potential and freedom, writes Jeremy D. Popkin, co-editor of *On Diary*, the English collection of Lejeune's work.

Lejeune also scrutinized diarists, including himself. Some three million French people over age fifteen kept a diary during the year, according to a 1988 survey by the country's Ministry of Culture. They represented 7 percent of the people surveyed. Lejeune brings this up in an article co-authored with Catherine Bogaert. In 1997, the percentage rose slightly to 8 percent, showing that diary writing was clearly "not outmoded," the co-authors argue. Further analysis showed that diary writing declines with age and that it is "more likely begun during adolescence," especially by girls. Among teens between age fifteen and nineteen, the co-authors report, there is a "huge" difference: 19 percent of girls reported keeping a diary versus 7 percent of boys. Beginning at age twenty-five, this difference narrows, "with a slight female predominance." Diary keeping is most common among educated or urban people, they write.

ooo

Sally MacNamara Ivey reads, collects, and sells other people's diaries for a living. An experienced diary dealer, she reports that she has read more than ten thousand unpublished handwritten diaries over the course of thirty-five years. She buys most of her diaries from sellers on eBay, who have found them at estate sales, garage sales, thrift shops, or antique shows, and then resells them on the same site. Dealers add value to their wares by reading and researching the diary to verify its authenticity and then learning about the diary's author (usually long deceased) to unearth the story that may make the manuscript valuable. "You mine the gold out of it, and that gold is what collectors are seeking," MacNamara Ivey told me from her Washington State home. Some of the most valuable items she has located include the

1912 diary of an original Machu Picchu explorer and the diary of an 1868 Missouri River voyager, each selling for about $9,000.

Drawn to the business as a diarist and diary lover, Ivey's favorite reads include: The late 1800s diary of a Civil War veteran turned railway baggage master, who encountered train wrecks, train robberies, and traveling circus performers. Two diaries, purchased ten years apart, by two girls in 1938 whom MacNamara Ivey later realized had both been written aboard the same ship traveling from New York to Europe (the girls became friends onboard). The diary of Sir Charles Middleton, a British Navy admiral, who wrote on September 1, 1793, "I have felt very gloomy of late on account of the loss of my companion, my friend, my wife."

Dealers participate in this small collectibles market with auction houses, antiquarian booksellers, and websites such as eBay. Diary sales have been on a "gentle incline" since 2007, says Rick Stattler, the in-house Americana specialist at Swann Auction Galleries in New York. Swann sells about a dozen diaries per year, valued starting at $600, most telling the stories of "overlooked Americans," reports Stattler. "Almost none of the manuscript diaries we've sold over the years have been by celebrities or household names. These diaries are by very ordinary people—in fact, their quotidian nature is, in many cases, at the heart of their appeal." But not all ordinary diaries are sale-worthy, Stattler told me. A Civil War soldier's account of the Battle of Gettysburg is not so interesting or valuable if the entry is short and mainly about the weather. In contrast, a Civil War diary written in 1863 by Lincoln Ripley Stone, a surgeon who served in the famed regiment of Black soldiers that inspired the 1989 film *Glory*, sold in 2023 for $40,000. A diary's market value hinges broadly on its historical content and writing quality, as well as variables including the author's background and the diary's visual appeal.

Independent rare-book dealer Glenn Horowitz also sells the papers of famous authors, which may include "intimate documentation, diaries and journals, that have never been disclosed," as he told the *New Yorker* in 2024. In 2009, Horowitz sold John Updike's papers to Harvard for $3 million on behalf of Updike's widow.

Diary buyers' interests vary. Some are individual collectors pursuing a hobby or passion. Some represent local historical societies that want diaries and other first-person documents offering a fresh source of regional information. Some buyers are from libraries and archives looking for diaries that can expand research in new directions, lure scholars from online sources back to physical ones, and burnish their institutional reputation, visibility, and status.

Strangers' diaries are sometimes bought not for their historical value but for their potential to provide unapologetically voyeuristic entertainment. "Inside this envelope are the private, personal thoughts and secrets of a random stranger," Joanna Borns says in a twelve-minute YouTube video as she gingerly unwraps a diary she bought for $32 on eBay. The diarist may or may not be dead, she notes as she prepares to read the diary for the first time—out loud. "I'm wondering if there will be scandals, a love story, murders," Borns, in her early twenties, says to the camera. Probably not, she decides, adding: "If you murder someone, you probably shouldn't write about it in your diary. That's just a tip from me." As she reads, a handwritten page fills the screen: "Tuesday, January 1, 1946: . . . This year is big for me for I graduate . . . after lots of trouble of having to go into the navy and then coming back and having to go through the junior year again. So happy I went back for today an education is something no one can take from me."

Borns continues to read select entries, struggles to decipher the handwriting ("cursive has been cancelled, as far as I'm concerned"), and shares her mounting discoveries about the diarist's identity. "I think we're dealing with the mind of a teenage boy," she says, as the camera zooms in on her wide-eyed, bespeckled face. Later she learns that the diarist was twenty and living in New Hampshire. She figures out his name (which she doesn't share), finds a census record about him, and is sobered to find his obituary. By the diary's end, on New Year's Eve, she's miffed that he hasn't revealed if he ended up with "Barbara" (oft-mentioned in his diary) and pronounces him a nerd. "I can't believe there's no more!" she exclaims. The video has received 250,000 views since it was posted in 2019.

In several posted videos, Borns reads strangers' diaries from 1908 to 1997. In another video she shares tips for diary buying on eBay and Etsy: when searching, use the words *handwritten*, *vintage*, and/or *antique* (otherwise you'll get an unused blank diary), and beware of fakes. Borns reports returning some diaries to the authors' families but says that most come from the families themselves.

Sally MacNamara Ivey sometimes reads from diaries on her *Diary Discoveries* podcast, primarily older ones from the 1800s to the 1930s. Beforehand, she researches to see if any family members or others might be affected if the diary becomes public. "The last thing I need is someone saying, 'Why did you say that about my grandmother?'" she told me. Due to privacy concerns, she also avoids handling unpublished diaries whose authors—or others mentioned in entries—may still be alive. Most of the diaries she buys or sells are pre-1920s, although they range from the 1800s to the 1970s. If she reads a diary that proves "extremely personal," she keeps it out of public view. Stattler, the Swann diary enthusiast, told me that "the more recent" a diary is, "the more cautious I try to be, regarding the provenance"—citing concerns over legal ownership, authenticity, and privacy.

On rare occasion, a bad actor peddles counterfeit or stolen goods. Perhaps the most high-profile diary hoax was that of the infamous "Hitler Diaries," published in 1983 by a German magazine and a British newspaper, soon after exposed as fakes—*bad* fakes, to boot. In 2024, two people were convicted for their roles in an August 2020 scheme to steal and sell the diary of presidential daughter Ashley Biden. The diary was sold to a right-wing group in a brazen attempt to hurt Joe Biden's 2020 campaign. Ashley Biden, whose diary mentions drug addiction recovery, called the theft and sale of her diary "one of the most heinous forms of bullying."

ooo

In 1994, students at a school in a racially divided California community beset by gangs, homicides, and drugs were assigned to read the diaries of Anne Frank and Zlata Filipović and write their own diaries. Erin Gruwell, their rookie teacher, hoped the diary assignment would teach tolerance and engage her students. In entries, the students aired their thoughts, writing about struggling with prejudice, abuse, violence, and dysfunction. This led to the 1999 book *The Freedom Writers Diary: How a Teacher and 150 Teens Used Writing to Change Themselves and the World Around Them*. The best-selling book, composed of entries by Gruwell's students, inspired a 2007 movie and a movement to replicate the effort in classrooms around the world. Gruwell's students all graduated from high school, and many attended college.

Another noble diary experiment was launched by American research psychologists Joshua Conrad Jackson and Michele Gelfand. "Can the Diaries of Ordinary People Be Used to Bridge Cultural Divides?" read the headline of their 2019 *Los Angeles Times* opinion piece. The researchers tested this by introducing a "diary contact technique," designed to improve relations between Americans and Pakistanis via positive contact, specifically by sharing journal entries between the groups that offer "mundane and humanizing details" about their everyday lives.

Surveyed before the diary reading, some Americans and Pakistani participants believed negative stereotypes about each other. Surveyed afterward, each group had developed a more tolerant and positive view of the other, reducing "perceived cultural distance." A control group showed no change. "Americans may be different than us in moral and religious values, but the life of a student in America is very similar to the life of a student here," wrote one Pakistani. An American wrote of the Pakistanis: "They are hardworking and selfless. They care about the greater good of their society and make sacrifices for others."

The diary's quotidian nature is its superpower, the researchers found. Unlike social media posts designed to grab attention, the diary entries were not written to be public or provocative. Instead, diarists offered their "naturalistic thoughts." Diaries have not yet brought about world peace. But the researchers conclude: "Diaries hold immense promise as a way of bringing cultures together, providing unfiltered access to the everyday lives of those we may know of only through the media."

9

Ordinary People

Why Save Diaries by Us All?

"Behind every diary there is a person—and every person counts in our archive," explained my guide, Giacomo Benedetti, as we walked through the Piccolo Museo del Diario (Little Diary Museum) in Tuscany's Pieve Santo Stefano. Tucked inside the faded elegance of a sixteenth-century palazzo, the high-tech museum holds many clever reproductions of the treasures stored nearby in the Archivio Diaristico Nazionale (National Diary Archive).

The museum introduced me to ordinary Italians through their written words: A ten-year-old girl in the 1980s, grappling with her parents' divorce in her "secret diary." Vincenzo Rabito (1899–1981), a semi-literate Sicilian who typed 1,027 pages of hard-to-read prose in a mishmash of dialects, misspellings, and odd punctuation, recalling his early "much-despised life" and later "good life" that spanned fifty years of Italian history. Clelia Marchi (1912–2006), a widowed northern Italian peasant who at age seventy-two began writing her life story as a tribute to her late husband, Anteo. She wrote in black felt-tip marker on the white sheet that covered the double bed the couple once shared. The original "bed sheet book" hangs in a room of its own.

The diary museum offered yet more evidence of Diary-land's reverence for ordinary writing by ordinary people about their ordinary lives, although the writing, the people, and their lives can be anything but ordinary. To find out why ordinary diaries are so valued, I visited some of Europe's diary archives, proud collectors and keepers of ordinary people's unpublished self writing. I learned about social research projects and living history initiatives that call on ordinary people to write and share their diaries. And I looked to diary scholars, historians, and cultural observers for insights.

ooo

"MASS OBSERVATION wants your story . . . Watch yourself. And watch your neighbor. Watch him with the detachment of a doctor examining a patient. May the 12th is going to be a field day for all of those who want to observe human behavior," reads a 1937 pamphlet for the first 12th May Diary Day. Seventy-seven volunteers across the UK submitted an hour-by-hour account of their day to Mass Observation, a fledgling British social research organization whose archive of diaries and other personal papers (letters, scrapbooks, photographs) is today housed at the University of Sussex in Brighton. Founded in London in 1937 by an anthologist, a journalist/poet, and an artist/documentary filmmaker, Mass Observation set out to create "an anthropology of ourselves" by gathering diaries and questionnaire responses from volunteers to learn about the everyday lives and opinions of ordinary Britons during an era of major social and economic change.

The May 12th Diary Day was Mass Observation's first large-scale project. Why May 12? Because that day in 1937 was King George VI's Coronation Day. George succeeded his brother King Edward VIII, who abdicated the throne following his marriage to an American divorcée. Mass Observation wanted to know ordinary people's thoughts about the abdication crisis. The May 12 Coronation Day diaries captured the public mood at the street level, offering views that might otherwise have gone unrecorded, including those from people not keen on the monarchy. A politically left-leaning divorcée reported that she spent Coronation Day catching up on her sewing instead of tuning in to radio coverage of the Big Event. She still offered sharp-eyed details of surrounding festivities: "9:30 p.m. . . . At last the fireworks start and there are cries of 'Ain't it lovely.' . . . We feel rather wet and bored with the fireworks and decide to go into town. . . . The public house at the bottom of the road is full of singing and dancing and [we] get the tram to Camden Town. The conductor is very friendly and jolly."

Diary Day became an annual event, providing a yearly snapshot of ordinary Britons until 1950, when the Mass Observation founders left and the organization became a private commercial market research firm. Mass Observation's archival material went to the University of Sussex, where it is available to researchers. Diary Day was revived in 2010, following the 1981 relaunch of Mass Observation's social research mission. In 2023, May 12th diarists wrote soon after King Charles III's May 6 coronation. In 1937, far fewer diarists openly discussed the Royals' legitimacy and relevance than in 2023, when the "fallibility of the monarch and monarchy was a more persistent theme."

Three years earlier, 2020 was a banner year for Diary Day, happening during the onset of the pandemic. Schools and pubs had shut. Travel ground to a halt. Non-essential shopping was restricted. The size of social gatherings was limited. Mass Observation received more than 5,000 diary responses, far more than the more typical 150 to 900 in a year. About 55 percent of diarists were female, while 21 percent were male, according to a diary sampling. (About 24 percent did not indicate a gender.) Almost 37 percent were age twenty or younger (students were encouraged to write); 14 percent were twenty-one to forty; 19 percent, forty-one to sixty; 18 percent, sixty-one to eighty; the rest were unknown. Diarists documented death and loss, grief and regret. "After she died, I fretted that I might not have been praying hard enough or in the right way or not asking God hard enough to keep her alive and let her recover from this terrible virus," wrote one diarist.

"There was an outpouring," recalled Kirsty Pattrick, Mass Observation's projects officer. "It just spoke to people, at that moment in time, that this was something unprecedented they were living through. And this was an opportunity to document that." Schoolchildren, nurses, architects, civil servants, and more wrote entries mentioning fear, job loss, panic buying, frustration, separation, heartache, and strange dreams. All was not gloomy. They also wrote about community spirit, homeschooling, baking, food-bank volunteering, nature appreciation, and being able to stay at home with newborns. *Everyday Life in the Covid-19 Pandemic*, a "democratic history" published in 2024, was based on Mass Observation's diaries.

Across the decades, the May 12th diaries have captured life experiences, views, and emerging concerns. Among the more recent: race, immigration, Brexit, gender identity, mental health, social media, and technology. Some of the entries include illustrations, ranging from a child's colorful drawing of flowers on May 12, 2013, to an inmate's black-and-white sketch of his cell. "What a day! Woke up and I was in prison! No surprise there but it always registers on first awakening!" he wrote on May 12, 2017.

The impetus for Mass Observation and its diary-keeping projects lay in Britain's emerging mass democracy after World War I, says Claire Langhamer, a Mass Observation trustee and director of the University of London's Institute of Historical Research. The electorate greatly expanded in 1918, when the right to vote was extended to all men over age twenty-one and to many women over age thirty. This prompted desire for a broader, more inclusive historical narrative that could be taught in school classrooms; a narrative including what people were thinking and experiencing. "That's what you get from a diary," Langhamer told me.

Mass Observation also is known for its many World War II diaries, collected for another project. The diarists' personal observations have been put to good use. An award-winning 2006 British television drama, *Housewife, 49*, dramatized one of the diaries. Simon Garfield showcased them in his 2006 book, *We Are at War: The Remarkable Diaries of Five Ordinary People in Extraordinary Times*. Erik Larson found evocative details to enrich his 2020 bestseller, *The Splendid and the Vile: A Saga of Churchill, Family, and Defiance During the Blitz*, which includes one diarist's report of an "extra noisy enemy plane" dropping a bomb that "puffed my curtains and made the house shiver."

In 2020, professors at Brown and the University of Connecticut recognized a similar opportunity to document history in the making and organized the Pandemic Journaling Project, requesting diaries. Their website declared: "Your Story Matters. . . . Usually history is written only by the powerful. When the history of COVID-19 is written, let's make sure that doesn't happen." Similar projects were launched at universities, cultural institutions, libraries, and news outlets—from Harvard and Arizona State to the Vermont Folklife Center, the Smithsonian, the Library of Congress, and NPR's StoryCorps.

Another outpouring. The Pandemic Journaling Project alone received almost 27,000 journal entries (writing, audio, and images) from more than 1,800 diarists in 55 countries. "Thick plastic separates me from my taxi driver," wrote a contributor on May 7, 2021. "He's taking me home from the airport where I just returned from my mother's funeral. She died of COVID a month ago, and with everyone's vaccine schedules this was the earliest we could have a service." Sarah S. Willen, the UConn project cofounder, told me: "We're interested in real people and their everyday lives. . . . Our impulses were deeply democratic."

The National Women's History Museum received 545 responses to its call for pandemic self writing by women, girls, and nonbinary people. Some were posted on the museum's website with now-familiar words as tags: social distancing, masks, quarantine, essential worker, lockdown (as well as misinformation, sadness, mental health, isolation). The *New York Times*' "Diary Project" asked well-known artists and writers "to help capture an extraordinary time." Cartoonist Linda Barry's offering was titled "Documenting All the Small Things That Are Easily Lost." Frustrated teenagers submitted written entries with artwork and even a ukulele song to Dispatches from Quarantine, author/educator Alexandra Zapruder's youth-focused project. One sixteen-year-old girl wrote: "I can hear the birds chirping all the time now. I never used to listen to the birds before; too busy. . . . So many things have been taken out of my life and replaced. Yes, by worry and fear, but also by time, my silver lining. For the first time in such a long while, I've been able to just stop and sit. I've been able to focus on myself and heal a bit, in a world that's so broken."

ooo

At the height of the pandemic, Europe's diary-rich archives had to close to visitors, but they also experienced an uptick in submissions as people suddenly had time to start a new diary—and unearth old ones. Diaries with "plague" in their title arrived at the Great Diary Project archive in London. In Italy, "people came back to writing about their life," reports my diary museum guide, Giacomo Benedetti. In Germany, baby boomers "had time to check their attics and closets" for old journals, Marlene Kayen, chair of the Deutsches Tagebucharchiv (German Diary Archive) told me. The pandemic also reinforced the value of digitizing documents (so some could be accessed as PDFs) and digital outreach. The German archive developed an online audio tour of its diary museum.

Europe has at least ten archives focused on collecting the unpublished diaries of ordinary people, Kayen told me. Many traditional archives collect a wide variety of documents but seldom diaries from non-prominent people, she explains: "Nobody collected the diaries of every Joe and Jane." Although these places are often collectively called "diary archives," this is a bit misleading. Only five include "diary" in their name and most, regardless of name, also collect other unpublished autobiographical forms (memoirs, autobiographies, letters). Some also collect life stories conveyed via, say, photographs rather than writing. These archives are located in seven countries. (Germany, Italy, and the Netherlands each have more than one.)

The European Diary Archives and Collections Network (EDAC) was established in 2015 to exchange archival best practices and promote scholarly research on diaries. Three years later, it tweaked its name to better reflect its members' diverse materials, swapping "Diary" for "Ego-Documents"—which is considered the "most modern comprehensive term," says Kayen. EDAC (the network's acronym didn't change) has grown from eleven to fourteen members across ten countries and holds periodic gatherings like the one I went to in Germany with the diary presentation. Most members have names or stated missions declaring their collecting focus as unpublished diaries, autobiography, life writing, or ego-documents. (One member is a private diary collector, and a few members collect diaries/ego-documents but have a broader mission.)

Regardless of name or scope, "diary archives" share a commitment to preserving unpublished diaries and other ego-documents by ordinary people of all social classes. They are dedicated to making these documents available to researchers and the public, and to promoting them as a valuable resource. Other commonalities: They primarily contain documents written in their national language, although they may welcome others. They operate as nonprofits, foundations, or as part of an academic or cultural institution, sometimes receiving government support such as grants. They tend to be founded not by professionally trained archivists but by people passionate about, say, diaries or history. They may or may not have archival staff, and several depend heavily on volunteers.

The archives also share concerns about sustainability, finances, aging volunteers, dwindling physical storage space, and keeping current in the digital age—grappling with whether to accept digital-born texts or digitize their handwritten texts, and with how to create and maintain a robust online presence. In Russia, the Prozhito Center for the Study of Ego-Documents, located at the European University in St. Petersburg, has shifted from collecting physical diaries and memoirs (written in Russian, Ukrainian, Belarusian, and Kazakh) to creating a digital library of entries.

EDAC's two Dutch members differ in what they collect and from whom. The Nederlands Dagboekarchief (Dutch Diary Archive) in Amsterdam collects unpublished diaries and memoirs by Dutch people or written in Dutch. In contrast, the Expatriate Archive Centre in The Hague collects "life stories"—shared via diaries/journals, letters, personal essays, photos, scrapbooks, and digital material—from anyone who lives temporarily in a country other than their home country. The center grew out of the quaintly named "Shell Ladies Project"—a 1990s effort by women married to far-flung Royal Dutch Shell employees. They collected oil company families' expat stories and published them in two anthologies. In 2008, the center became an independent foundation with a global outreach (equipped with a Shell endowment) and now has more than 130 family archival collections.

ooo

My grand European tour of diary-rich archives took me to the UK, France, Germany, and Italy. I began in London at the Great Diary Project, which I visited several times because I often visit London friends. The project was cofounded in 2007 by former journalist Polly North and classics professor and diary collector Irving Finkel, who early on personally stored the diaries collected. North became the project's director. In 2009, the project found permanent housing and archival support (while remaining a separate entity) within another archive at Bishopsgate Institute, a calm cultural oasis in London's bustling financial district. Established in 1895 to serve people from "non-privileged backgrounds," Bishopsgate seemed a perfect home for a diary archive. "We believe everyone's history should be valued," proclaims Bishopsgate's website. The Great Diary Project *does* focus on collecting unpublished diaries, rather than other ego-documents—holding more than nineteen thousand diary volumes, the oldest from 1735. Most are by not-famous diarists from the British Isles and written in English. Its impressive public outreach includes co-curating a 2017 exhibition celebrating diaries and "their digital descendants" at King's College in London. Two years later, the project lent diaries for display in a New York City exhibit to mark Women's History Month.

By mid-2023, with the British economy ailing, Bishopsgate was struggling financially and later cut costs. North assured me that the project was not in jeopardy. When I visited Bishopsgate's charming Victorian building in fall 2024, the main library study space that I'd visited earlier was shuttered indefinitely, and the project was now limiting diary submissions to those written in English by people from the British Isles. But Bishopsgate's helpful staff quickly got me the diaries I requested to read and reported that they are still processing newly arrived diaries.

In France, I visited what's often called APA, a common stand-in for its grand proper name: Association pour l'autobiographie et le patrimoine autobiographique (Association for Autobiography and Autobiographical Heritage). APA is located in Ambérieu-en-Bugey, a workaday city of about fifteen thousand people near Lyon. Like Italy's Pieve Santo Stefano, Ambérieu is a small, out-of-the-way place with a big sign. Ambérieu's reads: Ville de l'Autobiographie (City of Autobiography). APA opened in 1992 to collect all forms of unpublished autobiographies and to study the "autobiographical impulse": why and how people write about themselves. Its literary and research bent is unsurprising, given that its cofounder is the veteran diary/autobiography scholar Philippe Lejeune. (The French author Annie Ernaux is also a longtime supporter.)

APA has seven "reading groups," spread throughout France, composed of volunteers who meet monthly to read, summarize, and index newly arrived diaries and other texts. Volunteers also help with fundraising, social media outreach, and public events. Elizabeth Legros Chapuis, a friendly veteran volunteer and one of four APA co-presidents, greeted me inside the bland office park that houses APA and the municipal archive. The city lets APA use the space free of charge and provides occasional grants. Legros Chapuis led me into a climate-controlled room with tall, compressed shelves on rollers, cranking one open to reveal rows and rows of archival boxes filled with some of APA's more than 4,500 texts, dating from the nineteenth century to modern day. APA collects unpublished autobiographical texts from any location; 30 percent of the collection are diaries, 10 percent letters, and the rest autobiographical narratives. There are roughly 1,200 diary volumes written by 800 diarists.

Legros Chapuis, a retired journalist, oversees APA's impressive scholarly publications, including the association's scholarly journal (published three times a year) and document collections by theme (including exiles, prisoners of war, and women in war). About a hundred researchers visit APA annually. Claudine Krishnan, a retired literature teacher and an APA volunteer who lives in Paris, used eight teenagers' diaries from 1915 to 1981, held at APA, to write a 2023 book sharing adolescent views that can be both of their time and timeless. APA also presents roundtables and conferences, including an annual gathering called Autobiography Days that in 2024 focused on personal journals, followed by an exceptionally large APA scholarly journal on the topic. Both explored diarists' motivations and practices, researchers' use of diaries, emerging digital diary forms, and growing respect for the personal journal. Two signs of this respect in France: the 2017 birth of an annual diary festival, held in Brittany, and the 2019 birth of an annual literary prize (4,000 euros!) for the best published French-language diary.

Next stop: Germany's Deutsches Tagebucharchiv, located in the stately Old Town Hall of Emmendingen (population about 27,000). The archive contains 28,852 documents written by 5,530 people; 73 percent are diaries, 14 percent memoirs, and 13 percent letter collections. There are so many details "to be found in our diaries," the engaging Marlene Kayen, a former teacher, told me. "It's so much fun to see what these researchers find out about our long, forgotten past." The archive's oldest document is a 1760 daily planner, of sorts, written during Europe's Seven Years' War. A more recent diary, written in the 1950s by fifteen-year-old "Annette B," reads: "I began this diary today, June 17, 1951, because I need someone to whom I can show my innermost being."

The archive has earned an official recognition as a "cultural monument of special importance" and received its first public funding in 2023, which now covers about one-third of its budget. The rest comes from its six-hundred-some members, donations, and "minor" project grants. With four paid employees, the archive relies heavily on about a hundred volunteers, some who have been trained to transcribe documents written in Kurrent, an old German cursive script, into a modern-day font that visitors can read. Diaries were often written in Kurrent until the Nazis banned its use. (I found various possible explanations for the ban: that Kurrent was deemed unattractive, hard to read, or of "Jewish origin.")

As with the French diary archive, volunteers across Germany participate in groups that read incoming documents. They create subject search terms that help researchers find what they need in the archive's database. University researchers, journalists, filmmakers, writers, and high school students and teachers have used the archive's collections to learn about history, politics, medical sociology, and psychology. The archive also has an on-site diary museum that displays "manuscript" diaries (the original texts). During my visit, I listened to an English-language audio tour on my cellphone while gazing into glass cases at splayed diaries written by children, workers, and men's club members.

In Italy, the Archivio Diaristico Nazionale's collection, dating back to 1541, includes more than ten thousand unpublished texts: 27 percent are diaries; 62 percent are memoirs or autobiographies; and 11 percent are letters. Europe's first diary archive, the Archivio Diaristico Nazionale has been around more than forty years, since 1984, and is run by a nonprofit foundation. The archive was the brainchild of left-leaning Italian journalist Saverio Tutino, who sought to showcase "everybody's life and also Italian history" by preserving common people's unpublished autobiographical writing. ("Diary" was intended as a catch-all term.) "We wanted to awaken interest in this literature of life," Tutino wrote.

The Italian archive created the Pieve Prize (more formal name: the Pieve Saverio Tutino Prize) to coax people to donate personal writing—theirs or often a relative's. The archive, museum, and annual festival have increased tourism to Pieve Santo Stefano, which is relatively unknown to tourists compared to famous eastern Tuscan cities (such as nearby Arezzo) with their dazzling art, notable architecture, high walls, and hilltop views. A record-breaking ten thousand people visited the Piccolo Museo del Diario in 2024, which marked the archive's fortieth anniversary, the archive reported. My guide, Giacomo Benedetti, told me, "It's our honor, our privilege. People come here to read the life of others."

Post-war "social reconciliation and cultural reconstruction" figured prominently in the rise of these European archives, writes British historian T. G. Ashplant. At the start of my diary museum tour in Italy, Benedetti showed us an enlarged photo of the town of Pieve Santo Stefano reduced to near rubble following World War II. The museum was one of the few buildings not destroyed. Francesca Venuto, the archive foundation's press contact, later told me: "Italy and Europe experienced the tragedy of war on their own territory: writing diaries was a way to survive, leave a trace, transmit, in a more or less conscious way, memories of one's life, and of the society of the time, to loved ones. Giving autobiographical memories to an archive is equivalent to contributing to the reconstruction of a person and of a country."

The archive began actively seeking migrants' autobiographical memories in 2012, launching a migrant "multimedia" contest with several partners, in part to counter anti-immigration sentiment prompted by a surge of migrants arriving in Europe from North Africa and the Middle East. The "multimedia" contest seeks unpublished life stories—in writing, drawing, photos, video, audio, emails, and postcards (no social media, including blogs)—from people who have migrated to Tuscany. In 2016, the contest expanded to include migrants throughout Italy. In 2024, the archive partnered with a European migration research consortium to create a similar contest for migrants throughout the Mediterranean region.

The festival that I attended in 2023 awarded prizes to submissions written by ten migrants in Italy. Most were in their thirties from Africa, but the winners also included a seventy-four-year-old from Sri Lanka and two nineteen-year-olds born in Italy to parents from Eastern Europe. The prize was publication in an anthology. When I toured the archive, located in a post-war building, Natalia Cangi, the longtime archive foundation director, told me that, usually, migrants "are talked about or talked for. We want to give them a voice."

ooo

Diary archives also have been linked to social history that takes a more inclusive approach to history, inspired by the social and protest movements of the 1960s. This is the so-called "history from below," which focuses on ordinary people's experiences rather than elites' and uses ordinary people's firsthand accounts in diaries and other ego-documents as historical sources. This "life writing from below" was produced by serfs, artisans, factory workers, common people, the working class, and refugees, writes the historian Ashplant.

Diary archives, although not typically government run, preserve a nation's heritage and culture by bolstering its sense of self, distinctive traditions, and shared history, writes Dutch historian Marijke Huisman. The archives also "empower and immortalize common people." In a 2016 journal article about diary archives in the Netherlands, Germany, France, and Italy, Huisman wrote that "they appear to fulfill an almost existential need: to save the common man and woman from oblivion through the elevation of their life narratives into national heritage and memory." (Some archives call their diary effort a "memory project." Italy's annual gathering has been billed as "a festival of memory.") Huisman also helpfully noted the archives' "very wide conception of the term 'diary,'" which she attributes to a desire to be inclusive. The Dutch Diary Archive in Amsterdam chose the word "diary" to be consistent with other similar European archives, she notes, and because *diary* is a more recognizable term for non-academics. (The Italian archive reportedly inspired the 1998 founding of Germany's Deutsches Tagebucharchiv, which inspired the 2009 founding of the Dutch Nederlands Dagboekarchief.)

The US does not have the same robust diary archive tradition as Europe. However, two separate efforts to create an American diary archive recently kicked off. In October 2022, Kate Zirkle, a thirty-nine-year-old marketing professional in Cleveland, launched the American Diary Project, which collects the unpublished diaries of "ordinary, everyday Americans." (Other life writing is sometimes accepted.) The mission: to "provide a free public education resource that supports diarists, archives history, and honors the full human experience." The project began as a web-based initiative, with handwritten diaries purchased to seed the effort and a public call for donations. By mid-2025, the project had amassed more than three hundred handwritten diary volumes, says Zirkle, who is now the project's executive director. Some are donated diaries written by the donor or a donor's relative; others were found or purchased. More than thirty have been posted online.

The project has no paid or professional archival staff, instead relying on more than seventy trained volunteers, Zirkle told me. It has also joined the Society of Ohio Archivists and has sought best practices from the Society of American Archivists (SAA), a professional organization. A registered nonprofit with a five-member board, the American Diary Project has raised more than $9,000 and, in June 2024, opened a brick-and-mortar archive to store and share physical diaries. The location seemed fitting: a rented space in a stately bank building on a once-faded Cleveland commercial strip that's being reinvigorated by entrepreneurs selling recycled bikes, books, haircuts, tattoos, pottery, soup, and Ethiopian food.

The other effort to create an American diary archive also began in 2022, this time by five diary collectors who are still looking for an institutional partner, seeking long-term stability and sustainability. The effort doesn't yet have a name or location, online or off. The group includes Sally MacNamara Ivey, the Washington State diary collector and dealer, and Robert K. Elder, forty-eight, of Chicago, a foundation president and CEO. The archive wants to collect diaries *and* letters by people "from all walks of life" and be "a cultural movement in the US," sparking conversation, donation, and preservation, Elder told me. Diaries will likely be available at both a physical location and posted online, when copyright and privacy considerations allow. Members stressed to me the need for guardrails to protect privacy, especially with a contemporary diary that may mention or affect people still living.

The two American diary archive efforts' interest in online archiving differs from the European archives I visited, which rarely, if ever, post an unpublished diary online, especially in full or with names, largely because European copyright, privacy, and authors' rights laws are stricter than those in the US. As a result, in Europe, a full unpublished diary often can be read only by visiting a physical archive. In the US, some longstanding archives (not diary archives per se) appear to be cautious about posting contemporary diaries in particular, due to copyright and privacy concerns.

The American Diary Project's collected volumes were written between 1859 and 2025, as of this writing. Of the thirty-one volumes I saw posted online, most include scans of handwritten pages and a transcription. Four date from 1859 to 1899, fourteen from 1900 to 1949, and another thirteen from 1950 to 2000. The two most recent are from 1995 and 2000, both containing "strong language" and "suicidal ideation," according to their descriptions on the project's site. The 1995 diary spans about two years (eighth to tenth grade), written by a California girl identified by first name only. The 2000 diary was written by an unnamed man, born in 1981, during several months of his New York college years. He requested anonymity, and the diary was made "available for public viewing with his permission," according to the description.

The project's website has a boilerplate SAA-informed disclaimer regarding online diary posting, noting the project's "education and research purposes," that it doesn't always know who holds a diary's copyright (and welcomes information), and that, if requested, it will remove online material "to address a rights issue." Zirkle said no such requests have yet been made and that the response to the project overall was positive. For the contemporary diaries posted online, the project has either received explicit permission to share them or determined that they were written over twenty-five years ago.

The project's blog includes grateful testimonials from relatives of the diarists whose writing has been posted. In one, a woman explained why she donated her late mother's diary, written in the 1980s when the diarist was a young adult. "She was so funny and charismatic," the daughter wrote. "I would love for it, and her, to be shared and live on." Yet this story has a dark side: the daughter detailed how she and her mother became estranged, and that her mother was homeless in her final years. The daughter described discovering the diary after her mother's death in 2018 while sorting through broken furniture, worn clothes, stuffed animals, food wrappers, and lumber (possibly for fire burning) in her mother's impounded van. "I was bewildered," the daughter wrote. "The woman who lost everything managed to hold onto her diary for over thirty years."

ooo

In Italy, the "cultural movement" that some American diary fans dream of is for real. Archivio Diaristico Nazionale's online store sells published diaries and other autobiographical writing, plus promotional blank notebooks, T-shirts, and tote bags. The archive also offers themed projects online featuring short excerpts from diaries and other texts. I had fun clicking through the "Italians Abroad" project, where I found often touching personal writing by Italian emigrants. "I don't know what to base my hopes on, but I hope," a young Sicilian immigrant in Brooklyn wrote on January 1, 1927. "My English progresses every day, I become more and more familiar with American ways, it won't take long and I will be able to move around without begging to be considered."

During Pieve Santo Stefano's bustling diary festival that I attended in 2023, I met visitors who'd traveled there from across Italy. They scooped up newspapers with coverage of the festivities and flocked to an exhibit of a Tuscan artist's terracotta sculptures inspired by the female world and diaries. An enthusiastic young volunteer I met, who greeted visitors to the exhibit, told me she'd spent a day traveling to the festival from the southern region of Puglia because of the "special bond" she developed with the archive when she did research there as a student. At a local restaurant, during a hearty family-style meal organized for the festival attendees, I chatted over pasta with two gregarious middle-aged schoolteachers from Milan. They were excited about the migrants' stories being presented. A professorial-looking man from Florence at our table had come to give a presentation, and an older man from nearby Siena had formerly served as a Pieve Prize judge. When I asked if the writing quality determined the winner, the woman beside him set me straight, telling me from across the table: "Oh, no. The story is what's important." Pointedly "not a literary prize," the award is for the year's most "worthy" submission of unpublished "personal testimony." "Original authenticity" is a main criterion, with submitters urged *not* to change, cut, or correct the original.

During the closing ceremony, a large audience cheered as Paola Tellaroli, a thirty-seven-year-old biostatistician and travel writer from Turin, wiped away tears and accepted the Pieve Prize. Her memoir was about her long recovery from a debilitating stroke she suffered in 2017 at age thirty-one. When I returned to downtown Pieve Santo Stefano the next morning, the festivities were over and the many visitors were gone. The tents had been taken down, and the animated conversations in the piazza were replaced by quiet. A few older men sat at a table outside a café. A young woman walked beside a boy peddling a wobbly bike on an otherwise empty street. Italy's City of the Diary had returned to ordinary life.

10

Herstory

How Do Diaries Help Write Women into History?

The toilet paper was packaged like a fancy gift—five rolls, each wrapped in crisp paper and bow-tied with a ribbon, nestled in a pale gray box, waiting to be read. Yes, read. WHENEVER I AM TOO POOR TO BUY PAPER, I WRITE ON ANYTHING HANDY. THIS TIME IT WAS TOILET PAPER, Eleanor Cash wrote in large block letters in 1988 on the pouch she used to donate her toilet-paper diary to the Schlesinger Library, in Cambridge, Massachusetts, a leading center for scholarship on the history of women in the United States.

Using care worthy of a Torah, Kathryn Jacob, the library's retired manuscripts curator, placed one roll onto an archival board and removed the wrapping. Underneath was cheap, single-ply toilet paper encircling a chunk of foam tubing. As she slowly unrolled the diary, we saw fragile white squares of thin toilet paper filled with the words that Cash wrote in ink during her 1986 stay at a Harlem shelter for battered women. The handwriting was orderly, calm. The world it described was not: "Today Rosa went berserk when her two early teen boys started a fight & she hit one and he hit her back. She started screaming. . . . This got our guard and counselor upset and so the hospital cops were called. They took Rosa & the boys to the psychiatric ward, let Rosa go & kept the boys."

The toilet-paper diary is part of Jacob's ambitious Diary Project, a volunteer effort she launched in 2021 after twenty-one years on staff at the

Schlesinger, part of the Radcliffe Institute for Advanced Study at Harvard. Sprinkled among the library's holdings are more than 3,500 diary volumes, most handwritten, authored by over 650 women and a few men. Jacob has been reading and producing a detailed written record of Schlesinger's underused diaries to help researchers explore women's lives and the broader culture. The toilet-paper diary is a poignant reminder of what Jacob discovered about the many women whose diaries she reads: they are driven by a powerful need to document their lives.

One of America's oldest and best-known women's archives, the Schlesinger Library is an imposing 1906 redbrick building that overlooks the former campus of Radcliffe, the women's college that officially merged with the all-male Harvard in 1999. I'd never heard of women's archives until 2018 when a friend, a newly minted archivist, mentioned them as a possible home for my diary. I quickly found the Iowa Women's Archives and many others across Diary-land. I soon set out to learn about these archives' histories, missions, and work. Along the way, I encountered stories of intrepid modern-day women scholars using diaries to introduce fascinating women from the past—including an eighteenth-century white midwife in Maine, a nineteenth-century white lesbian landowner in England, and a Civil War–era Black seamstress in Philadelphia.

ꝏ

At the Iowa Women's Archives, tucked inside the University of Iowa's massive main library, the unmistakable dark eyes of Frida Kahlo caught my own, gazing at me from a reproduction of her 1947 *Self-Portrait with Loose Hair*. Fittingly badass décor, I thought. The reproduction also proved to be a reminder of the archives' creation story. In 1991, Louise Noun, a philanthropic Iowa feminist activist, historian, and civil libertarian, sold the real Kahlo painting at auction to create a $1.5 million permanent endowment for the archives, which opened a year later.

"Women do not have the funds that men who are corporation heads do," Noun recalled about why she sold her favorite and most valuable painting. "Meanwhile, I had this Frida Kahlo that was becoming increasingly valuable every year and I just thought, I've got an endowment hanging on my wall."

A Des Moines native, Noun got the idea for an archive while conducting research for her 1969 book, *Strong-Minded Women: The Emergence of the Woman-Suffrage Movement in Iowa*. Unable to find much in the state's archive about Iowa women's efforts to win the vote, Noun had to travel from Des Moines to the women's archive at Radcliffe—her grad school alma mater—to do her research. "Iowa needed something like that," said Noun. "If we do not consciously collect these bits and pieces of Iowa's history as seen through women's eyes, a very valuable part of our state's heritage will be lost." Noun, a Democrat, shared her idea with her friend Mary Louise Smith, an Iowan who became a national Republican leader. The two strong-minded women cofounded the archives.

Smith died in 1997; Noun in 2002. Today they are among the more than 1,200 women whose documents are housed at the Iowa Women's Archives. It is one of about thirty-five women's archives—or archives with substantial women's collections—dotting the American landscape, as of 2013, the most recent count I found. Most are in major cities or college towns; a few are in cyberspace. About twenty-three are run by universities, while another eight are managed by women's professional or social groups. Three archives focus on lesbians, while others are dedicated to women of a specific ethnicity (Black, Armenian, Latina), place (Nevada, the Houston area, Oklahoma), occupation (musicians, artists, engineers), or community (Maine women writers, Native American women playwrights, Georgia's women's movement).

Learning about the variety of women's archives, I couldn't help but wonder: *Where else might my diary have gotten in, if Iowa had turned me down?* Archives can't accept everything offered. A donation must match the archives' collecting bents, and even then, physical storage space is limited. My nine years as a *Des Moines Register* reporter got my diary into the Iowa Women's Archives, which wants to bolster its holdings from Iowa women journalists. If I'd had to play the archives admissions game, maybe the University of Missouri's National Women and Media Collection would have said yes, given my years of sweat and toil in journalism. Or the Midwest Women's Historical Collection at the University of Illinois, since I've lived in four Midwest states. Or the collection of the Jewish women's organization, Hadassah.

I also could have tried a more traditional, non-gendered archive—these predate women's archives in America by about 150 years. The nation's first historical society opened in Massachusetts in 1791, said to be the first archive in the US. Early US archives were male-centric because the practice of history was male-centric—focused on wars, politics, and business led by the powerful, who were usually white men.

The rise of women's archives in the 1930s followed the latest achievement of the US women's movement: the 1920 passage of the Nineteenth Amendment, granting women the right to vote. Suffragists proceeded to fight for their rightful inclusion in written history, which couldn't happen without documents—or archives to house them. In 1935, Mary Ritter Beard, a suffrage activist and historian, began efforts to create a World Center for Women's Archives. "Without knowledge of women in history as actual history, dead women are sheer ghosts to living women—and to men," Beard argued. Officially launched in 1937, the center's mission was to start a "systematic search" for women's history sources, share those sources, and recognize "women as co-makers of history." Its motto was "No documents, no history" (coined by a nineteenth-century French male historian). Supporters included Eleanor Roosevelt and Georgia O'Keeffe. With offices in New York and Washington, DC, the center started by identifying and publicizing valuable sources for the study of women, as well as promoting exhibits of women's collections at the Library of Congress.

But the center closed in 1940, unable to "build a permanent future" due to a lack of financial support and cohesive leadership. (The onset of World War II didn't help either.) Instead of giving up, Beard encouraged women's colleges to create women's archives. The Sophia Smith Collection of Women's History opened at Smith College in 1942, followed in 1943 by Radcliffe's Women's Rights Collection, renamed as the Schlesinger Library in 1965.

Spurred by second-wave feminism and the rise of social history, women's history courses started appearing on American campuses in the 1970s but were marginalized. "Women's history was not recognized as a legitimate field and to admit that one worked in it was considered the kiss of death professionally," recalled Gerda Lerner, who developed the nation's first graduate women's history program in 1972 at Sarah Lawrence College. To gain more acceptance for their field, women's history scholars, many of them women, needed to publish but faced another obstacle: they needed *more* documents.

In one giant leap for womankind, *Women's History Sources: A Guide to Archives and Manuscript Collections in the United States* was published in 1979. The 1,095-page guide listed thousands of documents "by and about women's lives and roles" held in archives and other repositories across the country. Its 391-page index, featured in a second volume, helpfully listed women's resources alphabetically by state, city, repository, and collection name. The guide resulted from a massive survey project launched in 1975 and led by Andrea Hinding, the curator of the University of Minnesota's Social Welfare History Archives. About eleven thousand repositories with archives nationwide were surveyed to see what women's documents they had, if any. The survey got about seven thousand responses from libraries and archives, large and small, public and private, at colleges, universities, and state and local historical societies. About two thousand initially reported having material on women. In 1976, twenty fieldworkers fanned across the country for follow-up visits to repositories.

The guide prompted a mindset shift for repositories from Walla Walla, Washington, to Holly Springs, Mississippi. Archivists who didn't think they had women's documents discovered that, yes, they did. Some hadn't known that their women's documents were of interest. Others pledged to do a better job of collecting material about women. *Women's History Sources* also destroyed the claim that there weren't enough documents to support women's history and helped legitimize the field. People in communities across the US used the guide to discover local women from days past. More women's archives opened, especially after 1990, when at least fifteen were established, including the Iowa Women's Archives, in 1992. More women's history programs, women's studies, and gender studies programs began, while others matured, gaining respect. Demand increased for a broader selection of women's documents that included more diverse ethnicities, religions, classes, occupations, geography, and views on everything from politics to pornography. Women's diaries were among the sources deemed valuable to write a new women's social history of *all* women, including the hidden and nonelite, and of *all* women's activities, including domestic work, that historians traditionally overlooked.

∞

"I've been sick for a year now," Frida Kahlo wrote in her journal in the early 1950s. "I don't feel any pain. Only this . . . bloody tiredness, and naturally, quite often despair. A despair which no words can describe. I'm still eager to live. I've started to paint again." In the ten years leading up to her death in 1954 at age forty-seven, the Mexican painter filled her diary with the emotional turmoil brought on by physical injuries, illnesses, and her tumultuous relationship with artist Diego Rivera. Her entries mix personal writing with visual art—including dramatic illustrations of amputated limbs and self-portraits that show her internal organs exposed, notably her heart.

Louise Noun also wrote a journal, which mentions selling her Frida Kahlo painting. The Iowa Women's Archives kindly digitized Noun's entries for me—the original seventy-two loose-leaf pages of spotless typed copy were converted into a PDF, accessed through a password-protected site. In those pages from her later years, I found a complicated and unguarded Noun, still sharp and intellectually hungry, yet vulnerable as she entered her nineties. "Empty, scared, fearful of the future," she wrote on June 2, 1997. Although she had become known beyond Iowa (she mentions in her diary an invite to Gloria Steinem's New York home), Noun wrote on April 4, 1998: "It is hard for me to realize I am now somebody, after all the years of self-doubt and of being ignored."

This was not the seemingly self-assured Noun I had long admired from afar but never met. When I moved to Des Moines in 1990, Noun was in her early eighties, a white-haired, bespectacled woman with a no-nonsense gaze and an outsize reputation for putting her intellect and family money to good use: promoting free speech and the arts, political participation, and the economic progress of women. I should have guessed she was behind the Iowa Women's Archives.

Noun's final act was staggering. Suffering from chronic pain at age ninety-four, she took a fatal dose of drugs and made sure the world knew about it, sending her suicide note to the *Des Moines Register*. "It has long been my intention to commit suicide whenever I decided that because of age and disability I no longer had the prospect of leading a full and useful life," read Noun's note, published in the *Register*, alongside news of her death in

2002. "The difficulties of achieving this goal are the laws and social customs designed to prevent me from finding the means to do so. Now that I have finally found the means, I happily take leave of you."

Five years earlier, Noun wrote in her diary that she and Mary Louise Smith were pleased with the archives that the Kahlo painting had bankrolled. But she wondered whether a concerted effort was needed to diversify its holdings so it included more "right-wing women" or, as she credited Smith with putting it, more women of "no especial prominence, i.e., farm women, small business women." The archives subsequently launched a campaign to collect more material on rural women, followed by efforts to step up collecting from its other underrepresented groups, including African American and Jewish women. In 2005, to document the underrecognized contributions of Latinas in Iowa, the archives kicked off the Mujeres Latinas (Latin Women) Project. Archives curators, librarians, community members, and graduate students visited Iowa Latinas in eight communities, recording over a hundred oral histories and soliciting donations. The impact: new educational resources are available, online and off, about the lives and roles in Iowa history of Latinas and their families.

Other women's archives have actively searched for material to diversify their collections. After Candice Vadala—also known as the 1970s porn star Candida Royalle—died in 2015 at age sixty-four of ovarian cancer, historian Jane Kamensky, then the Schlesinger Library's faculty director, wondered if Royalle had documented her life. The library already had the papers of feminist anti-porn leaders. Royalle would offer a different perspective, that of a staunch feminist, porn star, and producer of adult movies designed for female audiences. Turns out Royalle kept a journal, which her friends had found and saved, along with other documents. "To me, those unseen pages were not relics but historical documents: vital *evidence*," writes Kamensky in her 2024 book, *Candida Royalle & the Sexual Revolution*. Determined to "get the goods" from Royalle's executor for the library, Kamensky found herself "stalking" Royalle's archive by attending her Greenwich Village memorial service and handing out her library business card to members of a crowd she described as "flamboyant." Diary quotes are aplenty in Kamensky's book, subtitled "A History from Below." "Still trying to unlock the key to myself," Royalle wrote in her diary in 2013 during chemotherapy, after her cancer recurred.

ooo

Five years before University of Iowa Hawkeye superstar Caitlin Clark would popularize women's basketball and women's team sports nationwide, the Iowa Women's Archives marked its twenty-fifth anniversary in 2018 by co-curating a traveling exhibit on the state's proud history of girl's and women's basketball (especially a high school version called six-on-six, which ended by the early 1990s). The exhibit featured old photos, letters, game ticket stubs, and programs for bygone Iowa girls' high school basketball state tournaments. As the exhibit toured six cities, from Iowa's 8th largest (Ames, population 67,962) to its 260th largest (Conrad, population 1,083), women brought their own memorabilia and stories to share, as the archives suggested. During an Iowa City gathering, a Hawkeye women's basketball coach read from her grandmother's 1920s diary about her high school basketball-playing days. Grandma's team won the 1921 state tournament—a very big deal in Iowa. Grandma was the MVP.

Traditional archives also have used exhibits and events to promote their resources on women and to lift up women's history and culture. In the late 1990s, the Library of Congress launched a major effort to identify the women's documents in its vast holdings and create a dedicated guide for visitors to find them. In 2001, after four years of work, the library published the 456-page *American Women* resource guide. Although the venerable institution's archive focuses on collecting the personal papers of "nationally eminent Americans" who have "significantly influenced" the United States, including First Lady Dolley Madison, suffragist Susan B. Anthony, and anthropologist Margaret Mead, it also holds lesser-known women's diaries, letters, and other documents. These items were often "buried in the papers of a more famous husband, father, or brother," writes Janice E. Ruth, a co-author of the guide and now chief of the library's manuscript division. The guide's resources "reflect the daily activities, concerns, and observations of American women from the colonial period through the twentieth century." A website soon followed, kicked off with a symposium keynoted by Supreme Court justices Sandra Day O'Connor and Ruth Bader Ginsburg, whose papers are at the library.

At the Schlesinger Library, Kathyrn Jacob has prioritized reading diaries by minority women for her project, including the diary of Robin Kilson, who was a history and women's studies professor at the Massachusetts Institute of Technology when she cosponsored a landmark conference there for Black women academics in 1994. Kilson's diary, written during her twenties and thirties, broadens her story with entries about depression, illness, suicide, and thwarted love. "I think that some lives, some people are just destined to be outside, always different and off-course. And I am one of them," Kilson wrote on February 27, 1984. She died in 2009 in her late fifties, after living for many years with multiple sclerosis. Jacob also read the diary of Mildred Jefferson, the first African American woman to graduate from Harvard Medical School. During a solo European road trip, driving a rented Peugeot, thirty-four-year-old Jefferson wrote on May 15, 1960, about Vienna: "Night club tour (expensive, tasteless, pointless, only waste of money)."

For each diary volume she reads, Jacob enters details about the diarist and the diary into an Excel spreadsheet designed to help researchers. The spreadsheet includes available information about the diarist's birth and death, life stages, race and ethnicity, gender identity and sexual orientation, religion, marital status, education, and occupation, as well as particulars about the woman's diary, including a content summary, the number of volumes, time span, physical description, language, subject heads, and salient quotes.

In the Schlesinger's reading room, Jacob and I sat under a portrait of a formidable-looking Anna Chen Chennault, a Chinese national who, while working as a journalist in China in the mid-1940s, interviewed the US general and World War II hero Claire Lee Chennault. They married in 1947. Offering a less varnished glimpse of her life, Chennault's diary covers the 1950s, when she and her husband divided their time between Taipei and the small Louisiana town of Monroe, near where Claire grew up. Louisiana's anti-miscegenation laws did not recognize their marriage. On January 21, 1957, Anna Chen Chennault wrote of Monroe: "I have made many friends here, but sometimes their conversations get so boring, so uninteresting, I want to scream!" As the general was dying of lung cancer, the Chennaults moved to Washington, DC, where their marriage was recognized and she would be able to inherit their estate. Anna Chen Chennault went on to become a prominent author, Republican, hostess, businesswoman, and citizen-diplomat in Washington, DC. (She died in 2018.)

ooo

In the 1970s, before women's history really existed as a field, Laurel Thatcher Ulrich was a newly minted historian of early America, struggling to find sources on the lives of women in the late 1700s. With help from *Women's History Sources*, she found Martha Ballard's 1785–1812 diary in the Maine State Library. Written when less than half of all American women were literate, Ballard's diary offers rare insights into a rural Maine woman's life and work as a midwife in the years after the American Revolution—as well as women's contributions to medicine and obstetrics beyond hearth and home. Ballard began her diary at age fifty and continued until her death at seventy-seven. "I was blown away," Ulrich told me. "It opened up a world that I had tried to understand without the diary . . . [and it] made a huge difference." Ulrich was not the first historian to discover Ballard's diary, but she valued entries that others dismissed as "trivia." To Ulrich, the diary's "details" and "dailiness" illuminate "the really important differences between the eighteenth-century world and our own, and what it means to be a woman in that world."

In 1990 came Ulrich's *A Midwife's Tale: The Life of Martha Ballard Based on Her Diary, 1785–1812*, a labor-intensive reconstruction, juxtaposing diary excerpts with analysis. Ulrich transcribed and interpreted unclear writing (near-illegible cursive, misspellings, cryptic mentions), using many sources (maps, government records, wills) to find missing pieces of the diary's puzzle and better understand Ballard's life. The diary offered an "approximation" of her life, not a "transparent record," Ulrich told me. She "had to constantly interrogate: What does this tell me, what doesn't it tell me?" Ballard's account of her daughter Hannah's eighteenth birthday on August 6, 1787, gained poignancy when Ulrich's research revealed that three of Ballard's other daughters had died during the 1769 diphtheria epidemic. In October 1, 1789, she wrote about rape: "Mrs. Foster has sworn a Rape on a number of men among whom is Judge North. Shocking indeed."

After the trial, Ballard wrote on July 12, 1790: "North acquitted to the great surprise of all I heard speak of it." Enhancing previous scholarship by adding a woman's voice, *A Midwife's Tale* not only became a staple of history classes but influenced the use of diaries as a historical source and inspired more diary excavation. The Rhode Island Historical Society, for example, compiled a guide in 1997 to its seventy-nine diaries by women.

In 1988, another determined twentieth-century diary researcher, Helena Whitbread, introduced the world to another remarkable woman, Anne Lister, via her early 1800s diary. A scion of a prominent family in the Yorkshire town of Halifax, Lister courted women at a time when homosexuality was widely condemned—and chronicled her love affairs in her diary. On January 29, 1821, she wrote: "I love, & only love, the fairer sex & thus beloved by them in turn, my heart revolts from any other love than theirs." Lister was also an assertive businesswoman, landowner, and world traveler who dressed in black. Locals knew her as Gentleman Jack.

Whitbread chanced upon Lister's diary in a local archive in 1983, when she was a fifty-two-year-old aspiring freelance writer in Halifax. "I thought, *This has to be published. This is such a slice of women's history that's been hidden for centuries*," Whitbread recalled. She spent five years transcribing Lister's diary. Beyond facing the usual challenge of transcribing a century-old handwritten diary, Whitbread had the added difficulty of deciphering passages that Lister wrote in a code she called "crypt hand." Lister used the code—concocted with alphabet letters, numbers, and Greek symbols—to chronicle details of her romances, masturbation, menstrual cycle, money matters, digestive health, and opinions about townspeople. Whitbread discovered a code key that had been developed by two men who'd found the diary in the 1890s but hid it again, due to its lesbian content. An estimated five million words, the full diary spanned thirty-four years: from 1806, when Lister was fifteen, to 1840, when she died at forty-nine.

Whitbread transcribed and edited Lister's diary into two volumes covering ten years (1816 to 1826, starting when Lister was about twenty-five); the first was published in 1988. In 2019, the BBC aired a drama based on Lister called *Gentleman Jack*. And, in 2022, Whitbread received a royal honor "for services in history and literature." "Little did I know that forty years on, I would still be so heavily involved in what has become a worldwide phenomenon," the ninety-three-year-old Whitbread told me via email.

ooo

Sometimes a single historical diary receives different treatments from different scholars. This was the case with the diary written by Emilie Davis, a free Black woman who lived in Philadelphia in the 1860s during her early twenties. Davis wrote in a small preprinted "pocket diary" from 1863 to 1865, producing brief entries about herself, her community, cultural activities, and the Civil War. In 2014, two academics—Judith Giesberg at Villanova University in Pennsylvania and Karsonya Wise Whitehead at Loyola University in Maryland—each published their own edited version of Davis's diary. To Giesberg, a historian, Davis's diary offers a rare perspective on how a Northern Black community experienced the Civil War in daily life. To avoid "talking over" Davis, Giesberg's version—*Emilie Davis's Civil War: The Diaries of a Free Black Woman in Philadelphia, 1863–1865*—features mostly original entries, with some footnotes and an introduction offering historical, cultural, and political context. A Villanova graduate-student team transcribed the entries primarily as written, with no added punctuation and few "spelling interventions." In contrast, Whitehead—a professor of communications and of African and African American studies—set out to write a "herstorical reconstruction" of Davis's life through a "black feminist lens." Whitehead's book, *Notes from a Colored Girl: The Civil War Pocket Diaries of Emilie Frances Davis*, is a broad analysis, using history, literary, and feminist studies perspectives. The original diary entries have been made reader-friendly, with added punctuation and some corrected spelling.

The two approaches produced subtly different versions of entries. Here is Giesberg's version of Davis's entry from April 22, 1865, when the body of President Abraham Lincoln lay in state in Philadelphia: "Lovely morning is the day long to be remembered I have bin very busy all morning the President comes to town this afternoon I went out about 3 in the afternoon it was the gravest funeral I ever saw."

And here is Whitehead's: "Lovely morning. To(day) is the day long to be remembered. I have bin very busy all morning. The President comes to town this afternoon. I went out about 3 in the afternoon. It was the grandest funeral I ever saw. The coffin and hearse was beautiful."

Taking a personal diary public—in effect, ushering a private life into public view—is a daunting responsibility and complicated task, as woman scholars seem particularly quick to note. The two versions of Davis's diary demonstrate the transcribing and editing challenges that scholars face. I found Whitehead's version more enjoyable and, yes, easier to read. Her analysis helped me appreciate the value of Davis's diary: that it offers the rare perspective of an "everyday" and "unremembered" free Black woman during the Civil War era; that most other accounts, written or oral, from that era were from Black women who were either "elite" or "enslaved." The Giesberg version seemed more authentic—more similar to holding and reading Davis's original diary. Giesberg notes that not much is known about the discovery of the diary, which the Historical Society of Pennsylvania purchased in 1999. But Davis's entries "open a small and very personal window into this vibrant black community," Giesberg writes.

Although both publications earned praise, the late scholar Ann D. Gordon, a Rutgers University history professor who edited the papers of nineteenth-century women's rights activists, questioned their approaches. "What is gained by publishing quite imperfect and wildly divergent editions of these diaries?" asked Gordon, in a review of the two, plus a third online version from Giesberg and Villanova. "Indubitably, the publications draw attention to a rich historical source, its companionable author, and the many revelations and insights about nineteenth-century life that she provides." Ultimately, though, Gordon concludes that the published versions fall short compared to the original. "After all this attention, if a student or scholar or curious person wants to quote from the diary or be certain what Emilie Davis wrote about her days, he or she must still go to the manuscript and read the diaries afresh," Gordon writes.

After my self-tutorial on herstory, I was left questioning the practice of using women's diaries from gender-based archives to write gender-based history, as I had earlier questioned categorizing and studying diaries by gender. Again, I concluded: *Why not—especially if diaries are understood in a more nuanced way?* I also have no problem with "women's history." But why not aim to produce a *history of us*, using a variety of diaries as one source? Yes, a history that recognizes and respects our differences, aiming for diversity, equity, and inclusion in the true, nonpoliticized sense of those terms. *Our-story*, anyone?

FROM MY DIARY

Our times and world, as documented from 1973 to 2020 (at ages 14 to 61)

September 23, 1973: We watched Billie Jean King beat Bobby Riggs in the Tennis Battle of the Sexes. It was a great game. I have tennis in school. I hope I get good.

December 8, 1980: John Lennon of the Beatles was murdered tonight. . . . I can [work] for gun control—it's a start but is there ever an end?

July 13, 1984: I'm excited. And so are a lot of other women . . . Walter Mondale has chosen Geraldine Ferraro . . . as his running mate. It's a first.

April 19, 1995: A day in history I would have preferred NOT to witness. This morning, the worst terrorist act in U.S. history occurred in Oklahoma City.

September 11, 2001: For a few frightening hours this morning, all of our safety was unclear. . . . Writing this now, it all sounds like a compact tidy story but as it unfolded it was just one stunning chaotic upheaval after another with no sense of when it would end or what was actually happening. . . . I raced to the television where I saw the World Trade Tower engulfed in smoke. I slumped into a chair, my hand to my mouth, my heart pounding, my eyes tearing. Like millions of other people watching today, I was stunned. . . . I tried to explain [to the kids] what was going on without frightening them. Who knows if I succeeded.

April 28, 2009: And now for the latest crisis—swine flu . . . There is talk of a "pandemic," of possible travel restrictions.

September 27, 2018: Dr. Christine Blasey Ford, a name few of us knew 10 days ago, stood in front [of] a national T.V. audience and told a wrenching story.

March 2, 2020: The coronavirus scare seems to be intensifying. I tried to get some Wet Wipes at the local Walgreens. . . . Sold out.

11

Reader Experiences

What Else Do We Gain?

"I'm never going to churn butter," Kerry Schauber told me. But she came surprisingly close while she was transcribing the nineteenth-century diary of a butter-churning Iowa farm woman. "You're typing it in the first person and you feel like you're putting yourself in her shoes," says Schauber, an upstate New York art museum researcher in her fifties.

One of many volunteers working to preserve historic documents and make them more accessible, Schauber transcribed the scanned pages of the Iowa farm woman's handwritten diary into digital text so they are easier to read online and can be searched. She found the diary on the website of DIY History, a transcription project run by the University of Iowa Libraries.

Transcribing a diary online is one of the weirder ways to not only read but experience someone else's diary. As diary readers shared how they use and learn from other people's diaries, I picked up on something else. They often described their reader experience, what it *feels like* to tap into another person's thoughts by reading their diary.

Recalling these experiences, including my own, led me to ponder the less utilitarian or tangible aspects of diary reading. What else do readers gain? How do we connect with diarists on a personal or emotional level? Does this differ when the diary is digital rather than paper? Or differ from reading a memoir or novel? Is there a wrong way to read a diary? Are diaries a good read—or a snooze? "I have read some diaries that, honestly, are very boring. I've read some that are really fascinating," a public radio host told me during an on-air interview.

ꝏ

On March 10, 1919, sixteen-year-old Jessie Greer attended a celebration in Cincinnati to honor African American soldiers returning home from war. "We all got up early this morning because we are going to see the colored boys parade. These are the first soldiers back that really fought on the firing line," she wrote in her diary. "Such a crowd of colored people I never saw before in my life."

Offering a priceless glimpse of a Black teenager's life at the close of World War I, Greer's handwritten diary is part of the Smithsonian's National Museum of African American History and Culture collection, but I didn't travel to Washington, DC, to read it. Instead, I read the transcribed digital version on the Smithsonian website from the comfort of my home. Talk about convenience—and easy access to a stranger's diary. Sitting at my computer, I clicked on a thumbnail image of one of Greer's diary pages and up popped two larger images: one with a scan of the yellowed handwritten original and another with the transcription. My reading experience was made possible by some of the more than four hundred "volunpeers" at the Smithsonian's Transcription Center, who typed out over a thousand pages from diaries written by Greer and seven other girls for an exhibit knowingly titled *Girlhood (It's Complicated)*.

Countless centuries-old handwritten diaries are available to read online, thanks to the many archives and other repositories that now offer "a digital library" (or similar resource) with documents that have been scanned and *sometimes* transcribed and tagged by subject. Given this thoroughly modern storage, "it is quite possible that the digital age will become the golden age of diary scholarship," write Batsheva Ben-Amos and Dan Ben-Amos, editors of *The Diary*. Want to read Mormon missionary diaries? Visit the digital collection of Brigham Young University in Utah, which offers approximately 575 diary volumes written by 220 diarists between the 1830s and 1920s. Curious about nineteenth-century Wisconsin diaries? When I clicked into the University of Wisconsin–Madison Libraries' digital "Pioneer Experience" collection, the second diary I found was a welcome surprise. It was written by John Archiquette, an Oneida tribe member who recorded life on his reservation near Green Bay, including tribal court. "The chiefs are now in conference, about old widow Jerusha Powless," he wrote on September 16, 1868, in an entry translated from the Oneida language to English.

Elsewhere online, I found an animated video version of a diary written by a young Japanese American incarcerated during World War II. (It's on the website of the Japanese American National Museum in Los Angeles.) I found more than 160 women's travel diaries, collected by Duke University's Sallie Bingham Center for Women's History and Culture. Alas, I found no diaries (yet) in the Digital Research Room of the Barack Obama Presidential Library, the first presidential library to be entirely online. Given the many born-digital Obama presidency records, a digital archive makes sense, although some historians fear it will become a "hard-to-navigate data dump." (The virtual Obama presidential library differs from the physical Obama Center that is rising on Chicago's South Side, which *will* have a library—a new branch of the Chicago Public Library—along with other community offerings, plus draws for visitors.)

While far from every diary has been digitized and posted online, a diary's physical existence often can be discovered because it has an online catalog record. This, plus the ability to search digitally for words within a document, is great for researchers. "Digital searches are phenomenal," historian Laurel Thatcher Ulrich told me. But, she added, "what you lose is the bigger picture within which the material is embedded. I love reading the whole thing, more than I like searching." Beyond scholarly diary reading, the reader experience with a diary, digital or not, can be akin to "reading a poem, a folktale, a piece of writing that happens to be daily," said Ulrich. As the diary unfolds over days, it has an "inherent suspense," which is "what's fun about it."

ooo

The first public transcription projects began around 2010 as a practical solution to a digital-age issue: libraries, keen to digitize their paper documents, wound up with far more scanned material than their staffs alone could transcribe and tag with keywords. Transcription projects also proved to be a successful public engagement strategy: they attracted press attention and built online camaraderie as volunteers took to social media to share their transcription tips and discoveries. With a transcription project, many volunteers pitch in, adding to each other's work, which explains the clunky term "crowdsourcing" attached to the projects. Volunteers check fellow transcribers' work for completeness and accuracy. "Volunteer peer review is the final vital step," read the instructions for the Library of Congress's By the People transcription project. Complex documents may go through this process several times.

Iowa's DIY History website has been recruiting volunteers since about 2012. So far they have transcribed 104,145 pages of text, including centuries-old diaries from the Iowa Women's Archives. The Smithsonian's 99,501 "volunpeers" have transcribed more than 1.5 million pages since 2013. The National Archives' "citizen archivists" have transcribed declassified Panama Canal records, eyewitness reports of UFOs, and records regarding reindeer meat.

Launched in 2018, By the People has attracted an estimated 49,027 volunteers who have transcribed over 997,000 pages. "What an impact! . . . You have truly helped make the Library more useable and accessible for everybody," Carla Hayden, the fourteenth Librarian of Congress, told volunteers in a video message marking the project's sixth anniversary, in January 2025. A "transcribe-a-thon" held on February 14, 2025, to transcribe nineteenth-century Black history documents proved a "website-breaker": the transcription platform got so much traffic that it crashed temporarily. Five months later, 1,475 transcribers had completed 10,858 pages from documents including *The Child's Anti-Slavery Book* (1860) and the 1865 annual report of the "National Association for the Relief of Destitute Colored Women and Children."

Clara Barton's diary and other papers were the focus of an early By the People campaign that proved popular. Almost 5,800 volunteers transcribed 41,488 pages associated with the Civil War nurse and American Red Cross founder, so people like me (a former seventh-grader at Clara Barton Junior High in Royal Oak, Michigan) can read them online. I was moved by this entry from her diary, written on December 7, 1862: "Went to the Old National

Hotel found some hundreds—perhaps 400, western men, sadly wounded, all on the floors—had nothing to eat. I carried a basket of crackers—and gave two apiece as far as they went. . . . A great number of them were to undergo amputations sometime, but no surgeons yet."

Will technology make people-powered transcribing obsolete? Perhaps. At the 2023 EDAC gathering that I attended in Emmendingen, Germany, I learned about Transkribus, a potentially game-changing AI-powered tool for transcribing handwriting. An older technology known as OCR (optical character recognition) is already used for transcribing typeset text but doesn't work well for handwriting (especially messy handwriting). After a presentation on Transkribus by Achim Rabus, a professor at the nearby University of Frieberg, some diary scholars shared that they were enthusiastic early adopters of the technology, which was developed in Europe. But they added that Transkribus is not yet affordable or free of errors (known as "hallucinations") and voiced ethical concerns about AI, in general.

For now, transcription projects are going strong. What drives volunteers to donate their time to read and transcribe? "People should have as much information as they can so they can form their own opinions," said one volunteer during a report on By the People featured on the morning show *Today* in 2024. "Especially in this day and age, truth has been undermined and we need to fight to maintain the truth." Christian Mobley, a Cincinnati church pastor and history buff in his late forties, told me that volunteering for projects run by institutions from Chicago's Newberry Library to the Getty Museum in Los Angeles keeps him mentally sharp, takes his mind off his chronic pain, and lets him give back to society by "transcribing history for future learning."

"Women are so underrepresented in historical writing," volunteer Kerry Schauber told me. By transcribing women's history documents, she is adding women's voices "to the mix. I'm happy to contribute to that." As for her reading experience, she told me that transcribing can be fun, relaxing, absorbing, time-melting, and "very Zen." I took this to heart when I tried transcribing but, sadly, my first attempt was frustrating. The diary page I chose on DIY History was filled with script written both horizontally and vertically, what pros call "cross writing." I worked so hard to make out the words that my experience didn't feel like reading. Next time, I'll try to find a less chaotic diary page.

Transcribing appeals to middle-aged and retired people who can make use of their cursive-reading ability, a skill that doesn't come as naturally to younger folks, who haven't learned cursive and view it as an ancient art. Jess Atkinson struggled with cursive reading as a twenty-one-year-old student at William & Mary College. For Atkinson's 2022 course on nineteenth-century African American women's diaries, the professor, Jennifer Putzi, assigned students to transcribe scans of Mary Virginia Montgomery's original 1871 diary, housed at the Library of Congress. "A lot of people who write in script, I can't read their handwriting," Atkinson told me. Eventually, Atkinson made sense of Montgomery's diary. "There was something exciting about being able to find a coherent sentence within the messy handwriting and squished words," says Atkinson. "There's a certain level of closeness or proximity that you feel toward someone when you read their diary." The students became invested in the diary and were excited to give their transcription to the Library of Congress for others to use. "They talked about how meaningful it was," recalls Putzi.

ꝏo

Online or off, diary reading can get intense. Karsonya Wise Whitehead, one of the scholars who published a version of Emilie Davis's Civil War–era diary, found that Davis "became real" while reading her diary, creating an almost too-close connection. "At some point her story and mine merged, and though I tried, it was very difficult for me to have (and maintain) a bird's-eye view," writes Whitehead. "Diaries have a way of doing that to you."

Diary scholar Suzanne L. Bunkers struggled to maintain an "appropriate professional distance" and be "objective about the lives described in the diaries and journals" she pored over in Midwestern historical-society archives. Given her own diary writing and appreciation of other people's diaries, "how could I have expected to remain uninvolved, unempathetic?" writes Bunkers. That empathy has proved valuable as a researcher, she argues, by helping her "reach beyond my own experiences and values toward a growing recognition of my limitations as I try to understand another person's reality."

Sometimes a diary can feel like a shared secret between diarist and reader. The British writer Alexander Masters said that while he was reading the found diaries of Laura Francis, he had "this wonderful sense that no one else had read them but me. It was as if I'd been given special access to this woman's mind. It was a feeling of enormous privilege and also great delicacy." What a relief, he added, to discover that the diarist was not famous and therefore her writing was not burdened by fame's constraints or artificiality.

Four years into her diary-reading project at the Schlesinger Library, Kathryn Jacob reported reading more than two hundred volumes written by thirty-five women, spanning the years 1754 to 1992. Jacob was particularly drawn to farm women's diaries and their "litany of labor"—all the pie-baking, potato-chopping, kitchen-sweeping, chicken-dressing, relative-tending, and hand-washing laundry in scalding water. "That window into the fatigue of these lives, the endless work, is astonishing. I'm exhausted myself when I read about some of these days," Jacob told me. She pointed to Lucy Clapp, single and twenty-seven, who worked long and hard on a small Ohio dairy farm yet somehow stayed awake at the end of her busy days to write short diary entries. "Washed 49 pieces, 11 fore Wing Helped clean the milk room. Im very tired indeed," she wrote on April 29, 1872.

Jacob sometimes felt like a "voyeur" while reading especially intimate diaries or entries marked "private," presumably by the diarist. (The diaries *are* available to the public.) While reading, Jacob got to know diarists' personalities and grew fond of some, not all. She found diarist Effie McGrew "spiteful," pointing to the Indiana farm woman's May 1, 1917, entry about a neighbor: "I intend to grease that store floor with her guts when I get hold of her." Long Island teenager Ruth Teischman came across as "sweet, bright, and self-aware," writing in her pink plastic-covered diary with a gold-colored lock and an embossed image of a diary-reading girl wearing capri pants. "Dear Diary, Today I bought you. I am going to tell you loads of personal things and I'm going to write in you all my feeling[s] and emotions," Teischman wrote on September 3, 1959. She emulated Anne Frank, writing: "I can't make this diary like hers because there's no Hitler (thank G-d) but I'll try. I'd rather there would be no Hitler and a fair diary than Hitler & a great diary."

ooo

A diary doesn't always captivate. The better the writing, the better my reading experience—and the stronger my connection to the diarist. An unusual life or dramatic event helps too. This doesn't mean that I necessarily prefer the canonical published "literary" diaries of, say, Anaïs Nin. I've been captivated by unpublished diaries of obscure diarists, especially when they wrote well about what mattered to them. Take, for example, a diary I was introduced to at London's Great Diary Project, written by a worldly middle-aged twentieth-century Londoner who I'll call Henrietta Bellhouse (the archive requested anonymization). Bellhouse pulled me in with her dramatic tone, poignant eloquence, and candid self-appraisal.

"Mother is dead," began the first entry that I read, dated May 1967. "And as I write these words, I know that part of me is dead too." I kept reading. How could I not? "I cannot come to terms with my loss. There seems no purpose in life. I drift from one interest to another, never really involved, and have to force myself to keep the house tidy and even to wash my own clothes." Bellhouse goes on to mention her father, whose "domination of his family reached out beyond the grave," and her complicated feelings about her ex-husband: "I see him now as he is. He goes out of his way to let me know of his . . . affairs. . . . And yet the very thought of seeing him in a couple of weeks sets me in such a whirl that I might be a girl again." Now I'm hooked.

Although I felt a little like I was trespassing in private waters, I reminded myself that I had permission—however, not technically from the diarist. Turns out her relatives donated the diary after her death. Bellhouse's entries revealed everything from her (once) private sorrows to her critique of the day's fashions. Some diary pages were like a scrapbook, with pasted-in photos and news clippings. The lack of captions inspired speculation. Was Bellhouse one of the well-heeled travelers photographed in exotic locales? Was her ex-husband the dashing young man in military uniform, pictured in another photo? A newspaper illustration of a skinny woman in a skimpy skirt took me back to my childhood—and my old miniskirts. Surely this was an ode to Twiggy, the Swinging Sixties London model whose body type we thought we must have (yet didn't). Beside the newspaper clipping, Bellhouse wrote: "The Changing Face of Fashion a La Mode 1967." Below it, she vented:

"It is surely the ultimate in 'non-dress' . . . a revolting garment known as a body stocking is about the only possible thing to go under the current dresses."

Amusingly acerbic and understandably cranky, Bellhouse had spunk. (I love spunk.) I judged her writing, and I suppose I judged her. As she wrote engagingly about fashion or her travels, I liked and respected her. As she wrote about the loss of her mother and her marriage, I felt for her. As can happen with a novel, Bellhouse's diary let me eavesdrop on a stranger's thoughts. Bellhouse wrote as if she anticipated my prying eyes and skillfully ushered me in.

Other diaries left me out in the cold: when their writers communicated with themselves, and I was not invited; when they offered dull dispassionate details. And I confess: these were the diaries I often found boring to read—until I discovered Jennifer Sinor's book, *The Extraordinary Work of Ordinary Writing*. A creative writing professor at Utah State University, Sinor passionately defends much-maligned ordinary writing, making her case by studying the "ordinary diary of an ordinary woman," written by her great-great-great-aunt, Annie Ray. "From the start, I was unwilling to see Annie as anything other than a complicated, accountable, and strategic writer. I was unwilling to see her diary as boring and unsophisticated," writes Sinor.

Typically disregarded and often discarded because it's plain, spare, not literary, "ordinary writing" can apply to notes, grocery lists, memos, letters, and, yes, diaries, Sinor argues. Diaries are not inherently ordinary writing but are so-called when they lack detail, reflection, a linear progression; when they aren't crafted or storied like *valued* "diary literature" by writers like Anaïs Nin, Virginia Woolf, or Charlotte Forten. A white settler in the Dakotas, Annie Ray started her diary in 1881. In almost daily entries spanning four years, she matter-of-factly writes about the weather, money matters, her husband Charley's activities, her chores. A representative sampling from 1882: "[April] Tuesday 4/Cooler. I made Bread a lot of it, and washed a little. Charley got some Paint and Painted the door."

In Sinor's defense of ordinary writing, she urges us to read and evaluate Annie Ray's diary on its own terms. My takeaway: focus less on what Ray's diary does, more on what Ray was doing as a diarist. She was *not* writing her diary for us to read. She was not telling a story, so we diary readers should resist our natural inclination to create one. Instead, Ray was writing a diary for her own use: to monitor household income, to store ordinary moments and activities that could easily pass unnoticed, to self-track her bodily functions and health. (Ray used an asterisk to denote menstruation, like I did. She used a flower to denote sexual intercourse. I do not.)

Other reading advice I gleaned from Sinor: Appreciate that, compared with a memoir, an ordinary diary's dailiness can produce more authentic autobiography because it chronicles the unmarked ordinary moments that make up most of our days. (However dull they may be.) Respect the diarist as a writer with agency. Ray *chose* to write in a blank book; she *chose* which moments to record. "If nothing else," Sinor writes, "my hope is that you will see the power and complexity of ordinary writing as well as the vigor of the writer who makes the ordinary text."

Sinor's detailed argument inspired me to give *ordinary* diaries more of a chance, to read with a greater awareness of their particulars—and of my shortcomings as a reader. Jennifer Putzi—a twenty-first-century white college professor studying the diaries of nineteenth-century Black women—told me that Sinor's work was an important reminder: that the ordinary kind of diary "wasn't written for you, the reader. You were never meant to be the audience. So even when you feel like you know this person so well, you have to always remind yourself that you're an outsider . . . that there's a part of this world you don't understand."

Still, I struggled with the "no story" part of Sinor's defense. Suzanne L. Bunkers offers a different take: "Like other forms of narrative, a diary tells a story; unlike many other forms, however, a diary need not be plot-driven." Many diaries in their original manuscript state are *not* plot-driven, she notes. And most that she has studied don't follow a traditional narrative pattern (rising action, conflict, climax, denouement). Bunkers shares another scholar's interesting question: Does a *published* diary have to follow a traditional narrative pattern to produce a successful narrative of a diarist's life? (I wonder this about *any* diary, published or not.)

Desirée Henderson echoes Sinor's concern about "storying" a diary—making the diary something it's not by speaking for the diarist, imposing a plot, accenting the unusual. Some diarists *do* story (yes, a verb) their diary by revising it for anticipated readers, Henderson notes. Challenged to make sense of long, rambling, repetitious or tedious diaries, scholars and critics sometimes succumb to other common misreads, Henderson reports.

"Snippetotomy" involves highlighting snippets and letting parts speak for the whole. "Psychologizing" means analyzing a diarist's mindset or subconscious desires without having the psychological know-how, claiming to know what a diarist is *really* saying.

ooo

Even if a diarist isn't telling a story, does that mean no story has been told? When I'm writing a diary entry, I'm not thinking about creating or maintaining a storyline. But when I finish another volume of my diary, it feels momentous. Holding the completed volume (a physical book!) in my hand, it feels like the latest tangible chapter of my life and, yes, my story. When I read my old diary volumes, I recognize them as my story, with that squiggly throughline.

When I read someone else's diary, ordinary or not, I doubt I can completely stop searching for a story. With diaries of people I know (or think I know)—say, my former self, my mom, a well-known person—I often arrive with a story that I'm looking to confirm. When I'm reading a *stranger's* diary, I look for hints of a story—or short of that, an interesting person. Otherwise, I lose interest in reading. With Annie Ray's diary, I was naturally drawn to snippets that seemed remarkable, interesting, and dramatic, such as this self-reflective one from 1881: "Feb[ruary] 27/Sunday/It has been severely cold today. Wrote a letter to Mrs. Ward and one to Miss Virgile. Some way I feel down-hearted and lonely. The way seems so hard and dark."

I had a similar experience with another nineteenth-century diary that I browsed through at the Iowa Women's Archives, written by Iowa Byington Reed. (Yes, a woman named Iowa who lived in Iowa City, Iowa.) The archives' description of Reed's diary offered at least one potential story arc: her long courtship with a farmer, followed by wedding preparations, married life, and finally inconsolable grief at her husband's death. Reed kept a diary for sixty-four years, from age twenty in 1872 to age eighty-four in 1936. Some entries were "ordinary." Dry, dutiful, dull writing. An accomplished seamstress, she wrote on January 25, 1878: "I was busy sewing all the forenoon, and in the afternoon did some mending and washed out a few things." Reading other entries I sensed a story brewing—and, even if story making wasn't Reed's intent, this anticipation made me want to keep reading. On April 18, 1878, she wrote: "The man brought the little girl today. We are to keep her two weeks on trial. She is rather an interesting child but woefully neglected." Tell me more.

Although I first encountered Reed's diary at the Iowa Women's Archives under Frida Kahlo's watchful eyes, when the pandemic started I had to switch to reading the digital version. Much as I appreciated that option—especially the transcriptions—it didn't pack the same visceral punch as holding the paper diary that Reed once held, admiring its marbled cover, seeing her neat script flowing across lined pages. Reed's sturdy diary volume was one of thirty-four, testifying to her long life, while the single diary volume of another nineteenth-century Iowa farm woman, Jennie Sies, whispered the opposite. Sies chronicled her chores, Bible readings, and social activities for eight months, then stopped suddenly on September 24, 1880, nine days before her death at age twenty. Accompanying the handwritten journal was a touching surprise: a typed transcription by Sies's descendants. I like to think they wanted to make sure Jennie Sies was known and, perhaps, understood.

On the Schlesinger Library's website, I found some impressive digitized diaries, including the 1837–1838 diary of woman's suffragist leader and abolitionist Susan B. Anthony! (There's also an online collection of digital material about the #MeToo movement, including social media posts and related hashtags.) But nothing beat the thrill of visiting the physical library with Kathyrn Jacob as my enthusiastic guide and seeing some of her favorite diaries in their papery flesh: The toilet-paper diary that had to be unrolled to be read. A 1917 diary written in barely legible cursive on a brittle pad of paper that turned out to be a book of wallpaper samples. (The diarist's husband sold wallpaper.) Ann Reeve's fragile Civil War diary, with its faded pages inside a worn tan leather-bound cover, inspired a certain awe—especially when it was carefully placed atop gray archival foam blocks to protect it during our reading. Reclining regally on that foam throne, the diary commanded attention: all hail an important historical document!

From diary scholars, I have learned to pay attention to a diary's "materiality" and physical details: the writing materials used, changes in handwriting, blank pages, doodles, and the "paratext," pre-printed supplementary material found in manufactured diaries that hint at the particulars and passions of the diarist's day. As I browsed through a woman's *1986 Dairy Diary for the Home* at the Great Diary Project, I became less interested in the entries than the pre-printed recipes (with photos!). Were Brits really eating kipper soufflé, kidneys in batter, pasta campania, and mandarin and ginger russe in the 1980s, or were these recipes aspirational? I learned that, in 1981, the UK Milk Marketing Board began selling the *Dairy Diary* (1.5 million in the first year!), delivered by milkmen. Today, the Milk Marketing Board is gone, but the *Dairy Diary* is still for sale (by a different owner) and even has an Instagram account.

The Dairy Diary inspired me to revisit my own 1967 diary to more closely read its paratext for Signs of the Sixties. I found lists for the Seven Wonders of the Ancient World and "Rules for Spelling." Were these important back then? The prize for "Most Poignant Paratext" went to Population of Principal Cities, 1960. A list followed (American cities only!) and eight-year-old Betsy drew a star next to her hometown, Detroit, Michigan. Hard to believe it ranked fifth, population almost 1.7 million. By 2025, Detroit was twenty-sixth, with an estimated population of 645,705. The "Most Amusing Paratext" was on the "IDENTIFICATION" page where I had found my fudged weight. Eight-year-old Betsy ignored most of the "SIZES TO REMEMBER" for Gloves, Hat, Shoes, Hosiery—filling in only Shoes.

ooo

My reading experience with the diaries at the Iowa Women's Archives was colored by my pending diary donation. Who would my diary bunk with some day? The archives' website listed eighty-seven diarists. Many of them seemed to be classic rural Iowa women with classic rural Iowa lives, such as "Keppy, Myrtle (1924–2009): champion hog breeder, farm woman, 4-H leader, and president of the Iowa Porkettes."

But I also found early- and mid-1900s diarists whose descriptions foretold the diversity and women's lib to come. Martina Morado Vallejo, who emigrated from Mexico to Kansas in 1910, kept a diary in Spanish during the 1950s that was later transcribed and translated by her Iowa daughter. Lois Laughlin, a "feminist and activist" in West Branch, Iowa, wrote forty diary volumes between 1953 and 2007. The archives also hold the diaries of professors, artists, nurse-midwives, community activists, social workers; of missionaries in Sudan, Nigeria, and the Belgian Congo; and of immigrants from France, Sweden, and Holland.

Some of the online diary descriptions hint at tragedy, adventure, grit, or accomplishment. Ida "Belle" Bandfield Holden, a schoolteacher from near Waterloo, witnessed the death of her husband from tuberculosis only weeks after her mother died in 1899. Her diary's description reads: "These deaths had a profound effect on Holden. She remarried in 1904 and shortly thereafter took her own life." Annette Cech, an "Iowa City housewife and mother," wrote a journal in 1989, the same year her son Thomas won the Nobel Prize in chemistry. How might I be described in the archives' online catalog someday? Maybe: "Diary, woman, Iowa, Jewish, journalist, neurotic."

Were any of the Iowa diarists *like* me? I never connected with any diarists the way that Sarah Gristwood reported she did while researching her 2024 anthology of women's diaries, *Secret Voices*. At the time, Gristwood's husband was dying. When she read diaries written by widowed women, she felt a sense of "recognition" and "familiarity," she wrote in a newspaper essay. She empathized with one diarist's feeling of "disconnectedness," and with another's sense of "numbness" and "relief" when her husband died after a long physical decline. "Their emotion seemed to license my own," writes Gristwood.

I did feel an unexpected kinship with Iowa Byington Reed: we were both determined multi-decade diarists. I also found a kinship of sorts with a few Jewish Iowans and journalist Iowans, although our stories differed. Judy Klemesrud, whose diary spanned the mid-twentieth century, went from writing for her father's small-town northern Iowa newspaper in Winnebago County to covering the women's movement for the *New York Times*. She kept a diary for the last seven years of her life, which ended in her mid-forties due to cancer. Her remains were returned to Winnebago County, buried in its rich black soil. "She is one of the people we can say thank you to," said the feminist leader Betty Friedan, after learning of Klemesrud's death.

Ruth Laughlin, another fellow journalist, had a heartbreaking story. Born in 1954 in Iowa City, she spent her short but intense young adulthood in Philadelphia, writing about politics and religion for a Quaker newspaper, briefly marrying an African immigrant, and joining every social justice movement around—peace, racial justice, feminist, anti-poverty, anti-nukes. She would have been all-in during the 2020 Black Lives Matter protests. But Laughlin never made it past 1986 or age thirty-one, when she was raped and murdered in her Philly apartment. Somehow her mother, Lois, found the strength to read her daughter's diaries—and penned an introduction to them for the archives record. Ruth's diary entries, she writes, "relay the feelings of a young woman in the turbulent mid-years of the twentieth century when the Vietnam War, the civil rights movement, and the feminist movement had a massive impact on the behavior and attitudes of just about everybody and every institution."

Beyond Iowa, another diary proved a gut punch. It was written by Yitskhok Rudashevski, a thirteen-year-old Jewish boy who lived in a Lithuanian ghetto during the Nazi era, in 1941. He was murdered in 1943. He wrote from a city that *my* ancestors left, well before the war. In an online exhibit about his diary, organized by a Jewish research institute in New York, I watched a short video of an actor reading entries. I also read other entries shared in graphic novel form, including this one from September 6, 1941: "There is an anxious feeling. A ghetto is being created for the Jews of Vilna. It is an image from the Middle Ages. A big black mass of people moves harnessed to their big bundles. People cry looking at the bundles. . . . The sun, as if ashamed of what people are doing down below, let the sky cloud over."

My most personally meaningful reader experience didn't happen in an archive, online or off, or with a stranger's diary. It happened at home, reading my mother's diary. After she died in 2004, I salvaged a few of her slim, scuffed diary volumes from my parents' garage. Most were about travel, and the volumes I chose were about places I hoped to visit. They seemed primarily factual accounts of what my parents had done, eaten, and seen. Skimming the entries for travel tips, I noticed little else. Years later, in 2018, when I went to Copenhagen equipped with travel tips from Mom's 1972 travel diary, she never steered me wrong. I even tried a restaurant's herring dish, which she reported my dad had loved. Not bad.

But five years after my trip to Copenhagen, after roaming in Diary-land and talking with people who valued the diaries of people they loved and lost, I returned to my mother's Copenhagen diary. It was wedged in the crowded bookshelf in my Chicago apartment. When I opened the diary this time I saw how the entries were written in my mother's inimitable left-handed cursive. In her writing, I heard her distinctive voice and recognized some of her best qualities: her sunny disposition (especially when traveling), her curiosity, optimism, excitement, discerning taste, artist's eye. Much of that seemed gone during in her final years, as dementia robbed her of the ability to write, speak, and read. This time, reading my mother's diary brought her back to me. "Danish Royal Ballet performed Coppelia, a premier in the . . . colorful Royal Theatre," she wrote on May 17, 1972. "An exciting part of the evening was the Queen was there with her handsome husband. Her father the sea king Frederick, just died. She's just become queen; that was very thrilling to see her in her box—she was dressed very simply."

On my bookshelf, I suddenly chanced upon my mother's 1959 diary, which was *not* about travel. I forgot it was among the few I'd salvaged. Flipping instinctively to April 26, I found that I was mentioned, along with my father: "Our little daughter was born all covered with dark brown hair and crying, beautiful—Allen saw her—What a joy!"

12

Self-Exposure

Should We Let Strangers Read Our *Diary?*

November 15, 1980: After a party in the ramshackle house I shared with my college friends, I went upstairs to bed. Propping a pillow behind my head, I reached, as always, for my diary on the nightstand. This time I grabbed air. No diary. I turned toward the nightstand to look closer. Nothing. I got out of bed and crouched down to look under the nightstand, and then under my bed. I searched around my desk and dresser. Nowhere. Giving up, I fumbled around for paper, any paper.

"What a creepy feeling," I scribbled on yellow notepad paper. "I cannot find my diary and it is always next to my bed. Funny, it seems all of a sudden very valuable, as if I've lost part of my life's record. I would hate to think that one of my friends—and that is who was at our party tonight—would take it." The next night, the diary was still missing and I was still writing on yellow paper. The night after that, I had a new blank notebook. I tucked the yellow paper pages inside.

The missing diary never turned up. I vaguely remember feeling exposed, almost violated, but I continued to leave my diary in plain view, as if to say: *Nothing to read here—if there was, I'd hide this.* Or: *I trust you not to read this.* But, in truth, I leave it out for convenience, so I can find it quickly. I am not inviting readers. Although that's changing. I know that readers will eventually be invited—when my diary becomes available in an archive. What I learned in Diary-land bolstered my resolve to donate responsibly. I keep thinking about the British man whose "found" journal was used by a filmmaker, years after his death. In his journal, the filmmaker reported, he wrote that he planned to give the journal to someone trustworthy to do whatever they wished with it—as long as no living person was hurt.

Increasingly jittery as I searched for a way to do good, not harm, I became hyperaware of other diarists' efforts to shield their writing from prying eyes and to limit what was revealed, limiting their self-exposure and exposure of others. With celebrated published diaries, I learned that exposure concern could influence publishing prep. Hearing that other diarists redacted sensitive material, I wondered if I should too or, instead, rely on archives' privacy-enhancing options. While mulling over my donating *and* mulling over why I write a diary, I realized that donating might jeopardize this "why."

ooo

Hiding, deleting, obscuring, locking, threatening: thwarting diary snoopers is another periodic hot topic in Diary-land (beyond diary burning). Diarists share their anxiety and strategy in advice columns and online journaling communities, posting discussion questions like: "How screwed would you be if someone read your journal?" A teenager writes at the front of her diary: "Get out! Keep out! Private Property! Trespassers punished by fine! A dollar a page!" Ideas shared online range from obvious to ingenious: Hide the journal inside a large box of tampons! Tuck the diary behind a canvas painting on the wall! Create a fake decoy journal full of falsities!

Using code or near-illegible script to disguise diary entries goes way back. The seventeenth-century diarist Samuel Pepys deployed hard-to-decipher shorthand symbols and foreign words when he wrote about his sexual escapades. Anne Lister used her "crypt hand" code to cloak diary accounts of her love affairs with women (among other things she wished to keep secret). On April 29, 1832, she wrote: "What a comfort my journal is. How I can write in crypt all as it really is and throw it off my mind and console myself. Thank God for it." Lister's code sent me back to my 1967 diary and eight-year-old Betsy's stab at using a less effective code: "I-A, PLAYED-A, LOVE-A GAME-A. I-A KISSED-A ROBEN-A AND-A SHE-A KISSED-A ME-A."

Both the British writer Beatrix Potter and Franklin Roosevelt disguised journal entries. The reason? Speculation lands on their mothers. (Of course.)

Roosevelt, at age twenty-one, wrote brief daily notes in a pocket diary that sometimes shifted to code. A sentence written on November 22, 1903, and decoded in the 1970s reads: "After lunch I have a never to be forgotten walk with my darling." Sleuths surmise that Roosevelt was hiding the proposal he made that day to nineteen-year-old Eleanor because his mother thought Franklin was too young for marriage.

Beatrix Potter kept her journal for about sixteen years, starting at age fourteen in 1881 and stopping about four years before the 1902 publication of *The Tale of Peter Rabbit.* Before she died, at age seventy-seven in 1943, Potter mentioned in a letter that she'd written a journal in "cipher shorthand." One theory is that Potter used concealed writing as a teenager to conceal her mischievous, Peter Rabbit–like nature from her strict mother. In her journal (and, all the better, in cipher shorthand), she could freely write about her life and thoughts about well-known people in London, where she was part of a well-to-do family. In 1952, a young relative of Potter's discovered the journal and gave it to a Potter superfan, who spent thirteen years deciphering it, which was relatively easy, unlike reading Potter's tiny writing. *The Journal of Beatrix Potter*, published in 1966, expanded Potter's reputation from a writer of "bunny rabbit tales" to a skilled author and an astute observer of Victorian life.

Devoted diarist Queen Victoria was the queen of redaction, commanding her daughter Princess Beatrice to strike passages in her 43,765-page journal (after Victoria's death) that might offend other royals. Beatrice obediently cut material—including mentions of the queen's friendship with her Indian clerk, teacher, and confidant Abdul Karim, which rankled some in the royal household and court. Victoria's early handwritten volumes and later transcriptions of others by Beatrice (who destroyed the originals) are in Windsor Castle's Royal Archives; they were posted online in 2012 to mark the diamond jubilee (sixty-year reign) of Victoria's great-great-granddaughter Queen Elizabeth. Entries by Victoria (whose diamond jubilee was in 1897) include skillful family drawings and grief-laden writing after her husband Prince Albert's death at forty-two in 1860: "I have been unable to write my journal since my beloved one left us, and oh with what a heavy broken heart I enter a new year without him."

Abdul Karim also kept a diary, which reportedly alluded to an intimate but not romantic relationship with the queen. After Karim's death in 1909, descendants spirited his diary to India and then Pakistan where, in 2010, London-based author Shrabani Basu tracked it down and used it to update her book on the pair, suggesting that theirs was a "remarkable love story," but they were not likely lovers. Her book informed the 2017 biopic *Victoria & Abdul.*

The original manuscript of the early-1800s journal of English diarist Dorothy Wordsworth—later published as *The Grasmere Journals*—includes two sentences crossed out of an entry by an unknown hand. Later restored, the sentences appear in a much-discussed entry about the wedding day of Dorothy's brother, the poet William. They are believed to read: "I gave him the wedding ring—with how deep a blessing! I took it from my forefinger where I had worn it the whole of the night before—he slipped it again onto my finger and blessed me fervently." Some speculate that William gave Dorothy the ring for safekeeping and the sentences were struck because they hinted at a too-intimate relationship between the siblings, who shared Dove Cottage in the Lake District village of Grasmere. Dorothy began this much-discussed entry: "On Monday 4th October, 1802, my Brother William was married to Mary Hutchinson." Dorothy was too distraught to attend the wedding, scholars intuit from another sentence noting that after learning that the wedding had concluded, "I could stand it no longer, and threw myself on the bed, where I lay in stillness, neither seeing nor hearing anything."

Why did Dorothy write about the ring? Who crossed out Dorothy's words, and why? Does Dorothy's journal record of William's marriage mark the "divorce" of siblings who shared "a strange love?" asked Frances Wilson, a Dorothy Wordsworth biographer, in 2009. Editorial notes in a 2008 edition of Dorothy's journal claim that the "incest theory" has waned and interpret Dororthy's entry to mean that she "fully accepted" William's marriage. Dorothy may have been the one who crossed out her words because she thought this "drama of tenderness" was "not for other eyes—not even perhaps for [William's]," a note reports. Another nagging question I had is also addressed by a note mentioning that the "actual ring" is displayed in the Wordsworth Museum in Grasmere and is known as Mary Wordsworth's ring—she got it!

Scholars also make much of the wedding entry because Wordsworth soon stopped writing her journal—"conjecturally because the relationship between brother and sister had fundamentally changed," writes Jeff Cowton, curator of Wordsworth Grasmere. First published in 1897, forty-two years after Dorothy's death, *The Grasmere Journals* feature the enigmatic Wordsworth's acclaimed nature writing, as well as entries about William's poetry and their shared country life. She started her journal "because I shall give William pleasure by it." Post-wedding, that purpose was lost, suggests Wilson. When Wordsworth's "life alone with her brother was shattered . . . she stopped writing, as if writing and William were bound up with one another."

ooo

"No editor can be trusted not to spoil a diary," British critic Arthur Ponsonby famously grumbled in his 1923 anthology, *English Diaries*. Whether that editor is a relative (as with Leonard Woolf), an academic (as with the Emilie Davis scholars), or the diarist (as with David Sedaris), they inevitably change a voluminous diary by shrinking and shaping it. Sedaris, in the introduction to his 2017 diary-entry collection *Theft by Finding*, mentions that he chose a fraction of the roughly eight million words he produced between 1977 and 2002. "An entirely different book from the same source material could make me appear nothing but evil, selfish, generous, or even, dare I say, sensitive," Sedaris writes.

Then there's the serial editing of one of the world's most widely read diaries. The original handwritten diary of Anne Frank contained sexual material that was cut from the initial published version, overseen by her father, Otto, including fourteen-year-old Anne's writing about her vagina on March 24, 1944: "You can barely find it, because the folds of skin hide the opening. The hole's so small I can hardly imagine how a man could get in there, much less how a baby could come out." This material returned in later published editions.

Otto Frank's weighty decision to publish his daughter's diary followed personal tragedy: Anne's death at age sixteen, as well as the deaths of her sister and mother, in the Holocaust's concentration camps. The diary revealed "quite a different Anne than I had known as my daughter," Otto recalled in a 1967 broadcast. Most of Anne's entries were written while she was in hiding with her family from the Nazis in Amsterdam between July 6, 1942, and August 4, 1944. After her death in 1945, Anne's diary was published in Dutch in 1947 (well reviewed as "a war document of striking density"), followed by the English translation, *The Diary of a Young Girl*, in 1952. The original edition excised up to 60 percent of Anne's original words. Gone were her mentions of menstruation, sexuality, reproduction, masturbation, and same-sex attraction. Gone were some harsh words about her mother, classmates, and her parents' "tepid" marriage. In shrinking the diary down to publishable size with acceptable content, Anne was, arguably, shrunk down to a less complex and more saintly teenager.

Although Otto was later faulted for censorial editing, Anne Frank was her diary's first editor. As an ambitious young writer aware that her diary might be published after the war, fifteen-year-old Anne started writing a revised version while continuing to write her original diary, which she started at age thirteen. Beyond trimming the original's sexual content, she rewrote some parts, expanded others, and obscured people's names. "Like countless other diarists, Anne Frank was determined to exert control over what would remain in her texts," writes Suzanne L. Bunkers.

Anne Frank's diary has a complicated publication history, with several forms, multiple editions, and many translations (seventy languages!), and has been overseen by various editors, as Bunkers details. Both Anne's original diary (three bound notebooks) and Anne's revision (330 loose-leaf pages) were found after her death and used to create the first published edition (1947). In 1986, a "critical" edition was published in Dutch, which includes Anne's two handwritten versions, the 1947 published diary, and scholarly information. In 1991, a "definitive edition" was published in Dutch and included restored material removed from the first published edition. An English translation of the definitive edition followed in 1995.

As subsequent diary editions were published, a more complex and adolescent Anne emerged. So did new arguments for censoring her diary. In 2013, a Michigan mother made international headlines by complaining that the definitive version is pornographic. A British journalist countered: "Instead of banning the diary from schools . . . we should teach girls not to be ashamed of their bodies." In 2023, amid a growing US book-ban movement, a critically acclaimed 2017 graphic adaptation based on the definitive version was pulled off shelves in Texas and Florida schools, condemned as pornography and even as anti-Semitic. The illustrator countered that he had labored to ensure nothing was too explicit for young readers.

Controversy surrounded the posthumous publication of the journal of the celebrated (and controversial) poet and novelist Sylvia Plath. Written from 1950 to 1962, the journal was first published in 1982—long after Plath's death by suicide in 1963 at age thirty. Plath's entries were heavily edited by her estranged husband and literary executor, the British poet Ted Hughes, who was accused of producing a dark, inaccurate, unbalanced, and self-serving version. Hughes admitted that he burned the journal volume covering Plath's last days, allegedly to protect their two young children. In 2000, two years after Hughes's death, an unabridged version of Plath's journal was published, with her estate's support, that includes more than four hundred previously unpublished pages. The preface promised: "Sylvia Plath speaks for herself."

This "exact" transcription was hailed for offering fresh insights into Plath's literary work and her intense struggles, personal and creative. Deeming the new edition "a genuine literary event," Joyce Carol Oates wrote in a newspaper review that the unexpurgated Plath diary contains "marvels of discovery" and provides a seemingly justified corrective to Hughes's edits. But she questions "the wisdom—and the ethics—of exposing a major writer's unrevised, inferior work." Oates advises readers to seek out the unedited journal's "stronger, more lyric and exhilarating passages," helpfully pointing to a "brilliant thumbnail sketch" of W. H. Auden that Plath wrote on April 27, 1953: "Auden tossing his big head back with a twist of wide ugly grinning lips, his sandy hair, his coarse tweedy brown jacket, his burlap-textured voice and the crackling brittle utterances—the naughty mischievous boy genius."

What I question about the Plath diary publication are the ethics of posthumously publishing the depths of a diarist's pain, especially when it was unclear whether the diarist wanted publication. This issue has bubbled up with other posthumously published diaries, including in 2025 with Joan Didion's published therapy notes, filled with candid passages about her depression, self-doubt, and anxieties at age sixty-five onward. "Literary

Gold . . . or Betrayal of Trust? Joan Didion Journal Opens Ethical Minefield" read a newspaper headline before the release of *Notes to John*. Didion left no instructions about what should be done with the notes, which were found in an unlabeled folder soon after her death in 2021. Is publication justified if the new information from "the journal" offers fresh insights into Didion's late-in-life acclaimed memoirs? Was it published too soon? Is publication an inevitable consequence of celebrity—or what the savvy Didion wanted, since she left it behind? "If the motivation is to line pockets rather than honour legacies, that hardly seems a good enough justification for invading someone's privacy in the most brutal of ways," writes British journalist Helen Coffey.

Anaïs Nin's sexually frank diary, written from the 1930s to the 1970s, was published in two multi-volume versions—cut and less-cut. Nin reportedly approved of both. The first began appearing in 1966, with most volumes edited by Nin and published during her lifetime. Publication of the second "unexpurgated" version began in 1986, after Nin's death in 1977. In the first version, Nin cut much of her diary's sexual frankness. Because "her [first] husband and some of her lovers were still alive at the time, she was forced to excise an entire side of her character—the erotic—from the text," explains Paul Herron, editor of *Mirages*, part of the unexpurgated version.

Rupert Pole, Nin's second husband and literary executor, writes that Nin "realized she could never publish the diary as she wrote it without hurting" others so she used real names but edited out her personal life, first husband, and extramarital lovers. "It was Anaïs's wish to have the full story told," explains Pole in the preface to *Henry and June*, another part of the unexpurgated version. Technically a more complete but not "raw" version, *Henry and June* was edited to focus on Nin's literary and sexual intimacy with Henry Miller, plus her deep attraction to his wife, June. "Henry and I are tasting each other's flesh," reads an entry from April 1932. "We fall together into our savage world. He bites me. He makes my bones crack. He makes me lie with legs wide open and digs into me. Our cravings grow wild. Our bodies are convulsed."

ooo

A five-foot-tall Art Deco-style cabinet dominates the front foyer of Helen Churko's one-bedroom New York apartment. Dozens of Churko's handwritten journal volumes are inside. "It felt worthy of holding my memories," she explains about the elegant cabinet, made of caramel-colored wood arranged in a V-shaped parquet pattern. Although Churko has secured her journal now, she doesn't know where those volumes—spanning more than forty-five years of her life—will go after she's gone. "What on earth do you do with all of this?" she asked me.

Should diarists make end-of-life plans for their diary? Even some baby-boom elders told me they have no plan for their diary's long-term future. Creating a plan—not unlike writing a will—requires contemplating mortality. Other diarists *do* have plans, which range from destroying their diary to handing it down to a relative or friend. One senior diarist told me that while she has held onto her diary volumes for herself, she made a pact with a diary-keeping friend: whoever dies first will burn the other's diary so others can't read it. (Her diary mentions difficult personal issues.) The millennial diarist Robert Ryan told me that he mentions his journal in the will that he and his wife recently "got around to writing." The journal will go to their children as adults. Ryan reported moving the volumes to a safe so his young kids won't find them "before they're supposed to." Another diarist plans to give her family a "curated" and "cleaned-up" version of her diary. My eighty-three-year-old friend Janet Levine in suburban Detroit plans to leave her diary, as is, for her family. Written over sixty-five years, the diary speaks of childbirths, travels, her husband of fifty-seven years, miscarriages, cancer, love-hate relationships. "I am not afraid for them to read these musings, many wrenching, many more endearing and loving," she told me.

When I asked digital diarists in Day One's Facebook group if they had made plans for their diary to outlive them, these rugged individualists of Diary-land offered a variety of responses:

- "I hadn't thought of that but now I am!"
- "I want mine to die with me. No one else needs to read my goofy ideas or my bad poetry, reactions to food or my boring to-do lists."
- "Handing mine down, of course!"

- "I waver between a bonfire for all the handwritten journals/deleting the last twelve years' worth of digital . . . and just letting the descendants deal with it. . . . What I dread most is that anyone in my family is hurt by something I wrote in the petulance of the moment. What I hope for most is that some would-be historian or family member will find clues as to what was going on in the world when I was alive. And that I cared enough to leave a record."

"Dread" of hurting others resonated with me. The Scottish poet and diarist William Soutar memorably wrote in 1934: "A diary is an assassin's cloak which we wear when we stab a comrade in the back with a pen." I was also reminded of a writing teacher's feminist lament to me that women's personal stories are too often left untold because they include unvarnished reports about family and friends (i.e., potentially back-stabbing words). Which explains, in part, why donating to an archive can be a hard sell.

The legendary Iowan "radio homemaker" Evelyn Birkby, whose syndicated "Kitchen Klatter" program on rural life aired for decades, began donating her letters, scrapbooks, and professional papers to the Iowa Women's Archives in 1993. "It seemed mindboggling to think that those papers that I just wanted to get out of the house had a value—and the value was historic," the charming Birkby told me during my memorable visit to her western Iowa house in 2021, about two years before she died at age 101. But, she added, "My little high school diary, I don't think [it] will ever see the light of day. I'd have to read it first because that's personal."

Beyond this, diarists I met were often surprised to learn that donating was an option. But people who *do* donate their own diary or personal writing to an archive often are motivated by a desire to be known and not forgotten. So says Marlene Kayen, chair of the German Diary Archive, by way of explaining why she dislikes the word "donation," as do some other European diary archives. They prefer "submission" or "deposit," because these words acknowledge that the diary submitter benefits as well.

People can also donate—or submit—an unpublished diary they didn't write. Darla Ewalt of Iowa hopes to hand down her ancestors' nineteenth-century diaries to the next generation of her family. If there are no takers, she wants the diaries to remain in Iowa (they're "Iowa history"), perhaps on loan (if possible) to an archive. Nancy Guri Duncan, an American expat in France, donated the journal of another American expat, Barbara Reed Valbot, to France's APA archive. Valbot took writing workshops that Duncan taught in Paris and died in 2004, days before her ninetieth birthday. "No descendants. No one else to care about her writings but me, her writing teacher," Duncan wrote to me. She was Valbot's estate executor, so the journal was hers to donate, she explained, adding: "Barbara would be glad her words were being preserved." "French butchers don't talk, they sing," Barbara Reed Valbot wrote in her diary on August 24, 1966. "They all sound the same, tho Mr. Salmon has large dark eyes and shiny black hair to go with the song."

ooo

During my husband's family reunion in Kansas about two decades ago, I spied a girlish 1960s-era diary in a pile of old photos, letters, and memorabilia on a card table—all available for the taking. I claimed the diary, a golden oldie with an illustration of a perky, pony-tailed girl on the red plastic cover. When I finally got around to reading it, I had to first jimmy the diary's little metal lock with a kitchen knife. (Not smart, I know.) I was soon reading about an unnamed teenage diarist's bra shopping—until I realized that the diary was likely written by my husband's aunt. I stopped reading—it didn't feel right—and returned the diary to its author at another family gathering. (She didn't know it had survived.)

I've thought about that experience while contemplating someone chancing upon *my* diary—not on a Kansas card table, not even on an archive shelf, but perhaps posted online. I've also thought about another experience: reading online the 1870s entries in Iowa Byington Reed's diary, which is physically housed at my chosen Iowa archives and was transcribed by DIY History volunteers. Diaries, in general, are popular with transcribers. And, yes, I've heard that the *future is digital* and that archival paper documents that aren't digitized may not be read. But does my diary have to be posted online?

What I learned from seasoned archives staff, including in Iowa, was reassuring—mostly. I was relieved to find that my diary can remain with me until I die and, afterwards, be sealed for a period, to protect the privacy of those mentioned in the diary who are still living. Donors also have a strong say about their documents' future use including digitization and posting, via the all-important "donor/gift" agreement they must fill out to specify preferences regarding access restrictions, privacy measures, copyright transfer, and more. Archives often ask donors to transfer copyright to them so documents can be more readily used, as in, copied and distributed, now often interpreted to include being digitized and posted online, although the law doesn't specify this. When an archive receives a diary (or another unpublished work), it owns the physical diary, *not* the copyright, which remains with the diarist creator, often for decades, depending on the particulars. (This holds true for found or purchased diaries too. Diary sellers sell physical diaries but often don't address copyright.)

I was also glad to glean that professionally run archives do not tend to post *contemporary* unpublished diaries online, in part because the content might affect still-living people. A diary's glancing mention of a secret lover, an abusive husband, or a child's mental illness, for example, could be damaging. It would be "irresponsible" to post "recent" diaries when the author and people mentioned are still alive, an Iowa archive curator told me, which means generally posting diaries that are more than a hundred years old. (Sometimes posting more contemporary papers happens, with the donor's permission.)

But archives don't follow a single playbook. Josh Kitchens, the director of Archival Services and Digital Initiatives at the Georgia Public Library Services, told me, "There really isn't 100 percent consensus on exactly what to do with diaries, especially personal information." Some archives can't afford to hire trained archival staff well-versed in copyright law and privacy concerns, although they may seek out best practices. An archive may not clearly mention digitization or online posting in a donor agreement or in conversation. Some archives may not accept a donation if too many access restrictions are requested, limiting its use. The good news is that seasoned archive staff have been discussing how to handle digitization and posting—and, increasingly, they talk to prospective donors about this.

"How we approach conversations with donors in a digital world has gotten ever more complicated," Janice E. Ruth, the manuscript division chief of the Library of Congress (LOC), told me. A helpful LOC document for prospective donors (often prominent public figures) addresses the frequently asked question: Will my papers be digitized? The answer: No. At least not immediately. Scanning or microfilming is not routine because it "is expensive and time consuming." Priority for digitizing goes to documents that need preservation and/or are heavily used. (This includes paper documents considered most important and/or fragile.) Posting documents online requires a "rights analysis that evaluates both copyrights and privacy rights, which often pose additional obstacles for modern collections." But the document collection *will* be described in an online catalog record.

Although donors are understandably tempted to engage in "personal curation"—such as ripping pages out of a diary before donating it—this is discouraged. "Please do not destroy any material because it appears sensitive or controversial," the LOC document cautions. "The passage of time tends to desensitize most subjects. The more complete your papers are, the more likely they will permit researchers to reconstruct and understand that past in an authentic way, most especially when controversial events and personalities are involved."

ooo

Long before the diary's digital dawn, archivists have strived to balance two noble and seemingly contradictory goals: provide timely public access to their documents so they can be used to expand public knowledge *and* protect the privacy of donors and third parties. Archivists "have both legal and ethical duties to respect privacy," writes Susan C. Lawrence, a University of Tennessee, Knoxville, history professor. She also points to professional guidelines from the Society of American Archivists (SAA), whose ethics code states: "Archivists recognize that privacy is an inherent fundamental right and sanctioned by law. They establish procedures and policies to protect the interests of the donors, individuals, groups, and organizations whose public and private lives and activities are documented in archival holdings." The code also appears to address third-party privacy: "As appropriate and mandated by law, archivists place access restrictions on collections to ensure that privacy and confidentiality are maintained, particularly for individuals and groups who have had no voice or role in collections' creation, retention, or public use."

Although archives often don't hold the copyright to a diary (or other works), researchers can typically still read them. And copyright law (especially its "fair use" clause) offers workarounds for archives and scholars to use material without copyright permission, under certain conditions. Archives, for example, may scan and send diary pages to a researcher via a password-protected website for a limited time. Or an archive or scholar can publish some material to varying degrees, depending on the particulars. Because fair use is vague and case-specific, using it risks a lawsuit, but a legal challenge is commonly considered unlikely. If there is one, though, courts provide more copyright protection to unpublished works (including unpublished diaries) than published works.

Keen to make their material available for research and learning, archives sometimes face a tough judgment call when weighing whether to use fair use to post unpublished works without the copyright holder's permission. SAA provided some guidance in 2011, endorsing recommendations that advise archives to do a risk assessment, be cautious about posting recent material not intended to be public, ask donors to pinpoint privacy concerns, and adopt a "liberal take-down policy" (removing material from public view if requested).

Here's the rub: Making only material with *known* copyright available (via digitizing, posting, or printing) would considerably limit resources for researchers. Although the digital age was expected to expand public access to valuable documents in archives, some lamented that instead, risk-adverse archives were still too focused on complying with copyright law rather than on improving access.

Beyond the copyright issue, when it comes to privacy risks "diaries are an obvious red-flag category," wrote Sara S. Hodson, a former president of the Society of California Archivists, back in 2006. Other "potentially sensitive material," such as letters, also warrant caution, online and off. "The advent of the Internet has significantly ratcheted up the potential for invasion of privacy, even as it has become an enormously useful tool," wrote Hodson. "Diaries contain frank statements and revelations about one's self and about other people. Should diaries held in an archival repository be opened for research, even when people mentioned in them are still alive? Or should they be sealed for a reasonable period? If so, what constitutes a reasonable period?" These issues become "enormous" when posting is a possibility, writes Hodson. Archivists should know the content of personal material they plan to post and consider redacting sensitive parts in the online version, she advised. (Archives are loathe to redact material in a physical document, which is considered tantamount to censoring or erasing history.)

I caught up with Hodson, long after her article. Retired after thirty-eight years as a literary-manuscripts curator at the Huntington Library, near Pasadena, California, she reiterated her concerns about privacy. Hodson nevertheless agreed with other archivists I talked with on one crucial point: privacy risks, in general, are low for diary donors *if* they donate to a professionally run archive, i.e., with trained archival staff. "They're going to be good stewards," says Ellen LeClere, the digital curation and preservation archivist at Wayne State University's labor archive in Detroit.

At archives, basic protection generally kicks in as soon as a donation starts to be processed. When my untidy heap of papers (the Iowa archives also requested my newspaper clips and other career-related material) is pruned to create an orderly "collection," any "personally identifiable information"—say, health details or education records—will be removed or restricted. The stray email address or Social Security number, for example, could enable identity theft.

As for would-be diary readers who visit an archive's physical or digital space, they may be required to register to use material. To publish short excerpts of unpublished diaries in this book, I had to figure out what was permitted—which meant searching an archive's collection record for any restrictions, interpreting complex copyright and privacy laws in the US and Europe (they differ), closely reading SAA's helpful publications, double-checking with the archive, and/or consulting with my editor.

ooo

Diary donors face many decisions—some new, thanks to our digital day. Beyond whether to permit our handwritten paper diaries to be digitized, posted online, and transcribed, there is the question of whether to donate our born-digital diaries, including social media posts and blogs, if archives want them. Some archives *do* request born-digital material (emails, text docs, databases, digital photos, audio and video recordings, social media posts).

Just as the never-ending rush of digital innovation will generate new ways to *create* a diary, so, too, it will generate new ways to *share* archived diaries. "Technology will change this conversation" in a few years, Ellen LeClere told me.

Until my thirties, when I hunkered down in Iowa to build a family and a career, I thought little about taking care of my diary—let alone about whether it should outlive me. I left the childhood diary volumes of my lost youth in my parents' basement, later rescuing whatever I could find before the house was sold. During my wandering twenties, when I lived in six cities, I carted an ever-growing collection of volumes in a flimsy cardboard box from Ithaca to Boston, Stamford, Wichita, and Kansas City. (I didn't schlep them to London.) Only after one too many floods in our Des Moines basement did I relocate them above ground to the drab-gray fireproof filing cabinet.

Given all that I've learned in Diary-land, I did question *why* I'm donating. I landed almost where I began: I can't bear the thought of my diary being destroyed, so let's put my words and memories to *good* use! By donating (or diary writing), I'm not seeking immortality. Destruction just seems like a waste, a shame—and, yes, a death. I'm now more aware of how historians and other researchers might use a diary like mine (by someone who isn't famous). They won't be interested in the personal stuff that donors fret most about being revealed but instead will read for more lofty reasons, archivists assured me. What those reasons are is hard to know now and strange to ponder. Will they be looking for what girls did for fun before TikTok, how women juggled career and family, what Iowa women experienced as newspaper reporters? (*Newspaper* already sounds obsolete.) Will my entries be viewed as testimony or the first draft of memory by researchers wondering how people coped during the pandemic or if they did enough to resist Trump? The thought of my diary becoming a stand-alone publication, thinly veiled fiction, or voyeuristic YouTube fodder is unnerving. What I hope most is that future readers will use my diary not to zero in on *me* but to pan out on *us*.

Determining *how* best to donate proved agonizing at times. I realized I don't care what strangers think of me. I'll be dead. Because I care most about my third parties, my plan in progress has them most in mind. A thoughtful Iowa archives curator offered helpful suggestions to navigate the push-pull of access versus privacy. I'm leaning toward sealing my diary until a date when people in it will be old or gone, requiring that personal names be anonymized if used in any public way, and limiting online posting. Because I appreciated being able to read my late mother's diary, I'm considering creating a shorter, curated version of mine to give to my adult children, if they want one.

But another unforeseen risk has appeared: pledging to donate my diary threatens to upend my ongoing relationship with my diary. For more than a half century, my diary has been a sanctuary, a safe place where I can be alone with my thoughts, freely interrogate life's challenges, and try to understand me-me-me and, sometimes, other people. By deciding to let other readers in, however distant the day, I risk losing that sanctuary.

Over thirty-five years ago, in a shared youth-hostel bunk bed in Telluride, Colorado, a friend ordered me *not* to mention her in my diary, which was disappointing: she was flamboyant, feisty, fun, and fascinating. I obeyed her, although I questioned why I had to censor myself, especially since no one else would ever read my diary. Now that I know someone else *may* read my diary, will I clam up and no longer write freely? I remain troubled by what one archival curator told me: when a donor pledges to donate a diary posthumously but intends to keep diary writing, the date of the pledge is noted in the archive record. The assumption is that entries written after that date will be less personal because the diarist *knows* there may be other readers.

I hadn't expected to feel other readers' presence so soon. Now, however, when I get in bed, prop a pillow behind my head, reach for my diary on the nightstand (it's there!), and start writing, I sometimes sense other readers looking over my shoulder. I have caught myself *not* writing honestly about a problem or argument; *not* working through confusion, fear, anger, sadness, or guilt; *not* digging too deep. But I have vowed to guard against creeping self-wcensorship. If I can't be myself, on any given day, I've lost my most powerful reason to keep a diary.

APPENDIX

An Informed Donor Is a Smart Donor

Advice on Donating a Diary

If you're considering donating your diary to an archive, ask yourself:

- Why do you want to donate?
- What are you donating: is your diary handwritten or born digital?
- What are the benefits and risks?
- How might your diary benefit readers, researchers, and our shared history?
- What is in your diary? Is there sensitive material about you or others still living?
- What are your alternatives to donating, if need be? Do you want your family to have it and/or does your family want it?
- When do you want to donate—while alive or posthumously?

If you pursue donating, consider the following:

- Look for an archive that is institutionally stable and professionally run, with trained staff (an archivist, curator, librarian, historian, records manager) or others who understand copyright, privacy, and ethical concerns, and who follow best practices and procedures.
- Look for an archive that collects documents to preserve the heritage of a place, institution, and/or population. Beyond

government archives, repositories with archives may include state and local historical societies, public and university libraries, museums, corporations, and headquarters of religious faiths. (The word *archive* also refers to a physical location where archival materials are kept.)

- Achives have collecting priorities and cannot accept all offers. Consider who might want your diary by thinking about who you are (ethnicity, religion, gender, education, profession, trade). Start local and personal.
- If your diary is born-digital, look for an archive that accepts digital material.
- Consider discussing your interest in donating with family.

Once you find a willing archive:

- Ask questions—about policies, procedures, and ethics regarding access, privacy, digitization, and online posting.
- Share any concerns about sensitive material and discuss privacy options.
- Take your donor agreement seriously. This is your chance to spell out your wishes.
- Consult a lawyer if need be. (Archives may advise this.)
- If the donation will happen posthumously, make sure your plan, wishes, and diary whereabouts are known to someone else. Consider mentioning the donation in your will or leaving a signed note with your diary, stating your intentions.
- Store your diary in a cool dry place, perhaps in an acid-free storage box or fireproof safe.

For more information on donating, consult the Society of American Archivists, which has two relevant webpages:

- www2.archivists.org/publications/brochures/donating-familyrecs
- www2.archivists.org/publications/brochures/deeds-of-gift

For information on preserving diaries and other family mementos (paper and digital), see the following:

- The National Archives, www.archives.gov/preservation/family-archives
- The Library of Congress, www.digitalpreservation.gov/personal archiving/
- The *New York Times*, www.nytimes.com/wirecutter/blog/get-your-digital-accounts-ready-in-case-of-death/

Acknowledgments

Susan Freinkel, a generous friend and talented author, got me started and bravely stayed the course, from challenging to calming me. Thank you, Susan. Friend-of-my-youth (and beyond) Paula Jo Kemler volunteered ideas, copyediting, and an invaluable intro to her friend Kathryn Jacob. Thank you both. "New, different, well told" (among Kathryn's critical early feedback) became my mantra. Thank you, women of Ames, Veronica Lorson Fowler and Maria Eichmans Cochran, for insightful reading; Myra, Merida and Chip, Kathy and Doug, Nell, Marion, Steve, Chris, Margery, Leslie, Jamie, Shelby, Janet, Francine, Una, Jemima, and other friends/family for advice, tips, and hand-holding. Thank you, Sarah Flynn and Patricia Cohen for encouragement and publishing know-how; Dara Kaye and Gail Ross at WME for seeing the potential and helping me go wide; editor Catherine Tung for making this happen and making it better; Haley Lynch, Susan Lumenello, Marcy Barnes, and the rest of the Beacon Press team for enthusiastic and skilled follow-through.

Thank you to Helen Churko, Betsy Edgerton, Pam Patton, Kerry Schauber, Adrienne Su, Eileen Tull, Maycie Vorrieter, and many other thoughtful diary writers and readers for sharing your experiences. Boiling down complicated information is a risky business. I own any errors. Many people took time to explain. Thank you, Ellen K. Baker, David Balota, Suzanne L. Bunkers, Andrew Butler, G. Thomas Couser, Robyn Fivush, Desirée Henderson, Rebecca Hogan, Lee Humphreys, Sally MacNamara Ivey, James W. Pennebaker, Jennifer Putzi, Julie Rak, Henry Roediger, Paula Vene Smith, Rick Stattler, Laurel Thatcher Ulrich, Leonieke Vermeer, Helena Whitbread, Sarah S. Willen.

Thank you, archive folks: Natalia Cangi, Elizabeth Legros Chapuis, Robert K. Elder, Li Gerhalter, Sara S. Hodson, Marlene Kayen, Josh Kitchens, Claudine Krishnan, Claire Langhamer, Ellen LeClere, Kären Mason, Polly North, Kirsty Patrick, Janice E. Ruth, Jessica Scantlebury, Francesca Venuto, Janet Weaver, Caitlin Wells, Jennifer Wolfe, Kate Zirkel. Shout-outs to the Chicago Public Library (Lincoln Park), the Des Moines Public Library (Franklin Avenue), and the interlibrary loan!

Thank you with love, Dad, Barbara, MAT, Michael, Laurie, Jill, extended family, sweet pup Millie; Noah, Lily, and Emma—and Dirck, my rock.

Notes

CHAPTER 1: DAYS OF OUR LIVES

this archive: Francesca Venuto, archive press contact, email, June 12, 2024.

"People tend to agree on the general idea": Julie Rak, phone interview, Feb. 23, 2022.

The late British scholar Robert Fothergill: Robert Fothergill, *Private Chronicles: A Study of English Diaries* (Oxford: Oxford University Press, 1974), 3.

Monica Soeting: Monica Soeting, in-person conversation, Emmendingen, Germany, Apr. 14, 2023.

A Palestinian reading: Newshour, BBC, Sept. 8, 2025; Lauren Mechling, "How Journaling Went from a Solo Activity to a Social One," *Wall Street Journal*, Aug. 20, 2025, https://www.wsj.com/arts-culture/books/journaling-clubs-suleika-jaouad-book-876a6b3c; Lulu Garcia-Navarro, "Sandra Oh Knows What's Great About Middle Age," *New York Times*, July 25, 2025.

"I think deep down": Timothy White, "Reading My Father's Diaries," *New York Times*, Feb. 16, 2025.

I read about a North Dakota woman: Cathy Free, "Woman, 100, Has Journaled Every Day for 90 Years," *Washington Post*, Feb. 9, 2025.

Smart online publications: Maria Popova, "16 Life Learnings," *The Marginalian*, www.themarginalian.org/2022/10/23/16-learnings/; Jillian Hess, *Noted*, jillianhess.substack.com/; Maham Javaid, "Millions Are Reading a Teen's Account of Life and War. It's from 1945," *Washington Post*, Dec. 5, 2024; Helaina Lainaravs (@lainaravs), "We love a primary source document," TikTok, Nov. 21, 2024, www.tiktok.com/@lainaravs/photo/7439953307163954474.

Acquaintances urged me: Robert Ryan, phone interview, Feb. 12, 2023; Dimitri Gordon, text, June 28, 2024.

the discussion platform Reddit: r/Journaling, Reddit, https://www.reddit.com/r/Journaling/, accessed May 26, 2025.

"the big baby": Tom Alex, Facebook post, posted March 29, 2023, since deleted.

"They're such a gift": Veronica Fowler, email, Oct. 18, 2024.

In the United Kingdom: "Children and Young People's Diary Writing in 2022," National Literacy Trust, Jan. 5, 2023, literacytrust.org.uk/research-services/research-reports/children-and-young-peoples-diary-writing-in-2022/; "Children and Young People's Writing in 2024," National Literacy Trust,

June 4, 2024, literacytrust.org.uk/research-services/research-reports /children-and-young-peoples-writing-in-2024/.

"The Internet has arguably": Clare Brant and Max Saunders, "The Narrative Self," *Ego Media: Life Writing and Online Affordances*, Stanford University Press online publication, egomedia.supdigital.org/themes/self/index.html, accessed May 20, 2025.

Author Lucy Sante: Lucy Sante, *I Heard Her Call My Name: A Memoir of Transition* (New York: Penguin Press, 2024), 38.

Betsy Edgerton, a fifty-something: Betsy Edgerton, phone interview, Dec. 19, 2022.

Diary readers *also do their own thing:* Batsheva Ben-Amos and Dan Ben-Amos, eds., "Introduction," *The Diary: The Epic of Everyday Life* (Bloomington: Indiana University Press, 2020), 3.

In the 1990s: Desirée Henderson, email, July 8, 2025.

"Diaries are so multifaceted": Desirée Henderson, *How to Read a Diary: Critical Contexts and Interpretive Strategies for 21st-Century Readers* (New York: Routledge, 2019), 7.

"day-to-day writing": Philippe Lejeune and Catherine Bogaert, "The Practice of Writing a Diary," trans. Dagmara Meijers-Troller, in Ben-Amos and Ben-Amos, *The Diary*, 26, 30.

The diary is a series: Lejeune and Bogaert, "The Practice of Writing a Diary," 27–28.

"In the journal": Susan Sontag, *Reborn: Journals and Notebooks, 1947–1963*, ed. David Rieff (New York: Farrar, Straus and Giroux, 2008), 164–65.

"turned to the past": Philippe Lejeune, "How Do Diaries End?" *On Diary*, ed. Jeremy D. Popkin and Julie Rak, trans. Katherine Durnin (Manoa: University of Hawai'i Press, 2009), 191; and Philippe Lejeune, "Composing a Diary," *On Diary*, 173.

"I'm lamenting that my book": Alexei Navalny, *Patriot* (New York: Knopf, 2024), 279–80, 404–6, 416; Alexandra Alter, "How Aleksei Navalny's Prison Diaries Got Published," *New York Times*, Oct. 20, 2024, www.nytimes.com/2024/10/20/books/booksupdate/aleksei-navalny-memoir-prison-diaries.html?smid=nytcore-ios-share&referringSource=articleShare.

"Unlike memoirs or letters": Paula Vene Smith, "Black Women Diarists Have Always Looked to Black Future Month," *Ms.*, Feb. 1, 2023, https://msmagazine.com/2023/02/01/black-women-writers-history-diary-journal/.

"No other kind of document": Dear Diary, exhibition guide, 2017, King's College London.

I followed British diary scholars: The organizers of the 2017 *Dear Diary* exhibit in London from Kings College and the Great Diary Project, *Dear Diary*, exhibition guide, https://www.kcl.ac.uk/artshums/assets/dde-exhibition-guide-a5-12pp-final.pdf. Also see "Diaries Timeline," Kings College, https://www.kcl.ac.uk/research/diaries-timeline.

Although almanacs were designed: Polly North, "Unlocking the Self in Self-Writing," doctoral thesis, University of Greenwich, UK, September 2016, p. 62, https://gala.gre.ac.uk/id/eprint/23608/1/Polly%20North%202016%20-%20secured.pdf.

As for the diary's selfiness: Henderson, *How to Read a Diary*, 9–14.

Other contemporary forms: Julie Rak, "The Diary Among Other Forms of Life Writing," in Ben-Amos and Ben-Amos, *The Diary*, 60.

Puritans, Quakers: Henderson, *How to Read a Diary*, 9–14.

The nineteenth century saw: Peter Gay, *The Bourgeois Experience: Victoria to Freud, Vol. I: Education of the Senses* (New York: Oxford University Press, 1984), 446.

Scholars also link: Roland Allen, *The Notebook: A History of Thinking on Paper* (Windsor, Ontario: Biblioasis, 2024), 57–71.

Florentine apothecary: Alexandra Johnson, *A Brief History of Diaries: From Pepys to Blogs* (London: Hesperus Press, 2011), 20–23.

Eighteenth-century New England: Laurel Thatcher Ulrich, *A Midwife's Tale: The Life of Martha Ballard, Based on Her Diary, 1785–1812* (New York: Vintage, 1991), 8.

During the 1800s: Allen, *The Notebook*, 259, 271.

One caveat: Henderson, *How to Read a Diary*, 13.

Among the Middle Eastern and Asian texts: Sei Shōnagon, *Pillow Book*, in *Remarkable Diaries: The World's Greatest Diaries, Journals, Notebooks & Letters*, ed. DK (New York: DK, 2020), 30.

"The difference": Laurel Thatcher Ulrich, phone interview, Mar. 25, 2022.

"an imaginary friend": Kate Kellaway, "Patti Smith: I Feel the Unrest of the World in the Pit of My Stomach," *The Guardian*, Sept. 20, 2020, www.theguardian.com/music/2020/sep/20/patti-smith-i-feel-the-unrest-of-the-world-in-the-pit-of-my-stomach.

some of the many teenage diarists: The Legacy of Anne Frank, Dec. 24, 1967, NBC, available at www.youtube.com/watch?v=AWRBinP7ans.

The bullet journal's initial purpose: Julie Rak, phone interview, Feb. 23, 2022.

The "bullet journal method": Bullet Journal, https://bulletjournal.com/, accessed June 16, 2025.

The notebook has: Allen, *The Notebook*, 5–7.

"idea book": Jillian Hess, "Re-Noted: Roald Dahl's Diaries & Idea Books," *Noted*, June 2, 2025, jillianhess.substack.com/p/re-noted-roald-dahls-diaries-and.

"At no point": Joan Didion, "On Keeping a Notebook," *Slouching Towards Bethlehem* (New York: Farrar, Straus and Giroux, 1968), 169, eBook 2013.

"I said I wasn't sure": Joan Didion, "What We Knew Without Knowing," *New Yorker*, Apr. 7, 2025, https://www.newyorker.com/magazine/2025/04/07/what-we-knew-without-knowing.

Writing in both: Barbara Goldsmith, *Obsessive Genius: The Inner World of Marie Curie* (New York: Atlas Books, 2005), 141–42.

Some scholars also describe: Ben-Amos and Ben-Amos, "Introduction," *The Diary*, 14.

"Contrary to popular conception": Lynn Z. Bloom, "'I Write for Myself and Strangers': Private Diaries as Public Documents," in *Inscribing the Daily: Critical Essays on Women's Diaries*, ed. Suzanne L. Bunkers and Cynthia A. Huff (Amherst: University of Massachusetts Press, 1996), 23.

The contemporary assumption: Margo Culley, "Introduction," *A Day at a Time: The Diary Literature of American Women Writers from 1764 to the Present*, ed. Margo Culley (New York: Feminist Press, 1985), 3; Clara Schumann, diary entry, Jan. 1841, in *Remarkable Diaries: The World's Greatest Diaries, Journals, Notebooks & Letters*, ed. DK (New York: DK, 2020), 132; Edmond and Jules de Goncourt, *Pages from the Goncourt Journal*, ed. and trans. Robert Baldick (New York: New York Review of Books, 1962), preface.

"Pa came for us": Emily and Sarah Gillespie diary entries, Sarah Gillespie Huftalen Collection, State Historical Society of Iowa, Iowa City, as quoted with analysis in Suzanne L. Bunkers, "Diaries and Dysfunctional Families," in Bunkers and Huff, *Inscribing the Daily*, 226–27.

More recently, in 2010: Caralee Adams, "Rockville Family Launches Line of Journals," *Moco360.media*, June 6, 2023, http://moco360media/2023/06/06/journaling-connected-this-rockville-family-now-have-their-own-line-of-journals/; "Introducing Shared Journals," Day One, dayoneapp.com/shared-journals/.

British cabinet minister Richard Crossman's: Richard Crossman, *The Crossman Diaries: Selections from the Diaries of a Cabinet Minister, 1964–1970*, 3 vols., ed. Anthony Howard (London: Hamish Hamilton, 1975); Simon Hoggart, "Your Next Box Set: Yes Minister," *The Guardian*, June 18, 2010, www.theguardian.com/tv-and-radio/2010/jun/18/yes-minister-your-next-box-set.

"I very foolishly tried to talk": *Silent Hattie Speaks: The Personal Journal of Senator Hattie Caraway*, ed. Diane D. Kincaid (Westport, CT: Greenwood Press, 1979), quoted in US Senate, "Senate Stories, Senate Diaries," Oct. 16, 2020, www.senate.gov/artandhistory/senate-stories/senate-diaries.htm.

"the authenticity": Lejeune and Bogaert, "The Practice of Writing a Diary," in Ben-Amos and Ben-Amos, *The Diary*, 27.

"My mom doesn't let me": Jessica Bennett, "Being 13," *New York Times*, Oct. 15, 2023, www.nytimes.com/interactive/2023/09/20/well/family/13-year-old-girls-social-media-self-esteem.html.

"kind of truth": Culley, "Introduction," in *A Day at a Time*.

"This is terrible": Avery Rowling, phone interview, Mar. 27, 2024.

CHAPTER 2: BORN DIGITAL

If all *of the world's:* Global Social Media Statistics, DataReportal, July 2025, https://datareportal.com/social-media-users; Pew Research Center, *Teens, Social Media and Technology 2024*, December 2024, www.pewresearch.org/internet/2024/12/12/teens-social-media-and-technology-2024/.

"Blog posts became longer": Jill Walker Rettberg, "Online Diaries and Blogs," in *The Diary: The Epic of Everyday Life*, ed. Batsheva Ben-Amos and Dan Ben-Amos (Bloomington: Indiana University Press, 2020), 412, 420.

"founding father": Jeffrey Rosen, "Your Blog or Mine?" *New York Times*, Dec. 19, 2024, www.nytimes.com/2004/12/19/magazine/your-blog-or-mine.html.

Hall was one of the first: overshare: the links.net story, https://overshare.links.net/, accessed May 20, 2025.

"Howdy": Justin's Home Page, www.links.net/vita/web/start/original.html/, accessed May 20, 2025.

27,000 daily readers: Lena Buford, "A Journey Through Two Decades of Online Diary Community," in Ben-Amos and Ben-Amos, *The Diary*, 430.

Hall's "Cool Shit": "Justin Hall, '93," Parker, www.fwparker.org/alumni-perspectives/justin-hall-93, accessed May 20, 2025.

His early shared finds: Justin's Home Page.

Lauded as a blogging pioneer: Stephen Holden, "'Home Page': In This Version of Cyberutopia, Show and Tell Lasts All Day," *New York Times*, film review, Nov. 19, 1999, https://archive.nytimes.com/www.nytimes.com/library/film/111999page-film-review.html.

Canadian Carolyn L. Burke: Carolyn Burke, Carolyn's Diary, 2000, www.diaryhistoryproject.com/recollections/1995_01_03.html.

"both private and public": Buford, "A Journey Through Two Decades of Online Diary Community," 433.

Word of the Year: BBC NEWS, "'Blog' Picked as Word of the Year," Dec. 1, 2004, http://news.bbc.co.uk/2/hi/technology/4059291.stm.

blogs became commercial: Rettberg, "Online Diaries and Blogs," 413; Tammy Yu, "The History of Blogs in Marketing," *Portent*, Dec. 20, 2023, https://portent.com/blog/content/history-of-blogs-in-marketing-use-cases.htm.

19.5 million blogs: Adam Volle, "Search Engine Optimization," *Britannica*, last updated May 22, 2025, https://www.britannica.com/topic/search-engine-optimization.

Online diaries began to vanish: Buford, "A Journey Through Two Decades of Online Diary Community," 429, 433–35.

So did the rise: Buford, "A Journey Through Two Decades of Online Diary Community," 433.

online diaries/personal blogs: Buford, "A Journey Through Two Decades of Online Diary Community," 426–33.

Word of the Year: "Word of the Year? 'App,'" CBS News, Jan. 28, 2011, www.cbsnews.com/news/word-of-the-year-app/.

the Day One journaling app: "The Next Chapter of Day One," *Day One* (blog), June 14, 2021, https://dayoneapp.com/blog/the-next-chapter-of-day-one-at-automattic/.

the digital journaling apps market: Market Research Future, "Digital Journal Market Apps Overview," Feb. 2025, https://www.marketresearchfuture.com/reports/digital-journal-apps-market-29194.

"while some remain uneasy": Desirée Henderson, *How to Read a Diary: Critical Contexts and Interpretive Strategies for 21st-Century Readers* (New York: Routledge, 2019), 146–47.

"The digital revolution has transformed": Batsheva Ben-Amos and Dan Ben-Amos, "Introduction," in Ben-Amos and Ben-Amos, *The Diary*, 13–14.

Some experts argued: Henderson, *How to Read a Diary*, 130.

"IT'S A FB STATUS": Quick Meme, "It's a FB Status Not Your Fucking Diary," quickmeme.com/meme/353hoy, accessed May 20, 2025.

50,363 followers: Kylie Cardell, *De@r World: Contemporary Uses of the Diary* (Madison: University of Wisconsin Press, 2014), 147.

Soon after launching: Jeremy D. Popkin, "Philippe Lejeune, Explorer of the Diary," in Philippe Lejeune, *On Diary*, ed. Jeremy D. Popkin and Julie Rak, trans. Katherine Durnin (Manoa: University of Hawai'i Press, 2009), 4–5; Julie Rak, "Dialogue with the Future: Philippe Lejeune's Method and Theory of Diary," in Lejeune, *On Diary*, 19–21.

"new frontier": Philippe Lejeune, "Diaries on the Internet: A Year of Reading," *On Diary*, 316.

Other scholars point: Lee Humphreys, phone interview, June 7, 2024.

Considering all this: Humphreys, phone interview.

"Facebook is totally": Wendy Whitcomb, email, Apr. 4, 2024.

Also falling into: Myra Shapiro, email, Sept. 11, 2024; Betsy Edgerton, email, July 10, 2024.

"I've written myself into being": Helen Churko, phone interview, Apr. 5, 2023.

Mark Koester: Mark Koester, phone interview, Sept. 7, 2023; Sarah Fitzgerald, email, Feb. 1, 2023; Elizabeth Grubgeld, phone interview, Jan. 30, 2023.

"I was just tired": Sarah Fitzgerald, "A Wheelie Wise Decision," *Wobbly Yummy Mommy* (blog), Mar. 21, 2023, wobblyyummymummy.com/2023/03/.

Kureishi started "a blog": Hanif Kureishi, "By the Book," *New York Times Book Review*, Feb. 2, 2025, www.nytimes.com/2025/01/30/books/review/hanif-kureishi-shattered.html; Hanif Kureishi, *Shattered: A Memoir* (New York: Ecco, 2024), 8.

"Always private": Dabble.Me, https://dabble.me/, accessed July 17, 2025.

"Privacy is our #1 concern": Penzu, https://penzu.com, accessed July 17, 2025.

"It's unsocial": Farhad Manjoo, "Why a Digital Diary Will Change Your Life," *New York Times*, June 12, 2019, www.nytimes.com/2019/06/12/opinion/digital-diary.html.

"All of that information": David Pierce, "My Impossible Search for the Best, Most Powerful, Most Private Journaling App Ever," *The Verge*, Mar. 29, 2023, www.theverge.com/2023/3/29/23660375/journaling-app-day-one-security-personal-space.

Journaling apps include: Dabble Me, https://dabble.me/, accessed July 18, 2025; Grid Diary, https://griddiaryapp.com/, accessed July 18, 2025; Daylio: Self-Care Bullet Journal with Goals Mood Diary & Happiness Tracker, https://daylio.net/, accessed May 20, 2025.

"Artificial Intelligence": Memairy: AI Powered Memory, https://memairy.com, accessed May 20, 2025.

"automatically identifies": Journey—Diary, Journal, https://apps.apple.com/us/app/journey-diary-journal/id1300202543, accessed May 20, 2025.

By 2024: Josephine Sittenfeld, "An Analog Library of All the Lives I've Lived," *New York Times*, Mar. 3, 2024, www.nytimes.com/2024/03/02/opinion/journaling-diary-iphone-app.html.

"a huge boon": Pierce, "My Impossible Search for the Best, Most Powerful, Most Private Journaling App Ever."

"You can journal": Koester, phone interview.

Grinnell professor Paula Vene Smith: Paula Vene Smith, "Handwritten Diaries May Feel Old-Fashioned, but They Offer Insights That Digital Diaries Can't Match," *Salon*, Aug. 21, 2022, www.salon.com/2022/08/21/handwritten-diaries-may-feel-old-fashioned-but-they-offer-insights-that-digital-diaries-cant-match_partner/.

"technologies of the self": "Urban Lives: Amsterdam Diaries and Other Stories of the Self," Vrije Universiteit Amsterdam, Oct. 26, 2023, vu.nl/en/events/2023/urban-lives-amsterdam-diaries-and-other-stories-of-the-self.

Digital fatigue is one reason: Robert Ryan, phone interview, Feb. 11, 2023; Peter Tomka, phone interview, Apr. 2, 2024; Madison Ollila, phone interview, Mar. 27, 2024.

"The reason Moleskine": John Naughton, "How Bruce Chatwin's Notebooks Continue to Shape the Virtual Word," *The Guardian*, Mar. 30, 2013, https://www.theguardian.com/technology/2013/mar/31/bruce-chatwin-notebook-shapes-virtual-word.

"life book/diary page": "How It's Used," Hobonichi Techo, https://www.1101.com/store/techo/en/collection/#/, accessed May 20, 2025.

"A waxy, anemic": Edmond and Jules de Goncourt, *Pages from the Goncourt Journals*, ed. and trans. Robert Baldick (1962; New York: New York Review of Books, 2006), 144.

So, I'm actually: Maycie Vorreiter, Facebook message, Aug. 3, 2023.

Vorreiter was among digital diarists: Day One users' replies to author's question posted on Day One Community Facebook page (https://www.facebook.com/groups/DayOneCommunity/), Mar. 13, 2023.

CHAPTER 3: ABOUT A GIRL

detractors castigated diaries: Philippe Lejeune, "The Diary on Trial," in *On Diary*, ed. Jeremy Popkin and Julie Rak, trans. Katherine Durnin (Manoa: University of Hawai'i Press, 2009), 147.

"like a diary": Matt Stieb, "J. D. Vance Can't Stop Saying the Dumbest Things Imaginable," *Intelligencer*, July 29, 2024, https://nymag.com/intelligencer/article/j-d-vances-vp-rollout-beta.html.

Between 2020 and 2022: Janis Whitlock, Cornell research scientist, phone interview, Mar. 23, 2023.

Women also accounted for: Sarah S. Willen, phone interview, July 21, 2023.

"higher female usage": Alexander Mimran, email, Mar. 13, 2023.

the Shakespeare of diarists: Patrick Huyghe, "Diary Writing Turns a New Leaf," *New York Times*, Nov. 9, 1981.

from "Eye to I": Alexandra Johnson, *A Brief History of Diaries: From Pepys to Blogs* (London: Hesperus Press, 2011), 25.

Pepys's entries ranged: Samuel Pepys, *The Diary of Samuel Pepys*, ed. Richard Le Gallienne (New York: Random House/Modern Library Imprint, 2003), 57, 187.

"The most celebrated": Desirée Henderson, *How to Read a Diary: Critical Contexts and Interpretive Strategies for 21st-Century Readers* (New York: Routledge, 2019), 54–55.

Lady Anne Clifford's diary: Anne Clifford, *The Diaries of Lady Anne Clifford*, ed. D. J. H. Clifford (Gloucestershire: History Press, 1993).

produced a historical: English Heritage, "Lady Anne Clifford," Women in History, https://www.english-heritage.org.uk/learn/histories/women-in-history/anne-clifford/, accessed July 18, 2025.

the longest firsthand account: DK, ed., *Remarkable Diaries: The World's Greatest Diaries, Journals, Notebooks & Letters* (New York: DK, 2020), 70–71.

Frances "Fanny" Burney: DK, ed., *Remarkable Diaries*, 92.

Fifteen-year-old Burney: Frances Burney, *Journals and Letters*, ed. Peter Sabor and Lars E. Troide (London: Penguin Classics, 2001), 1.

Burney ignored: Peter Sabor and Lars E. Troide, "Introduction," in Burney, *Journals and Letters*, xiii–xiv.

For the first ten years: Sabor and Troide, "Introduction," in Burney, *Journals and Letters*, xiii–xxii.

One chronicles: Burney, *Journals and Letters*, 281.

Twenty-three years later: Burney, *Journals and Letters*, 442.

"I hate to be idle": Arthur Ponsonby, "Queen Victoria's Diaries," 1923, Victorian Web, https://victorianweb.org/authors/diarists/1.html.

Beatrix Potter: Beatrix Potter, journal, in Jillian Hess, "Re-Noted: Beatrix Potter's Naturalist Notes," *Noted*, Aug. 19, 2024, https://jillianhess.substack.com/p/re-noted-beatrix-potters-naturalist.

The British socialist reformer: Beatrice Webb, diary entry, in DK, *Remarkable Diaries*, 160.

Another *Abigail Adams:* H. Merrifield Forbes, *New England Diaries, 1602–1800* (Topsfield, MA: privately printed, 1923), vii, https://catalog.hathitrust.org/Record/001168352.

about "sea journals": Forbes, *New England Diaries*, vii.

The sea-journal writers: "Abigail Adams' Diary of Her Voyage from Boston to Deal, 20 June–20 July 1784," *Founders Online*, National Archives, https://founders.archives.gov/documents/Adams/01-03-02-0003-0001.

"Some matters": Forbes, *New England Diaries*, 18.

Initially thought a masterpiece: Kenneth S. Lynn, "The Masterpiece That Became a Hoax," review of *Mary Chesnut's Civil War*, ed. C. Vann Woodward, *New York Times*, Apr. 26, 1981.

"Right after": Carolyn L. Burke, "Virtually Yours," *Carolyn L. Burke*, Jan. 1995, https://diary.carolyn.org/Overview.html.

"As all the standard bibliographical": Margo Culley, "Introduction," *A Day at a Time: The Diary Literature of American Women Writers from 1764 to the Present*, ed. Margo Culley (New York: Feminist Press, 1985), xii, 3.

"very few white women": Suzanne L. Bunkers and Cynthia A. Huff, "Issues in Studying Women's Diaries: A Theoretical and Critical Introduction," *Inscribing the Daily: Critical Essays on Women's Diaries*, ed. Suzanne L. Bunkers and Cynthia A. Huff (Amherst: University of Massachusetts Press, 1996), 5–6.

"Working-class diaries": Kathryn Carter, "Feminist Interpretations of the Diary," in *The Diary: The Epic of Everyday Life*, ed. Batsheva Ben-Amos and Dan Ben-Amos (Bloomington: Indiana University Press, 2020), 42–43.

"Historically, women's diaries": Carter, "Feminist Interpretations of the Diary," 40.

"bundle of papers": Pepys, *The Diary of Samuel Pepys*, 87.

"Evidence from around": Carter, "Feminist Interpretations of the Diary," 40.

"He became outrageous": Sarah Welch Hill, 1844 diary entries, University of Guelph Rural Diary Archive, Province of Ontario Archives, Toronto, F634, https://ruraldiaries.lib.uoguelph.ca/transcribe/files/show/7899.

"from well before": Margo Culley, "Preface," *A Day at a Time: The Diary Literature of American Women Writers from 1764 to the Present*, ed. Margo Culley (New York: Feminist Press, 1985), xi.

Culley also notes: Culley, "Preface," *A Day at a Time*, xii.

"Whether a diary": Suzanne L. Bunkers, "Introduction," *Diaries of Girls and Women: A Midwestern American Sampler*, ed. Suzanne L. Bunkers (Madison: University of Wisconsin Press, 2001), 26.

large 1957 anthology: Citing Philip Dunaway and Mel Evans, eds., *A Treasury of the World's Great Diaries* (New York: Doubleday, 1957), in Bunkers, "Introduction," 36.

the 1974 collection: Mary Jane Moffat and Charlotte Painter, eds., *Revelations: Diaries of Women* (New York: Random House, 1974).

Culley's 1985 anthology: Culley, "Preface," xiii.

By 1996: Bunkers and Huff, "Issues in Studying Women's Diaries," 2.

In the twentieth: Culley, "Introduction," *A Day at a Time*, 3–7.

Women were all in: Culley, "Introduction," *A Day at a Time*, 3–7.

"to the diary as one place": Culley, "Introduction," *A Day at a Time*, 3–7.

"Oh! but there arises": Marie Bashkirtseff, diary entry, July 23, 1880, quoted in *Assassin's Cloak: An Anthology of the World's Greatest Diarists*, ed. Irene and Alan Taylor (Edinburgh: Canongate Books, 2000), 363.

"Many women have found": Rebecca Hogan, "Engendered Autobiographies: The Diary as a Feminine Form," *Autobiography and Questions of Gender/Prose Studies* 14, no. 2 (Sept. 1991): 105.

After digesting four hundred years: Sarah Gristwood, "Foreword," in *Secret Voices: A Year of Women's Diaries*, ed. Sarah Gristwood (London: Batsford Books, 2024), Kindle ed.

"her independent and secret identity": Judy Simons, "Invented Lives: Textuality and Power in Early Women's Diaries," in Bunkers and Huff, *Inscribing the Daily*, 252–55.

"Far from being isolated": Marilyn Ferris Motz, "The Private Alibi," in Bunkers and Huff, *Inscribing the Daily*, 191.

"perfectly acceptable": Cynthia A. Huff, "Textual Boundaries," in Bunkers and Huff, *Inscribing the Daily*, 128–29.

"subversive autobiography": bell hooks, *Remembered Rapture: The Writer at Work* (New York: Henry Holt, 1999), 3.

"It's as if Sarajevo": Zlata Filipović, *Zlata's Diary: A Child's Life in Sarajevo* (New York: Viking Penguin, 1994), 132–33.

Bunkers's study of diaries: Bunkers, "Introduction," *Diaries of Girls and Women*, 15–16.

"In their journals": Mary Pipher, *Reviving Ophelia: Saving the Selves of Adolescent Girls* (New York: Riverhead Books, 1994), 347.

Margo Culley illustrates: Mary Vial Holyoke and Mary MacLane, diary entries, in Culley, "Introduction," *A Day at a Time*, 4–8.

"Random Thoughts": Barbara Smith, "Black, Woman, Lesbian . . . ," in Culley, *A Day at a Time*, 307.

"We are a poor, oppressed": Charlotte Forten Grimke, *The Journals of Charlotte Forten Grimke*, ed. Brenda Stevenson (Oxford: Oxford University Press, 1988), 163. The 1953 edition featured some, not all, of Forten's journal entries. The next edition, in 1988, is a fuller version.

the next published: Audre Lorde, *The Cancer Journals* (New York: Penguin Books, 1980), 4.

"To be a BLACK WOMAN": Dorothy Sterling, ed., *We Are Your Sisters: Black Women in the Nineteenth Century* (New York: W. W. Norton, 1984), 453.

"distinct literary tradition": Paula Vene Smith, "Refashioning Diary Studies: The Tradition of Black Women's Diaries," *Auto/Biography Studies* 38, no. 1 (2022): 189–210, doi.org/10.1080/08989575.2022.2135892. For the diary publication count and chronology, Smith notes scholars' conflicting accounts, over time, as more diaries have been found and published. She points to the relatively little-known Black American Juanita Harrison's 1920s diary, which became a bestseller after it was published in 1936 but

faded from view and wasn't rediscovered until 2020, and to the 1960 publication of Brazilian journalist Carolina Maria de Jesus's diary. The other diarists are American.

In an arresting 1974 essay: Alice Walker, *In Search of Our Mothers' Gardens: Womanist Prose* (New York: Amistad, 2023), 241.

In 1984, the: Gloria T. Hull, "Introduction," in Alice Dunbar-Nelson, *Give Us Each Day: The Diary of Alice Dunbar-Nelson*, ed. Gloria T. Hull (New York: W. W. Norton, 1984), 14.

"O God is there": Ida B. Wells, *The Memphis Diary of Ida B. Wells: An Intimate Portrait of the Activist as a Young Woman*, ed. Miriam Decosta-Willis (Boston: Beacon Press, 1995), 141.

Montgomery wrote her: Virginia Montgomery, diary excerpt, in Sterling, *We Are Your Sisters*, 463, 466.

"a place where": Mary Helen Washington, "Introduction," in *The Memphis Diary of Ida B. Wells*, ix–x.

"From the moment": Carole Ione, *Pride of Family: Four Generations of American Women of Color* (New York: Harlem Moon/Broadway Books, 2004), 7.

In 2025, Rollin's diary: Jennifer Putzi, email, Apr. 19, 2024.

"invariably document unremitting": Joycelyn K. Moody, "Negotiating National Identity and Well-Being in US Black Women's Diaries," in *The Divided States: Unraveling National Identities in the Twenty-First Century*, ed. Laura J. Beard and Ricia Anne Chansky (Madison: University of Wisconsin Press, 2023), 39, 51.

"surprisingly forward-looking vision": Paula Vene Smith, "Black Women Diarists Have Always Looked to Black Future Month," *Ms.*, Feb. 1, 2023, https://msmagazine.com/2023/02/01/black-women-writers-history-diary-journal.

"structurally unjust": Smith, "Black Women Diarists Have Always Looked to Black Future Month."

"the terrible curse": Grimke, *The Journals of Charlotte Forten Grimke*, 174.

"signals an intent to record": Smith, "Black Women Diarists Have Always Looked to Black Future Month."

"private glimpses": Gloria T. Hull, "Introduction," in Dunbar-Nelson, *Give Us Each Day*, 30.

"Suppose the ticket seller": Dunbar-Nelson, *Give Us Each Day*, 69.

"often-unwelcoming world": Morgan Jerkins, "Black Women Writers and the Secret Space of Diaries," *New Yorker*, Mar. 4, 2016, www.newyorker.com/books/page-turner/Black-women-writers-and-the-secret-space-of-diaries.

The first book: Jeff Kinney, *Diary of a Wimpy Kid* (New York: Amulet Books, 2007), 1.

Desirée Henderson presents: Henderson, *How to Read a Diary*, 3, 13.

Philippe Lejeune points to: Beatrice Didier, *Le Journal Intime* (1976), quoted in Philippe Lejeune, "The Diary on Trial," *On Diary*, ed. Jeremy Popkin and Julie Rak, trans. Katherine Durnin (Manoa: University of Hawai'i Press, 2009), 150.

Growing up during the 1960s: Jane Kamensky, *Candida Royalle and the Sexual Revolution: A History from Below* (New York: W. W. Norton, 2024), 52.

"We are still": Thomas Mallon, *A Book of One's Own: People and Their Diaries*, 3rd ed. (1984; St. Paul, MN: Hungry Mind Press, 1995), 210.

"a lady's accomplishments": Culley, "Introduction," in *A Day at a Time*, 4.

Among the more sinister: Henderson, *How to Read a Diary*, 56–57.

"systematically pushed": Phillipe Lejeune and Catherine Bogaert, "The Practice of Writing a Diary," in Ben-Amos and Ben-Amos, *The Diary*, 26.

the "most elegant": Allen, *The Notebook*, 257–59.

"The old dichotomy": Suzanne Bunkers, email, May 7, 2022.

Ironically, feminine: Carter, "Feminist Interpretations of the Diary," 45–51.

"I would stick to my guns": Rebecca Hogan, email, June 19, 2024.

"The diary accommodates": Henderson, *How to Read a Diary*, 57.

"queer archival reading": Julie Rak, "The Diary Among Other Forms of Life Writing," in Ben-Amos and Ben-Amos, *The Diary*, 61–62.

Bechdel was nineteen: Andrew Meacham, "Cartoonist Alison Bechdel Talks 'Fun Home,' Growing Up Around Death and Coming Out," *Tampa Bay Times*, Nov. 27, 2017, https://www.tampabay.com/things-to-do/stage/Cartoonist-Alison-Bechdel-talks-Fun-Home-growing-up-around-death-and-coming-out_163039108/.

Bechdel had her diary: Rak, "The Diary Among Other Forms of Life Writing."

"restore value": Henderson, *How to Read a Diary*, 54–55.

"the pejorative characterization": Henderson, *How to Read a Diary*, 54–55.

CHAPTER 4: SELF-HELP

How to explain: Alexandra Alter, "How a Self-Published Book 'Broke All the Rules,'" *New York Times*, May 30, 2024, www.nytimes.com/2024/05/30/books/booksupdate/keila-shaheen-shadow-work-journal-TikTok.html.

"face your shadows": Marketing copy for Keila Shaheen, *The Shadow Work Journal: A Guide to Integrate and Transcend Your Shadows* (privately published, 2021), https://www.amazon.com/Shadow-Work-Journal-Integrate-Transcend/dp/B09KN2QCML.

"transform your life": Dabble Me, https://dabble.me/; "The Five Minute Journal," Intelligent Change, www.intelligentchange.com/products/the-five-minute-journal, accessed May 20, 2025.

Launched by Toronto entrepreneurs: Lindsay Gellman, "They Think You Should Be Grateful," *New York Times*, May 16, 2024, www.nytimes.com/2024/05/16/style/five-minute-journal-ikonns.html.

The thirty-year-old British actor James Phoon: "James Phoon, a New Face on 'Bridgerton,' Is Team Ariana Grande," *New York Times*, June 23, 2024, https://www.nytimes.com/2024/06/15/arts/television/james-phoon-bridgerton.html; "Jay Ellis Considers Colson Whitehead His Literary GOAT," *New*

York Times, June 29, 2025, https://www.nytimes.com/2025/06/21/theater/jay-ellis-duke-roya-off-broadway.html.

"Perfection of character": Marcus Aurelius, *Meditations*, Book 7, trans. Robin Hard (Oxford: Oxford University Press, 2011), 69 (ebook).

The Roman emperor: "Diaries Timeline," Kings College London, https://www.kcl.ac.uk/research/diaries-timeline.

"There is, therefore": Saint Augustine, *City of God*, trans. Marcus Dods, Box XIV, Chapter 13, Logos Library (ebook), www.logoslibrary.org/augustine/city/1413.html.

In 1656: Kylie Cardell, "From Puritans to Fitbit: Self-Improvement, Self-Tracking, and How to Keep a Diary," in *The Diary: The Epic of Everyday Life*, ed. Batsheva Ben-Amos and Dan Ben-Amos (Bloomington: Indiana University Press, 2020), 401–2.

"how-to instructional diary": Cardell, "From Puritans to Fitbit," 403.

Traction became major momentum: Xaiojuan Gao, "Research on Expressive Writing in Psychology: A Forty-Year Bibliometric Analysis and Visualization of Current Status and Research Trends," *Frontiers in Psychology* 13 (Oct. 2022): 1–2.

"intrusive and avoidant thinking": James W. Pennebaker, phone interview, Jan. 3, 2023.

Expressive writing works: Pennebaker, phone interview.

"Everything is wrong": Hua Hsu, *Stay True: A Memoir* (New York: Doubleday, 2022), 118.

Research on "expressive writing": Gao, "Research on Expressive Writing in Psychology," 2–4; Karen Baikie and Kay Wilhelm, "Emotional and Physical Health Benefits of Expressive Writing," *Advances in Psychiatric Treatment* 11, no. 5 (2005): 338–46, doi.org/10.1192/apt.11.5.338.

Other research using MRI imaging: Christina M. Karns, William E. Moore, and Ulrich Mayr, "The Cultivation of Pure Altruism via Gratitude," *Frontiers in Human Neuroscience* (Dec. 12, 2017): 1, https://pubmed.ncbi.nlm.nih.gov/29375336/.

"online positive affect journaling": J. M. Smyth et al., "Online Positive Affect Journaling in the Improvement of Mental Distress," *JMIR Mental Health* 5, no. 4 (Dec. 10, 2018): 1, mental.jmir.org/2018/4/e11290/.

Michelle Obama: Katie Kindelan, "Michelle Obama Releasing Journal," ABC News, Oct. 8, 2019, abcnews.go.com/GMA/Culture/michelle-obama-releasing-journal-pair-memoir/story?id=66111538.

An app called Stoic: Stoic, "How to Improve Your Productivity by Improving Your Mental Health: The Ultimate Guide," May 9, 2025, https://www.getstoic.com/blog-posts/productivity-mental-health-guide; Inquiry Health, "Clarity: CBT Self Help Journal," App Store Preview, https://apps.apple.com/us/app/clarity-cbt-thought-diary/id1010391170, accessed May 26, 2025.

The Anti-Anxiety Notebook *emphasizes:* Hod Tamir et al., *The Anti-Anxiety Notebook: Cognitive Behavioral Therapy to Reframe and Reset* (Therapy Notebooks, n.d.), https://shop.therapynotebooks.com/products/anti-anxiety-notebook.

"spiritual journey": Alter, "How a Self-Published Book 'Broke All the Rules.'"

"It can be risky": Alter, "How a Self-Published Book 'Broke All the Rules.'"

"Feeling Anxious?": Valeriya Safronova, "Feeling Anxious? Journaling Might Help," *New York Times*, Oct. 7, 2021, www.nytimes.com/2021/10/07/style/therapy-notebooks-anxiety-depression-mindfulness.html; Lisa Tams, "Journaling to Reduce COVID-19 Stress," Michigan State University Extension, Nov. 11, 2020, https://www.canr.msu.edu/news/journaling_to_reduce_stress; David Allan, "Pandemic Diaries: Why Journaling Now Is the Best Time to Start or Restart," CNN.com, Dec. 17, 2020, www.cnn.com/2020/12/14/health/start-a-journal-diary-wellness-wisdom-project/index.html.

"Expressive writing is not": James W. Pennebaker and Joshua M. Smyth, *Opening Up by Writing It Down: How Expressive Writing Improves Health and Eases Emotional Pain* (New York: Guilford Press, 2016), ix, 24–26.

Progoff bluntly stated: Ira Progoff, *At a Journal Workshop: Writing to Access the Power of the Unconscious and Evoke Creative Ability* (New York: Dialogue House Library, 1975), 16, 23–26.

But this journaling: Patrick Huyghe, "Diary Writing Turns a New Leaf," *New York Times*, Nov. 9, 1981.

It's easy to chalk up: Progoff, *At a Journal Workshop*, 26.

While diary writing: Henderson, *How to Read a Diary*, 160–66.

The amiable Pennebaker: Pennebaker, phone interview, Jan. 3, 2023.

"Diary writing, at its best": Pennebaker, phone interview, Mar. 17, 2022.

"you have to be": Pennebaker, phone interview, Jan. 3, 2023.

The absence of scientific proof: Ellen K. Baker, phone interview, Nov. 8, 2023.

"happy and carefree": Zlata Filipović, "Foreword," in The Freedom Writers with Erin Gruwell, *The Freedom Writers Diary: How a Teacher and 150 Teens Used Writing to Change Themselves and the World Around Them*, 2nd ed. (New York: Broadway Books, 2009), xvi.

"I found journaling": Kristina Baines, "It's Normal to Admit You're Not Okay," *SSM-Mental Health* 2 (Dec. 2022): 1–4, doi.org/10.1016/j.ssmmh.2022.100119.

"clearly overwhelmed": Baines, "It's Normal to Admit You're Not Okay," 4.

The mental health community: Sarah S. Willen, phone interview, July 21, 2023.

In her 1994 anthology: Patricia Bell-Scott, "Introduction," in *Life Notes: Personal Writings by Contemporary Black Women*, ed. Patricia Bell-Scott (New York: W. W. Norton, 1994), 19.

"During my years": R. H. Douglas, "Writing, Screaming, and Healing," in Bell-Scott, *Life Notes*, 249–50.

"I owe a good deal": Anne Lister, *The Secret Diaries of Miss Anne Lister*, ed. Helena Whitbread (London: Virago Press, 2010), 171.

"the first modern lesbian": "The Lesbian 'Dead Sea Scrolls,'" *Los Angeles Public Library* (blog), June 29, 2021, www.lapl.org/collections-resources/blogs/lapl/lesbian-dead-sea-scrolls-anne-lister-diaries.

"If I get into the habit": Alice James, *The Diary of Alice James*, ed. Leon Edel (Boston: Northeastern University Press, 1999), 25.

"the most important diary": Steven Kagle, "The American Diary Canon," in Ben-Amos and Ben-Amos, *The Diary*, 114.

"It may prove impossible": May Sarton, *After the Stroke: A Journal* (New York: W. W. Norton, 1988), 15.

"individualistic and introspective": Desirée Henderson, *How to Read a Diary: Critical Contexts and Interpretive Strategies for 21st-Century Readers* (New York: Routledge, 2019), 154–56.

Writer Suleika Jaouad: Suleika Jaouad, Instagram, Dec. 30, 2024, www.instagram.com/p/DENbBTFOPev/?img_index=1l; Suleika Jaouad, *Between Two Kingdoms: A Memoir of a Life Interrupted* (New York: Random House, 2021), 106; "Caught in Pandemic Limbo?" NPR, Nov. 11, 2021, npr.org/transcripts/1053569597.

disability rights activists: G. Thomas Couser and Susannah B. Mintz, "Introduction," in *Disability Experiences: Memoirs, Autobiographies, and Other Personal Narratives*, ed. G. Thomas Couser and Susannah B. Mintz (Farmington Hills, MI: Macmillan Reference USA, 2019), 1–2.

"terrible little notebook": C. S. Lewis, *A Grief Observed* (New York: HarperCollins, 1961), 9–10.

"a defense against": Lewis, *A Grief Observed*, 59–60.

Manguso's probing 2015 memoir: Sarah Manguso, *Ongoingness: The End of a Diary* (Minneapolis: Graywolf Press, 2015), 8–10.

"I wanted to live": Tara Westover, "A Visit to Madam Bedi," *New Yorker*, Feb. 17 and 24, 2025.

"Is it good?": Philippe Lejeune and Catherine Bogaert, "The Practice of Writing a Diary," trans. Dagmara Meijers-Troller, in Ben-Amos and Ben-Amos, *The Diary*, 33–35.

They worry that: Julie Rak, "The Diary Among Other Forms of Life Writing," in Ben-Amos and Ben-Amos, *The Diary*, 62.

Lejeune and Bogaert counter: Lejeune and Bogaert, "The Practice of Writing a Diary," 35.

"journaling comes as naturally": Lejeune and Bogaert, "The Practice of Writing a Diary," 33–35.

An overabundance: Henderson, *How to Read a Diary*, 140.

In June 2024: Ellen Barry and Cecilia Kang, "Surgeon General Calls for Warning Labels on Social Media Platforms," *New York Times*, June 18, 2024, https://

www.nytimes.com/2024/06/17/health/surgeon-general-social-media-warning-label.html.

Armstrong's blog Dooce: Chavie Lieber, "She Was the 'Queen of the Mommy Bloggers.' Then Her Life Fell Apart," *Vox*, Apr. 2019, www.vox.com/the-highlight/2019/4/25/18512620/dooce-heather-armstrong-depression-valedictorian-of-being-dead.

Armstrong died: Alex Williams, "Heather Armstrong, 'Queen of the Mommy Bloggers,' Is Dead at 47," *New York Times*, May 10, 2023, https://www.nytimes.com/2023/05/10/us/heather-armstrong-dead.html.

For Burke, blogging: "Carolyn's Diary," *One Year: 1995* (podcast), season 2, episode 7, aired Jan. 13, 2022, *Slate*, https://slate.com/transcripts/QXJKaDMoSjZyUWtTa2hUVnRuNnllWlpqTjJjVzIrbnZPOW5DZGhQaDhLMDo=.

However, because Burke: Carolyn L. Burke, "Carolyn's Diary Republished," Carolyn's Diary Museum, May 30, 2004, https://diary.carolyn.org/.

"Do [diaries] promote": Henderson, *How to Read a Diary*, 166.

CHAPTER 5: MEMORABLE

"thoughts, manners": Frances Burney, *Journals and Letters* (London: Penguin Classics, 2001), 1.

"partly because": Alice Walker, *Gathering Blossoms Under Fire: The Journals of Alice Walker, 1965–2000*, ed. Valerie Boyd (New York: Simon & Schuster, 2022), 504.

"I'm documenting": Aubrie Kiesling, phone interview, Mar. 27, 2024.

"common memory aid": "Memory Aids and Tools," Alzheimer's Society (UK), www.alzheimers.org.uk/get-support/staying-independent/memory-aids-and-tools; Dementia Diaries, https://dementiadiaries.org/; Dementia Activity Studio, "Grateful Journal: A Simple Daily Gratitude Log Book for Dementia and Alzheimer's Patients," 2019, Amazon.com, www.amazon.com/Grateful-Journal-gratitude-Alzheimers-happiness/dp/1081054913, accessed May 21, 2025.

"When I have a profound experience": Madeleine L'Engle, *Herself: Reflections on a Writing Life*, ed. Carole F. Chase (Colorado Springs: Shaw Books, 2001), 85.

Science has determined: Kathleen B. McDermott and Henry L. Roediger III, "Memory (Encoding, Storage, Retrieval)," Noba, 2024, https://nobaproject.com/modules/memory-encoding-storage-retrieval.

"That's the beauty": Henry L. Roediger, phone interview, May 28, 2022.

"big picture takeaways": Andrew Butler, phone interview, Jan. 4, 2023.

"the motor and sensory memory": The Economist, "The Importance of Handwriting Is Becoming Better Understood," Sept. 14, 2023, www.economist.com/culture/2023/09/14/the-importance-of-handwriting-is-becoming-better-understood.

a much-reported 2014 study: P. A. Mueller and D. M. Oppenheimer, "The Pen Is Mightier Than the Keyboard: Advantages of Longhand over Laptop Note Taking," *Psychological Science*, 25, no. 6 (2014): 1159–68, https://doi.org/10.1177/0956797614524581.

"Taking lecture notes": Roediger, phone interview, May 28, 2022.

It "probably makes": Andrew Butler, email, May 16, 2024.

a 2021 study: "Don't Ditch the Laptop Just Yet," Association for Psychological Science, Apr. 30, 2021, https://www.psychologicalscience.org/observer/writing-.

"The memory is constantly changing": McDermott and Roediger, "Memory (Encoding, Storage, Retrieval)."

"especially if they're": Butler, phone interview, Jan. 4, 2023.

"Memories are continuously": Scott A. Small, *Forgetting: The Benefits of Not Remembering* (New York: Penguin Random House, 2021), 81.

Then there's the pioneering: Discussed in Elizabeth J. Marsh, "Retelling Is Not the Same as Recalling: Implications for Memory," *Current Directions in Psychological Science* 16, no. 1 (Feb. 2007): 16–17.

memories change: Marsh, "Retelling Is Not the Same as Recalling," 16–20.

"Stories are": Robyn Fivush, phone interview, Feb. 9, 2022.

Between 1952 and 2020: Igor Sotgiu, "Eight Memory Researchers Investigating Their Own Autobiographical Memory," *Applied Cognitive Psychology* 35, no. 6 (Nov.–Dec. 2021): 1631–40.

Marigold Linton: Marigold Linton, "Transformations of Memory in Everyday Life," in *Memory Observed: Remembering in Natural Contexts*, ed. Ulric Neisser (San Francisco: Freeman, 1982), 77–91.

Inspired by Lingold's: Avril Thorne, "Using What to Remember When: Studies of 450 Daily Diaries," review of *Autobiographical Memory: Remembering What and Remembering When*, by Charles P. Thompson et al., *American Journal of Psychology* 111, no. 3 (1998): 480–82, doi.org/10.2307/1423455.

Why do we recall: Butler, phone interview, Mar. 24, 2022.

As we acquire more: Harry P. Bahrick, "Long Term Maintenance of Knowledge," in *The Oxford Handbook of Memory*, ed. Endel Tulving and Fergus I. M. Clark (Oxford: Oxford University Press, 2005), 247–61.

Some cues work: James Pichert and Richard C. Anderson, "Taking Different Perspectives on a Story," *Journal of Educational Psychology* 69, no. 4 (1977): 309–15.

Martha Hodes's absorbing 2023 memoir: Martha Hodes, *My Hijacking: A Personal History of Forgetting and Remembering* (New York: HarperCollins, 2023), 93, 109, 256.

Young Martha didn't: Hodes, *My Hijacking*, 256–57, 288.

During a radio interview: "An 'Exvangelical' on Loving, Leaving and Reporting on the Culture of Christianity," *Fresh Air*, NPR, Mar. 18, 2024, npr.org/2024/03/18/1239122282/sarah-mccammon-exvangelical-christianity-trump.

"Unfortunately, research": Jen Wirth, Alzheimer's Association, email, Mar. 31, 2022.

Dementia caused by Alzheimer's: Alzheimer's Association (US), "Alzheimer's & Dementia," accessed May 21, 2025.

Regardless of what disease: Alzheimer Society of Canada, "The Difference Between Alzheimer's Disease and Other Dementias," https://alzheimer.ca/en/about-dementia/what-alzheimers-disease/difference-between-alzheimers-disease-other-dementias, accessed May 21, 2025.

During the early stage: Alzheimer's Society (UK), "Memory Loss and Dementia," https://www.alzheimers.org.uk/about-dementia/symptoms-and-diagnosis/symptoms/memory-loss, accessed May 21, 2025.

But the suggestion: David Balota, email, Apr. 26, 2023.

I was pleased: David Balota, email, Apr. 13, 2024.

People with a parent: Alzheimer's Association, "Is Alzheimer's Genetic?" www.alz.org/alzheimers-dementia/what-is-alzheimers/causes-and-risk-factors/genetics, accessed May 21, 2025.

"horror story": Greg O'Brien, *On Pluto: Inside the Mind of Alzheimer's* (Brewster, MA: Codfish Press, 2014), 18, 72, 137.

O'Brien's candor, clarity: O'Brien, *On Pluto*, 73–74.

Begun in 1986: Kathryn P. Riley et al., "Early Life Linguistic Ability, Late Life Cognitive Function, and Neuropathology: Findings from the Nun Study," *Neurobiology of Aging* 26, no. 3. (2005) 341–47.

The sisters who produced: Jad Abumrad, "Agatha Christie and Nuns Tell a Tale of Alzheimer's," NPR, June 1, 2010, npr.org/2010/06/01/127211884/agatha-christie-and-nuns-tell-a-tale-of-alzheimers.

Typical age-related memory: Alzheimer's Association, "10 Early Signs and Symptoms of Alzheimer's and Dementia," www.alz.org/alzheimers-dementia/10_signs, accessed May 21, 2025.

With typical aging: Ranganath, *Why We Remember*, 199.

Can a brain-stimulating activity: Melinda Wenner Moyer, "Will Stimulating Your Brain Help Keep It Sharp as You Age?" *New York Times*, Apr. 27, 2025.

Typical forgetting may: Small, *Forgetting*, 38, 174.

"I wrote down": Sarah Manguso, *Ongoingness: The End of a Diary* (Minneapolis: Graywolf Press, 2015), 4, 11, 86.

CHAPTER 6: CREATIVES

For Anaïs Nin: Anaïs Nin, The Early Diary of Anaïs Nin: 1923–27, vol. 3 (New York: Houghton Mifflin *Jovanovich*, 1983), 32–33, quoted in Elizabeth Podnieks, *"The Literary Author as Diarist," in The Diary: The Epic of Everyday Life*, ed. Batsheva Ben-Amos and Dan Ben-Amos (Bloomington: Indiana University Press, 2020), 274.

"[This] diary writing": Virginia Woolf, "Monday, January 20th," *A Writer's Diary: Being Extracts from the Diary of Virginia Woolf*, ed. Leonard Woolf (New York: Harcourt Brace, 1954), 7.

Nathaniel Hawthorne's idea: "The Diary: Three Centuries of Private Lives," exhibition, Morgan Library, 2011, www.themorgan.org/exhibitions/the-diary.

Albert Camus's journal: Thomas Mallon, *A Book of One's Own: People and Their Diaries*, 3rd ed. (St. Paul, MN: Hungry Mind Press, 1995), 144–45.

Playwright Tennessee Williams: "The Diary: Three Centuries of Private Lives," exhibition, Morgan Library.

Novelist Louisa May Alcott: Meredith Mann, "Louisa May Alcott, in Her Own Words," New York Public Library (blog), Sept. 28, 2015, www.nypl.org/blog/2015/09/28/louisa-may-alcott-own-words.

"Oh hell": Alice Dunbar-Nelson, *Give Us Each Day: The Diary of Alice Dunbar-Nelson*, ed. Gloria T. Hull (New York: W. W. Norton, 1984), 429.

"communed with herself": Leonard Woolf, "Preface," in Woolf, *A Writer's Diary*, 13.

She also charted: Elizabeth Podnieks, "The Literary Author as Diarist," in Ben-Amos and Ben-Amos, *The Diary*, 277.

Of diary writing itself: Woolf, "Easter Sunday, April 20th," *A Writer's Diary*, 13.

Woolf distinguished: Podnieks, "The Literary Author as Diarist," 276–80.

"I daresay": Woolf, *A Writer's Diary*, 88.

Leonard Woolf caught flak: Elizabeth Bowen, "The Principle of Her Art Was Joy," review of *A Writer's Diary*, ed. Leonard Woolf, *New York Times*, Feb. 21, 1954.

Over two decades: Rebecca Hogan, review of *Becoming Virginia Woolf: Her Early Diaries and the Diaries She Read*, by Barbara Lounsberry, *Auto/Biography Studies* 37, no. 2 (2022): 349–52, doi.org/10.1080/08989575.2022.2027653.

Contemporary authors' diaries: Adrienne Su, phone interview, Jan. 26, 2023; Adrienne Su, "The Days," *New Yorker*, Dec. 26, 2022, www.newyorker.com/magazine/2023/01/02/the-days.

Brooklyn writer Tyler: Tyler Wetherall, "Portal to a Forgotten Land: Finding Your Character's Voice in Old Diaries," *Literary Hub*, Oct. 23, 2024, https://lithub.com/portal-to-a-forgotten-land-finding-your-characters-voice-in-old-diaries.

"the lines between": Sarah Durn, "How to Start and Keep a Journal," *New York Times*, Jan. 6, 2025, www.nytimes.com/article/journaling-tips.html.

"While I was writing": Alice Walker, *Gathering Blossoms Under Fire: The Journals of Alice Walker, 1965–2000*, ed. Valerie Boyd (New York: Simon & Schuster, 2022), 495, 504.

For journalists who: DK, ed., *Remarkable Diaries: The World's Greatest Diaries, Journals, Notebooks & Letters* (New York: DK, 2020), 216.

"The Barnsley public baths": George Orwell, diary excerpt, "The Road to Wigan Pier Blog," Orwell Foundation, https://theroadtowiganpier.wordpress.com/, accessed May 21, 2025.

Singer-songwriters also: Rachel Syme, "Alanis Morissette Isn't Angry Anymore," *New York Times*, Nov. 26, 2019, www.nytimes.com/2019/11/26/magazine/alanis-morissette-jagged-little-pill-musical.html; Wendy Goodman, "A

Trip to Stevieland," *Harper's Bazaar*, Nov. 1997, available at https://www.fleetwoodmac-uk.com/articles/FMart26.htm; Jon Caramanica and Joe Coscarelli, "Taylor Swift's Diary Entries Are a Must-Read Companion to 'Lover,'" *New York Times*, Aug. 26, 2019, www.nytimes.com/2019/08/26/arts/music/taylor-swift-lover-journals.html.

The diary entries: Caramanica and Coscarelli, "Taylor Swift's Diary Entries Are a Must-Read Companion to 'Lover.'"

Critic Jon Caramanica: Caramanica and Coscarelli, "Taylor Swift's Diary Entries Are a Must-Read Companion to 'Lover.'"

Singer-songwriter Lucy: Rebecca Bengal, "Lucy Dacus Takes Confessional Songwriting to a New Level," *New York Times*, June 21, 2021, www.nytimes.com/2021/06/21/t-magazine/lucy-dacus-home-video.html.

Comedy writer Merrill Markoe: Merrill Markoe, *We Saw Scenery: The Early Diaries of Merrill Markoe* (Chapel Hill, NC: Algonquin Books, 2020), 50.

Not every successful creative: Zadie Smith, "Life Writing," *Rookie*, Feb. 16, 2015, www.rookiemag.com/2015/02/life-writing/.

Among the diarists: Benjamin Anastas, "The Most Ambitious Diary in History," *New Yorker*, Nov. 8, 2021, www.newyorker.com/magazine/2021/11/08/the-most-ambitious-diary-in-history-claude-fredericks.

Unable to get a publishing deal: Anastas, "The Most Ambitious Diary in History."

One opportunity: Anastas, "The Most Ambitious Diary in History."

"Perhaps no one": Podnieks, "The Literary Author as Diarist," 284.

"Anaïs Nin, Author": C. Gerald Fraser, "Anaïs Nin, Author Whose Diaries Depicted Intellectual Life, Dead," *New York Times*, Jan. 16, 1977.

"literary accomplishment": Podnieks, "The Literary Author as Diarist," 284–86.

On June 10, 1931: Anaïs Nin, *The Early Diary of Anaïs Nin, Vol. 4, 1927–1931* (London: Peter Own, 1995), 433.

Nin's novella Djuna*:* Anaïs Nin, *Incest: From "A Journal of Love"* (Orlando, FL: Harvest, 1992), 280. *Djuna* was included in the first edition of Nin's *The Winter of Artifice* (Paris: Obelisk Press, 1939) but removed from later editions.

Nin the novelist: Rupert Pole, "Preface," Anaïs Nin, *Henry and June* (Orlando, FL: Harvest, 1986), viii–ix.

To some, Nin: DK, *Remarkable Diaries*, 214; Sady Doyle, "Before Lena Dunham, There Was Anaïs Nin," *The Guardian*, Apr. 7, 2015, https://www.theguardian.com/culture/2015/apr/07/anais-nin-author-social-media.

Nin was criticized: Fraser, "Anaïs Nin, Author Whose Diaries Depicted Intellectual Life, Dead."

Predating Nin was: Sonia Wilson, "How Marie Bashkirtseff Rewrote the Route to Fame," *Public Domain Review*, Sept. 2, 2020, https://publicdomainreview.org/essay/marie-bashkirtseff/.

"If I should not": Marie Bashkirtseff, *The Journal of a Young Artist 1860–1884*, trans. Mary J. Serrano (New York: E. P. Dutton, 1919), xiv.

"immense egotism": Margo Culley, "Introduction," in *A Day at a Time*, 7–8.

More recently: Wilson, "How Marie Bashkirtseff Rewrote the Route to Fame."

Bashkirtseff's diary was read: Wilson, "How Marie Bashkirtseff Rewrote the Route to Fame."

"I of womankind": Mary MacLane, diary entry, in Culley, *A Day at a Time*, 188.

Although MacLane: Culley, *A Day at a Time*, 187.

Imagine uploading: Sheila Heti, "A Diary in Alphabetical Order," *New York Times*, Mar. 23, 2022, www.nytimes.com/interactive/2022/03/23/opinion/sheila-heti-alphabetized-diary-wxyz.html

An early version: "Sheila Heti," *New York Times*, Mar. 22, 2023, www.nytimes.com/column/sheila-heti.

Heti reports: Sheila Heti, "A Diary in Alphabetical Order."

The American diarist: Heidi Julavits, *The Folded Clock: A Diary* (New York: Anchor Books, 2015), 21.

Twentieth-century French writer: Simone de Beauvoir, *After the War, Force of Circumstance, I* (New York: Paragon House, 1992), 7, quoted in Francoise Simonet-Tenant, "The Contemporary Personal Diary in France," in Ben-Amos and Ben-Amos, *The Diary*, 236–37.

Tina Brown's 2017: Tina Brown, *The Vanity Fair Diaries, 1983–1992* (New York: Henry Holt, 2017), 2, 417.

Although diary purists: Lejeune, "The Diary as 'Antifiction,'" *On Diary*, 201.

In her personal diary: Helen Fielding, "Bridget Jones and the Subtle Art of Diary Keeping," *LitHub*, Jan. 26, 2024, https://lithub.com/helen-fielding-on-bridget-jones-and-the-subtle-art-of-diary-keeping/; Helen Fielding, *Bridget Jones's Diary* (New York: Penguin, 1996), 24.

"idea of using": Kylie Cardell, *De@r World: Contemporary Uses of the Diary* (Madison: University of Wisconsin Press, 2014), 38–43.

"huge collection": Helen Fielding, "By the Book," *New York Times Book Review*, Feb. 16, 2025.

For better or worse: Rachel Thompson, "Calling Bridget Jones One of the Most Influential Women of the Past 70 Years Is Problematic," *Mashable*, Dec. 14, 2016, https://mashable.com/article/bridget-jones-influential-woman.

"Now I know *I am":* Sue Townsend, *The Secret Diary of Adrian Mole, Aged 13¾* (1982; New York: HarperTempest, 2003), 8.

"I prefer to keep": Alex Clark, "A Life in . . . Sue Townsend," *The Guardian*, Nov. 6, 2009, www.theguardian.com/books/2009/nov/07/sue-townsend-interview-alex-clark.

"keep an honest": Aaron S. Rosenberg, *Madeleine L'Engle* (New York: Rosen, 2006), 74.

"immensely helpful": Joyce Carol Oates, "Journals: Observing the World," Masterclass video, www.masterclass.com/classes/joyce-carol-oates-teaches-the-art-of-the-short-story/chapters/journals-observing-the-world, accessed May 21, 2025.

"When you start writing": "David Sedaris on Keeping a Diary in the Age of Over-Sharing," video, *The Atlantic*, Oct. 19, 2017, www.theatlantic.com/video/index/543267/david-sedaris-video-interview-writing-advice/.

"It's sort of": "David Sedaris on Keeping a Diary in the Age of Over-Sharing."

becoming "overproduced": David Sedaris, *Carnival of Snackery Diaries* (New York: Little, Brown, 2021), 4–5.

"I was writing": Lulu Garcia-Navarro, "Rick Steves Refuses to Get Cynical About the World," *New York Times Magazine*, Dec. 22, 2024, 12.

Some professionals offer: Julie Thalund et al., Diary School, email, Mar. 31, 2023; "Workshops for Businesses," Allswell, allswellcreative.com/pages/workshops-for-businesses, accessed May 21, 2025; Ellen K. Baker, phone interview, Nov. 8, 2023.

Grinnell College English professor: Paula Vene Smith, phone interview, Feb. 10, 2023; Martha McPhee, "Why I (Still) Carry a Notebook Everywhere," *Wirecutter*, Apr. 3, 2020, www.nytimes.com/wirecutter/blog/carry-a-notebook-everywhere/; Angela Hooks, "Bringing the Diary into the Classroom," *Currents in Teaching and Learning* 11, no. 2 (Sept. 2020): 47–54.

Sometimes a best-selling: "Morning Pages," The Artist's Way, juliacameronlive.com/basic-tools/morning-pages/, accessed May 21, 2025; Amazon entry for Julia Cameron, *The Artist's Way: 30th Anniversary Edition* (2016), https://www.amazon.com/Artists-Way-25th-Anniversary/dp/0143129252, accessed July 2025.

"I could write": Helen Churko, phone interview, Apr. 5, 2023.

In 2007 came: wreckthisjournal, Instagram, www.instagram.com/wreck.this journal/.

"the art of journaling": Suleika Jaouad (@Suleikajaouad), "The news is out!" Instagram, Oct. 17, 2024, www.instagram.com/suleikajaouad/p/DBPAa8NJKmW/?img_index=1.

A gathering in Jaouad's: Lauren Mechling, "How Journaling Went from a Solo Activity to a Social One," *Wall Street Journal*, Aug. 20, 2025.

Alexandra Johnson's 2001: Alexandra Johnson, *Leaving a Trace* (Boston: Little, Brown, 2001), book jacket, 12, 66, 84–85.

"I perceived": Annie Ernaux, *Getting Lost*, trans. Alison L. Strayer (New York: Seven Stories Press, 2022), 9.

When Ernaux won: "Annie Ernaux Facts," Nobel Prize, 2022, www.nobelprize.org/prizes/literature/2022/ernaux/facts.

During her all-consuming: Ernaux, *Getting Lost*, 8.

"I wanted to make": Ernaux, *Getting Lost*, 178.

"For me, words": Ernaux, *Getting Lost*, 9.

CHAPTER 7: HINDSIGHT

Standing onstage: Eileen Tull, *Mortified Live*, Music Box Theatre, Chicago, May 4, 2023.

Thus unfurled another: WBEZ Facebook post, 2023, https://www.facebook.com/events/music-box-theatre/wbez-presents-mortified-chicago/715949673221842/.

Some variation of this question: "Does Anyone Here Destroy Their Journals?" Reddit, 2018, r/Journaling, www.reddit.com/r/Journaling/comments/9epj6e/does_anyone_here_destroy_their_journals/.

But other destroyers: "Readers Respond on Destroying Diaries," Ask Amy, *Chicago Tribune*, Sept. 2, 2011, www.chicagotribune.com/things-to-do/#nt=taxonomy-article.

Elsewhere on the internet: Taymiya R. Zaman, "Riffat's Diary," *Cagibi*, July 16, 2019, https://cagibilit.com/riffats-diary/.

In the media: Dani Shapiro, "I Don't Want Anyone to Read My Diaries, Yet I Can't Burn Them," *New York Times*, Mar. 16, 2025, www.nytimes.com/2025/03/16/opinion/diary-didion-writing.html.

"My journals nearly": Ruth Estelle, "My Journals Nearly Destroyed Me So I Nearly Destroyed Them," *Medium*, June 14, 2019, medium.com/swlh/my-journals-nearly-destroyed-me-so-i-nearly-destroyed-them-cefc8fbf8593.

Another catchy headline: Helen Garner, "My Early Diaries Filled Me with So Much Shame I Burned Them," *The Guardian*, Oct. 29, 2019, https://www.theguardian.com/books/2019/oct/30/my-early-diaries-filled-me-with-so-much-shame-i-burned-them-im-publishing-the-rest.

British journalist Helen Coffey: Helen Coffey, "If Someone Published My Diary After I Died, I'd Die Again—of Shame," *The Independent*, Feb. 25, 2025, www.independent.co.uk/life-style/joan-didion-diary-therapy-notes-to-john-b2703678.html.

But bell hooks: bell hooks, *Remembered Rapture: The Writer at Work* (New York: Henry Holt, 1999), 5.

"Don't Burn Your Diary!": Desirée Henderson, "Don't Burn Your Diary!" *The Diary Index*, Feb. 5, 2017, diaryindex.com/2017/02/05/dont-burn-your-diary/.

Joan Didion argued: Joan Didion, "On Keeping a Notebook," in *Slouching Towards Bethlehem* (New York: Farrar, Straus and Giroux, 1968), 175, eBook 2013.

Postscript: Soon: Sheila McClear, "Goodbye to All That," *Los Angeles Magazine*, Nov. 17, 2022, https://lamag.com/news/goodbye-to-all-that-joan-didion-estate-hits-the-auction-block.

Maybe the secret: Eileen Tull, phone interview, Apr. 14, 2024.

Granted, some diaries: Ellen K. Baker, phone interview, Nov. 8, 2023.

"If you think": James W. Pennebaker, phone interview, Jan. 3, 2023.

Rosalie Deer Heart and Alison Strickland: Rosalie Deer Heart and Alison Strickland, *Harvesting Your Journals: Writing Tools to Enhance Your Growth & Creativity* (Santa Fe, NM: Heart Link Publications, 1999), 14–15.

psychologist Ira Progoff: Journal Feedback Process, https://www.intensivejournal.org/AboutMethod_JournalFeedback.php, accessed July 20, 2025.

Other therapists argue: Emma Loewe, "Want to Use Your Journal for Self-Discovery? Be Sure to Read It," Sept. 10, 2024, mindbodygreen, www.mindbodygreen.com/articles/why-this-therapist-wants-you-to-read-through-old-journal-entries.

An interesting twist: Roland Allen, *The Notebook: A History of Thinking on Paper* (Windsor, Ontario: Biblioasis, 2024), 337–44.

Destroying a diary: Patrick Huyghe, "Diary Writing Turns a New Leaf," *New York Times*, Nov. 9, 1981.

Diary burning is: Henderson, phone interview, Mar. 16, 2022.

the don't destroy *camp:* Baker, phone interview.

"to remember": Lee Humphreys, *The Qualified Self: Social Media and the Accounting of Everyday Life* (Cambridge, MA: MIT Press, 2018), 13.

One possible answer: Michael Ross and Anne E. Wilson, "Autobiographical Memory and Conceptions of Self: Getting Better All the Time," *Current Directions in Psychological Science* 12, no. 2 (Apr. 2003): 66–69, doi.org/10.1111/1467-8721.01228.

Thomas Mallon proposed: Thomas Mallon, *People and Their Diaries*, 3rd ed. (St. Paul, MN: Hungry Mind Press, 1995), 2–6, 19–21, 29–34, 44–45, 54–56, 76–87, 125–28, 135–40, 166–67, 184, 207–10, 251–57.

CHAPTER 8: OTHER EYES

My friend Pam: Pam Patton, phone interview, Feb. 20, 2023.

She did find: John Patton, diary entries, Apr. 9, 1992, Private Collection of Pam Patton, Windsor Heights, IA.

a rare and amazing family history: Darla Ewalt, phone interview, Dec. 8, 2023.

The diaries hold: Ewalt, phone interview.

On Sunday, December 31, 1899: Mary Caroline Coffin, diary entry, Dec. 31, 1899, Private Collection of Darla Ewalt, Ames, IA.

"It's so intimate": Amy Elbert, phone interview, Dec. 6, 2023.

"Thanksgiving day": Blanche Ford Hardin, diary entry, Nov. 28, 1915, Private Collection of Amy Elbert, Des Moines, IA.

The journal volumes: Becky Edmunds, "What to Do with a Diary?" webinar, Centre for Life History and Life Writing Research, University of Sussex, UK, Dec. 1, 2020; Dick Perceval, diary entry, Jan. 1, 1932, from the *(to be continued)* web series, episode 1, https://www.tobecontinued.online/.

On September 3, 1939: Dick Perceval, diary entry, Sept. 3, 1939, from the *(to be continued)* web series, episode 1.

On July 21, 1969: Dick Perceval, diary entry, July 21, 1969, from the *(to be continued)* web series, episode 16.

On December 31, 1972: Dick Perceval, diary entry, Dec. 31, 1972, from the *(to be continued)* web series, episode 27.

With help from a detective: Laura Francis and Alexander Masters, "Love, Death & Trousers," *Paris Review* 221 (Summer 2017), https://www.theparisreview.org

/letters-essays/6964/love-death-trousers-laura-francis-alexander-masters; Alexander Masters, "What to Do with a Diary?" webinar, Centre for Life History and Life Writing Research, University of Sussex, UK, Dec. 1, 2020.

Rather than use: Rachel Aviv, "Alice Munro's Passive Voice," *New Yorker*, Dec. 23, 2024, www.newyorker.com/magazine/2024/12/30/alice-munros-passive-voice.

Then there's "bad boy": Will Self, *Elaine* (New York: Grove Press, 2024), epigraph, book jacket.

For the book: Elisabeth Egan, "He Read His Dying Mother's Diaries, and Spun Them into a Novel," *New York Times*, Sept. 16, 2024, www.nytimes.com/2024/09/16/books/elaine-will-self.html.

about an Elaine: Sandra Newman, review of *Elaine*, by Will Self, *The Guardian*, Aug. 29, 2024.

"Diaries can tell": Leonieke Vermeer, presentation, "Researchers Using Diaries," Deutsches Tagebucharchiv, Emmendingen, GER, Apr. 14, 2023.

Vermeer searched: Leonieke Vermeer, "Tiny Symbols Tell Big Stories: Naming and Concealing Masturbation in Diaries (1660–1940)," *European Journal of Life Writing* 6 (2017): 101–34, doi.org/10.5463/ejlw.6.209.

For another study: Leonieke Vermeer, "From Diaries to Data Doubles: Self-Tracking in Dutch Diaries (1780–1940), *Life Writing* 19, no. 2 (2022): 215–40, doi.org/10.1080/14484528.2021.1971057.

Vermeer told me: Leonieke Vermeer, email, May 1, 2024.

"Tiny symbols": Vermeer, "Tiny Symbols Tell Big Stories," 102, 124–26.

Like the modern-day: Vermeer, "From Diaries to Data Doubles," 216–17, 221, 231.

Secretly recording: Vermeer, "Tiny Symbols Tell Big Stories," 101, 125.

Although far more men: Leonieke Vermeer, email, Apr. 24, 2024.

One woman who did: Vermeer, "Tiny Symbols Tell Big Stories," 114.

While some women track: Vermeer, "From Diaries to Data Doubles," 228–30.

Li Gerhalter, a senior scientist: Li Gerhalter, presentation, "Researchers Using Diaries," Deutsches Tagebucharchiv, Emmendingen, GER, Apr. 14, 2023; Li Gerhalter, "Publications: A History of Diary Research," Deutsches Tagebucharchiv, German Diary Archive website, tagebucharchiv.de/eine-geschichte-der-tagebuchforschung/; Li Gerhalter, email, Apr. 25, 2024.

"The Jews are": Dutch diary entries, from NIOD Institute for War, Holocaust and Genocide Studies in Amsterdam, translated and quoted by Nina Siegal, *The Diary Keepers: World War II in the Netherlands, as Written by the People Who Lived Through It* (New York: Ecco/HarperCollins, 2023), 110–12.

These three Dutch: Siegal, *The Diary Keepers*, 30–32, 301–2.

The Dutch Nazi policeman's: Siegal, *The Diary Keepers*, 304–5.

In his defense: Siegal, *The Diary Keepers*, 300–302, 310–11.

For diarists who write: Siegal, *The Diary Keepers*, 33, 294–305, 311.

I recalled this discussion: Catherine Porter and Ségolène Le Stradic, "French Doctor Who Sexually Abused Hundreds of Children Is Sentenced," *New York*

Times, May 28, 2025, www.nytimes.com/2025/05/28/joel-le-scouarnec-france-doctor-abuse-sentence.html.

Diary-based scholarship: Siegal, *The Diary Keepers*, 12, 381.

After reading 164: Siegal, *The Diary Keepers*, 381–84, 391–92.

It was Van der Boom's: Siegal, *The Diary Keepers*, 381–84, 393–94.

All this further bolsters: Siegal, *The Diary Keepers*, 20, 381–82, 392–94. Beyond the Nazis and the debated culpability of Dutch bystanders, other factors have been linked to the high death rate of Dutch Jews during World War II, including a late-starting resistance movement, proximity to Germany, and other geographical and topographical factors.

In the 1950s: Siegal, *The Diary Keepers*, 440–43.

Presser once memorably: M. Bosch et al., "Gender and Life Writing Today," *Tijdschrift voor Genderstudies* 19, no. 3 (2016): 291–99.

Siegal concludes: Siegal, *The Diary Keepers*, 456–57.

Historians have long: Siegal, *The Diary Keepers*, 18–30.

On March 28, 1944: Siegal, *The Diary Keepers*, 22.

The "secret archive": Siegal, *The Diary Keepers*, 25, 427.

So, too, diaries: Alexandra Alter, "How Aleksei Navalny's Prison Diaries Got Published," *New York Times*, Oct. 20, 2024, www.nytimes.com/2024/10/20/books/booksupdate/aleksei-navalny-memoir-prison-diaries.html; Alexei Navalny, *Patriot* (New York: Knopf, 2024), 405–6.

the unearthed diary-like manuscript: Andrew E. Kramer and Maria Varenikova, "The Buried Book That Helped Ukraine's Literary Revival," *New York Times*, July 20, 2024, https://www.nytimes.com/2024/07/20/world/europe/ukraine-publishing-buried-book.html.

a twenty-four-year-old Syrian man's: Samer, *The Raqqa Diaries: Escape from Islamic State* (Northampton, MA: Interlink Books, 2017).

For scholars of modern China: John Ruwitch, "In Battle over Its Past, China Wages Courtroom Fight in California," NPR, Oct. 1, 2024, npr.org/2024/10/01/nx-s1-5123277/in-battle-over-its-past-china-wages-courtroom-fight-in-california.

Since the 2023 start: Atef Abu Saif, *Don't Look Left: A Diary of Genocide* (Boston: Beacon Press, 2024), 35.

Israeli American historian: Saul Friedländer, *Diary of a Crisis: Israel in Turmoil* (Brooklyn, NY: Verso Books, 2024), 2.

Friedländer's diary account: Ruth Margalit, "How Oct. 7 Upended One Man's Diary," review of *Diary of a Crisis: Israel in Turmoil*, by Saul Friedländer, *New York Times*, Oct. 7, 2024, www.nytimes.com/2024/10/07/books/review/diary-of-a-crisis-saul-friedlander.html.

"It's important": Kimberly Katz, presentation, online launch for Batsheva Ben-Amos and Dan Ben-Amos, eds., *The Diary: The Epic of Everyday Life*, Feb. 18, 2021, available at www.youtube.com/watch?v=8AjXJABq_vw.

Makdisi argued: George Makdisi, "The Diary in Islamic Historiography: Some Notes," *History and Theory* 25, no. 2 (May 1986): 173–85, http://www.jstor.org/stable/2505304.

Not that there's: Katz, presentation.

In her essay: Kimberly Katz, "Writing the Self, Writing History in Palestine," in Ben-Amos and Ben-Amos, *The Diary*, 247–48; Katz, presentation.

Both men's diaries: Katz, "Writing the Self, Writing History in Palestine," 248–52; Katz, presentation.

The survival of these diaries: Katz, "Writing the Self, Writing History in Palestine," 250–56.

What both men wrote: Katz, presentation.

They also represent: Katz, "Writing the Self, Writing History in Palestine," 250–56.

The Diary *anthology's:* Batsheva Ben-Amos and Dan Ben-Amos, "Introduction," in Ben-Amos and Ben-Amos, *The Diary*, 1–2.

"How I detested": Philippe Lejeune, "Composing a Diary," *On Diary*, ed. Jeremy Popkin and Julie Rak, trans. Katherine Durnin (Manoa: University of Hawai'i Press, 2009), 168–69.

The diary was often: Philippe Lejeune, "The Diary on Trial," in *On Diary*, ed. Jeremy Popkin and Julie Rak, trans. Katherine Durnin (Manoa: University of Hawai'i Press, 2009), 147.

Deeming his own: Philippe Lejeune, "The Practice of the Private Journal," *On Diary*, ed. Jeremy Popkin and Julie Rak, trans. Katherine Durnin (Manoa: University of Hawai'i Press, 2009), 31.

But in the 1980s: Jeremy Popkin, "Preface," *On Diary*, ed. Jeremy Popkin and Julie Rak, trans. Katherine Durnin (Manoa: University of Hawai'i Press, 2009), 2–5.

Lejeune also scrutinized: Philippe Lejeune and Catherine Bogaert, "The Practice of Writing a Diary," trans. Dagmara Meijers-Troller, in Ben-Amos and Ben-Amos, *The Diary*, 25–26.

Some three million French people: Lejeune and Bogaert, "The Practice of Writing a Diary," 25–26.

Sally MacNamara Ivey reads: Sally MacNamara Ivey, phone interview, Feb. 2, 2023.

Drawn to the business: Sally MacNamara Ivey, "What I've Learned from Reading over 10,000 Diaries," TEDx Talk, Jan. 7, 2022, available at www.youtube.com/watch?v=CIopFzbIPJw.

The diary of Sir Charles Middleton: Charles Middleton, diary entry, Sept. 1, 1793, Private Collection of Sally MacNamara Ivey, Issaquah, WA.

Dealers participate: Rick Stattler, phone interview, June 27, 2023.

"overlooked Americans": Rick Stattler, "Old Diaries Tell the Stories of Overlooked Americans," Swann Auction Galleries, Mar. 23, 2020, www.swanngalleries.com/news/books/2020/03/collectors-guide-manuscript-diaries/.

But not all: Stattler, phone interview.

Independent rare-book dealer: Tad Friend, "A Controversial Rare-Book Dealer Tries to Rewrite His Own Ending," *New Yorker*, Oct. 21, 2024, www.newyorker.com/magazine/2024/10/28/a-controversial-rare-book-dealer-tries-to-rewrite-his-own-ending.

Strangers' diaries are: Joanna Borns, "I Bought a Stranger's Diary from eBay," YouTube video, June 20, 2019, www.youtube.com/watch?v=RFcp_EawOQw.

Borns continues to read: Joanna Borns, "My Embarrassing Teen Diary," YouTube video, Mar. 11, 2023, www.youtube.com/watch?v=hOK_aHthYcE; Joanna Borns, "How to Buy a Stranger's Diary Q&A," YouTube video, Jan. 30, 2020, www.youtube.com/watch?v=toZLMuLtGM4.

If she reads: MacNamara Ivey, phone interview May 21, 2024, and email Jan. 2025; Stattler, phone interview.

the infamous "Hitler Diaries": Kieran Fogarty et al., "Hitler Diaries," *Britannica*, https://www.britannica.com/topic/Hitler-Diaries, accessed July 21, 2025.

In 2024, two people: Adam Goldman, "Women Sentenced to Month in Prison over Theft of Ashley Biden's Diary," *New York Times*, Apr. 26, 2024, https://www.nytimes.com/2024/04/09/us/politics/project-veritas-ashley-biden-diary.html.

Another noble diary experiment: Joshua Conrad Jackson and Michele Gelfand, "Opinion: Can the Diaries of Ordinary People Be Used to Bridge Cultural Divides?" *Los Angeles Times*, Oct. 25, 2019, www.latimes.com/opinion/story/2019-10-25/study-foreign-cultures-prejudice-diaries-pakistan; J. C. Jackson et al., "Together from Afar: Introducing a Diary Contact Technique for Improving Intergroup Relations," *Behavioral Science & Policy* 5, no. 1 (2021): 15–33.

Surveyed before: Jackson et al., "Together from Afar."

The diary's quotidian: Lauren Silverman, "A Pocket-Size Time Machine," *The Atlantic*, Nov. 28, 2022, www.theatlantic.com/technology/archive/2022/11/read-strangers-diary-book/672199/.

But the researchers: Jackson and Gelfand, "Opinion: Can the Diaries of Ordinary People Be Used to Bridge Cultural Divides?"

CHAPTER 9: ORDINARY PEOPLE

"Behind every diary": Author's visit to diary museum, Pieve Santo Stefano, Sept. 14, 2023.

The museum introduced: "The Little Museum of Infinite Memories," Piccolo Museo del Diario and Archivio Diaristico Nazionale, https://www.piccolomuseodeldiario.it/, accessed May 21, 2025; Elizabeth Povoledo, "A Trove of Diaries," *New York Times*, Aug. 19, 2019.

"MASS OBSERVATION wants": "MO85: The 12th May Diary Project," Mass Observation, Apr. 27, 2022, available at www.youtube.com/watch?v=cKhIAehVi9E.

The May 12th Diary Day: Diary entry, May 12, 1937, Mass Observation Archive, University of Sussex, Brighton, UK.

Diary Day became: Emily Calcraft, "Similarities and Dissimilarities in Mass Observation's 12 May Diaries from 1937 & 2023," Mass Observation, Apr. 12, 2024, https://massobs.org.uk/2024/04/12/i-am-not-interested-in-the-coronation/.

Three years earlier: Jessica Scantlebury, Mass Observation Archive, email, July 15, 2020; Chloe Daniel, "12th May 2020 an Introduction to the Diaries," University of Sussex, Mar. 25, 2021, blogs.sussex.ac.uk/librarycollections/2021/03/25/12th-may-2020-an-introduction-to-the-diaries/.

"There was an outpouring": "MO85," Mass Observation; Kirsty Pattrick, email, Apr. 30, 2024; Nick Clarke, ed., *Everyday Life in the Covid-19 Pandemic: Mass Observation's 12th May Diaries* (London: Bloomsbury, 2024).

Across the decades: Ella Beales, "Reviewing Mass Observation's 12th May Day Diaries," *The Keep* (blog), May 12, 2020, www.thekeep.info/reviewing-mass-observations-12th-may-day-diaries-we-are-more-alike-than-we-think/; Prison diary entry, May 12, 2017, Mass Observation Archive, University of Sussex, Brighton, UK.

The impetus for: Claire Langhamer, phone interview, Mar. 17, 2022.

2006 British television drama: Stephanie Billen, "Housewife, 49," *The Guardian*, Dec. 11, 2006, https://www.theguardian.com/culture/tvandradioblog/2006/dec/11/youreviewhousewife49.

Simon Garfield showcased: Simon Garfield, *We Are at War: The Diaries of Five Ordinary People in Extraordinary Times* (London: Ebury Press, 2005).

Erik Larson found: Erik Larson, *The Splendid and the Vile: A Saga of Churchill, Family, and Defiance During the Blitz* (New York: Crown, 2020), 308.

In 2020, professors: "Your Story Matters," Pandemic Journaling Project, pandemic-journaling-project.chip.uconn.edu.

Another outpouring: "Featured Entries," Pandemic Journaling Project, pjp-featuredentries.core.uconn.edu/; Sarah S. Willen, phone interview, July 21, 2023.

National Women's History Museum: Amelia Nierenberg, "The Quarantine Diaries," *New York Times*, Mar. 30, 2020, www.nytimes.com/2020/03/30/style/coronavirus-diaries-social-history.html.

Frustrated teenagers: Lori Ann Terjesen, museum vice president, email, May 17, 2024; Alisha Haridasani Gupta, "The Caretakers of Women's Pandemic Stories," *New York Times*, Apr. 21, 2022, www.nytimes.com/2022/04/21/arts/design/women-coronavirus-pandemic-journals.html; Farah Eltohamy and Phil Harrell, "Dispatches from Quarantine," NPR, Apr. 16, 2021, npr.org/2021/04/16/986927761/dispatches-from-quarantine-how-young-people-are-documenting-history.

Diaries with "plague": Great Diary Project, blog, https://thegreatdiaryproject.co.uk/collections/covid-19-diaries-of-human-truth/, accessed July 21, 2025.

"people came back": Author visit to Italy's Little Diary Museum, Sept. 14, 2023.

In Germany, Marlene Kayen: Marlene Kayen, phone interview, Feb. 13, 2024.

The European Diary: Marlene Kayen, email, Feb. 15, 2025.

EDAC's two Dutch members: Expatriate Archive Centre, "About the Collection," https://xpatarchive.com/collection/about-the-collection/, accessed July 21, 2025.

The project: Great Diary Project, "About Us," https://thegreatdiaryproject.co.uk/about-us/, accessed July 21, 2025.

"We believe": Bishopsgate Institute, "What We Do," www.bishopsgate.org.uk/charles-goss, accessed May 21, 2025.

The Great Diary Project does *focus:* Great Diary Project, "The Oldest Diary in the Collection," https://thegreatdiaryproject.co.uk/collections/the-oldest-diary-in-the-collection/, accessed July 21, 2025.

not-famous diarists: Polly North, email, Feb. 16, 2024.

Its impressive public outreach: Great Diary Project, "A Selection of the Talks and Exhibitions We Have Provided," 2023, https://thegreatdiaryproject.co.uk/events/, accessed July 21, 2025.

By mid-2023: Polly North, email, May 30, 2024.

In France, I visited: Association for Autobiography and Autobiographical Heritage (APA), "Who Are We?" https://autobiographie.sitapa.org/qui-sommes-nous, accessed May 21, 2025.

Elizabeth Legros Chapuis: Author visit to APA, Jan. 17, 2023.

APA collects unpublished: Elizabeth Legros Chapuis, email, May 3, 2024.

There are roughly: Claudine Krishnan, email, May 2, 2024.

Next stop: Kayen, phone interview; German Archives for Diaries, tagebucharchiv.de/the-german-archives-for-diaries/, accessed May 21, 2025; Annette B. diary, June 17, 1951, DTA 448, Deutsches Tagebucharchiv, Emmendingen, accessed May 21, 2025.

The archive has: Marlene Kayen, email, Apr. 7, 2024.

Kurrent was deemed: Walden Font Co., "On the History of Old German Script," https://www.waldenfont.com/OntheHistoryofOldGermanScript.asp, accessed July 21, 2025.

In Italy, the Archivio: Saverio Tutino, "The Archives of Pieve Santo Stefano," Archivio Diaristico Nazionale, http://archiviodiari.org/index.php/archivio/421.html, accessed May 21, 2025.

A record-breaking: Email blast from Fondazione Archivio Diaristico Nazionale, Jan. 29, 2025.

Post-war "social reconciliation": T. G. Ashplant, "Life Writing 'from Below' in Europe," *European Journal of Life Writing* 7 (2018): 237–42, doi.org/10.5463/ejlw.7.237; Francesca Venuto, Archivio Diaristico Nazionale press officer, email, May 8, 2024; Saverio Tutino, "The Archives of Pieve Santo Stefano," Archivio Diaristico Nazionale, http://www.archiviodiari.it/index.php/archivio/421-the-archives-of-pieve-santo-stefano.html, accessed July 21, 2025.

The archive began: The two contests (Italian and international) are referred to as the DiMMi project ("Diari Multimediali Migranti" or "migrant multimedia diaries"). For more information, see www.archiviomemoriemigranti.net /projects/dimmi-diari-multimediali-migranti/, accessed May 21, 2025.

The festival that: Francesca Venuto, email; Natalia Cangi, on-site interview, Pieve Santo Stefano, Sept. 18, 2023.

Diary archives also: Ashplant, "Life Writing 'from Below' in Europe."

Diary archives, although: Marijke Huisman, "Monuments for the Common (Wo)man: Diary Archives in Europe," *Tijdschrift voor Genderstudies* 19, no. 3 (2016): 373–85, www.aup-online.com/content/journals/10.5117/TVGN 2016.3.HUIS.

the American Diary Project: American Diary Project, "The Diary Archive for Everyday Folks," https://americandiaryproject.com/, accessed July 21, 2025.

The mission: American Diary Project, "About Us," https://americandiaryproject .com/about-us/, accessed July 21, 2025.

By mid-2025: Kate Zirkle, phone interview, May 16, 2024.

The project has: Author visit to American Diary Project, Cleveland, Sept. 9, 2024.

The other effort: Robert K. Elder, email, May 28, 2024; Sally MacNamara Ivey, phone interview, May 21, 2024.

The American Diary Project's: "Collection of U.S. Diaries," American Diary Project (website) https://americandiaryproject.com/collection/ accessed Apr. 25, 2025; Kate Zirkle, email, Apr. 25, 2025.

The project's blog: "Daughter Gains More Than Just a Diary," American Diary Project, Aug. 27, 2023, americandiaryproject.com/2023/08/27/daughter -shares-what-it-was-like-finding-her-late-mothers-diary/.

In Italy, the "cultural movement": F.L.R. diary entry, Jan. 1, 1927, Archivio Diaristico Nazionale, Pieve Santo Stefano (Arezzo) Italy, www.idiariracontano .org/estratti/buoni-popositi/.

CHAPTER 10: HERSTORY

Using care worthy: Eleanor Skelton Cash, diary entry, Feb. 11, 1986, Roll #2, MC 716, Eleanor Skelton Cash Papers, Arthur and Elizabeth Schlesinger Library on the History of Women in America, Harvard Radcliffe Institute, Cambridge Massachusetts (hereafter Schlesinger Library).

a poignant reminder: Kathryn Jacob, on-site interview, Schlesinger Library, Nov. 3, 2023.

In 1991, Louise Noun: University of Iowa Libraries, "IWA Timeline," www.lib .uiowa.edu/iwa/timeline, accessed July 21, 2025.

"Women do not": University of Iowa Libraries, "IWA Timeline."

Smith died in: Kären M. Mason and Tanya Zanish-Belcher, "A Room of One's Own," in *Perspectives on Women's Archives*, ed. Tanya Zanish-Belcher with Anke Voss (Chicago: Society of American Archivists, 2013), 140–42.

Learning about the variety: Fernanda Perrone, "From Annals to Heritage Centers: The Archives of Women's Religious Communities," in Zanish-Belcher and Voss, *Perspectives on Women's Archives*, 204.

The rise of women's archives: Anke Voss-Hubbard, "'No Documents—No History': Mary Ritter Beard and the Early History of Women's Archives," in Zanish-Belcher and Voss, *Perspectives on Women's Archives*, 31–56.

Spurred by second-wave feminism: Kären M. Mason, "A Grand Manuscripts Search," in Zanish-Belcher and Voss, *Perspectives on Women's Archives*, 71–96.

"Women's history": Gerda Lerner, *Living with History/Making Social Change* (Chapel Hill: University of North Carolina Press, 2009), 46.

In one giant leap: Mason, "A Grand Manuscripts Search," 71–95.

The guide prompted: Mason, "A Grand Manuscripts Search," 71–95.

More women's archives: Kären M. Mason and Tanya Zanish-Belcher, "A Room of One's Own," in Zanish-Belcher and Voss, *Perspectives on Women's Archives*, 123–32.

Women's diaries were among: Eva S. Moseley, "Sources for the 'New Women's History,'" in Zanish-Belcher and Voss, *Perspectives on Women's Archives*, 103–16.

"I've been sick": Frida Kahlo, *The Diary of Frida Kahlo: An Intimate Self-Portrait* (New York: Abrams, 2005), 252.

"Empty, scared": Louise Noun, diary entry, June 2, 1997, Box 31, Louise Noun Papers, Iowa Women's Archives (hereafter IWA), University of Iowa Libraries, Iowa City.

Although she had: Louise Noun, diary entry, Apr. 4, 1998, Box 31, Louise Noun Papers, IWA, University of Iowa Libraries, Iowa City.

Noun's final act: Jason Clayworth, "Louise Noun: She Feared a Botched Suicide," *Des Moines Register*, Mar. 19, 2016, www.desmoinesregister.com/story/news/health/2016/03/19/louise-noun-she-feared-botched-suicide/81653288/.

Five years earlier: Louise Noun, diary entry, May 27, 1997, Box 31, Louise Noun Papers.

Other women's archives: Jane Kamensky, *Candida Royalle & the Sexual Revolution: A History from Below* (New York: W. W. Norton, 2024), 10–11, 429, 433.

In 2001, after four years: Sheridan Harvey, ed., *American Women: Library of Congress Guide for the Study of Women's History and Culture in the United States* (Washington, DC: Library of Congress, 2001).

"buried in the papers": Janice E. Ruth, "Collecting, Describing, and Promoting Women's History at the Library of Congress," in Zanish-Belcher and Voss, *Perspectives on Women's Archives*, 341–71.

At the Schlesinger Library: Robin W. Kilson, diary entry, Feb. 27, 1984, MC 877, Robin W. Kilson Papers, Schlesinger Library; Mildred Jefferson, diary entry, May 15, 1960, Mildred Jefferson Papers, MC696, Schlesinger Library.

In the Schlesinger's reading room: Anna Chennault, diary entry, Jan. 21, 1957, MC 552, box 5, Anna Chennault Papers, Schlesinger Library.

In the 1970s, before women's history: Laurel Thatcher Ulrich, phone interview, Mar. 25, 2022.

Ulrich was not: A Midwife's Tale, dir. Richard Rogers, written by Laurie Kahn-Leavitt, aired Jan. 19, 1998, PBS, www.pbs.org/wgbh/americanexperience/films/midwife/#transcript.

The diary offered: Ulrich, phone interview.

"Mrs. Foster": Martha Ballard, diary entry, in Laurel Thatcher Ulrich, *A Midwife's Tale: The Life of Martha Ballard, Based on Her Diary, 1785–1812* (New York: Vintage, 1991), 102.

"North acquitted": Martha Ballard, diary entry, in Ulrich, *A Midwife's Tale*, 126.

On January 29, 1821: Anne Lister, *The Secret Diaries of Miss Anne Lister*, in 2 vols., ed. Helena Whitbread (London: Little, Brown, 1988), 161.

Whitbread chanced: "Helena Whitbread—Decoding the Diaries," interview by Sherry Thomas, Apr. 9, 2019, available at https://www.youtube.com/watch?v=JrFQcrYn604.

Whitbread transcribed: Helena Whitbread, email, June 11, 2024.

Sometimes a single historical: Emilie Davis, *Emilie Davis's Civil War: The Diaries of a Free Black Woman in Philadelphia, 1863–1865*, ed. Judith Giesberg (University Park: Pennsylvania State University Press, 2014), xxiii–xxxiv; Karsonya Wise Whitehead, *Notes from a Colored Girl: The Civil War Pocket Diaries of Emilie Frances Davis* (Columbia: University of South Carolina Press, 2014), x, xiii, xvi, 4.

The two approaches: Davis, *Emilie Davis's Civil War*, 158; Whitehead, *Notes from a Colored Girl*, 187.

Her analysis: Whitehead, *Notes from a Colored Girl*, 3, 14–17.

Giesberg notes: Davis, *Emilie Davis's Civil War*, 13.

Although both publications: Ann D. Gordon, "Getting History's Words Right: Diaries of Emilie Davis," *Pennsylvania Magazine of History and Biography* 139, no. 2 (Apr. 2015): 214, https://www.jstor.org/stable/10.5215/pennmaghistbio.139.2.0197.

CHAPTER 11: READER EXPERIENCES

"I'm never going": Kerry Schauber, phone interview, Apr. 3, 2019.

On March 10, 1919: Jessie Greer, diary entry, Mar. 10, 1919, Smithsonian Digital Volunteers, Smithsonian National Museum of African American History and Culture, Washington DC, transcription.si.edu/view/26292/NMAAHC-2019_18_2_023.

Countless centuries-old: Batsheva Ben-Amos and Dan Ben-Amos, "Introduction," in *The Diary: The Epic of Everyday Life*, ed. Batsheva Ben-Amos and Dan Ben-Amos (Bloomington: Indiana University Press, 2020), 14; John Archiquette, diary entry, Sept. 16, 1894, University of Wisconsin–Madison Libraries, Madison, SC53, search.library.wisc.edu/digital/AVBF57DFGFOH248Q/pages/A26EL4SHRMYIH48Q.

some historians fear: Jennifer Schuessler, "The Obama Presidential Library That Isn't," *New York Times*, Feb. 20, 2019, https://www.nytimes.com/2019/02/20/arts/obama-presidential-center-library-national-archives-and-records-administration.html.

Elsewhere online: Japanese American National Museum, "A Life in Pieces: The Diary and Letters of Stanley Hayami," video, www.janm.org/exhibits/a-life-in-pieces/video; Jennifer Schuessler, "The Obama Presidential Library That Isn't," *New York Times*, Feb. 20, 2019, https://www.nytimes.com/2019/02/20/arts/obama-presidential-center-library-national-archives-and-records-administration.html.

"Digital searches": Laurel Thatcher Ulrich, phone interview, Mar. 25, 2022.

The first public transcription: Jie Jenny Zou, "Civil War Project Shows Pros and Cons of Crowdsourcing," *Chronicle of Higher Education*, June 14, 2011, www.chronicle.com/blogs/wiredcampus/civil-war-project-shows-pros-and-cons-of-crowdsourcing.

"Volunteer peer review": Library of Congress, By the People (website) https://crowd.loc.gov/get-started/how-to-review/, accessed June 14, 2025.

Iowa's DIY History: DIY History, https://diyhistory.lib.uiowa.edu/, accessed July 21, 2025.

The Smithsonian's 99,501: Smithsonian, Smithsonian Digital Volunteers: Transcription Center, transcription.si.edu, accessed July 2, 2025.

Launched in 2018: Library of Congress, "About By the People," https://crowd.loc.gov/about/, accessed July 2, 2025.

"What an impact!": Carla Hayden, "Celebrating Six Years of By the People," Library of Congress Blogs, Jan. 10, 2025, blogs.loc.gov/thesignal/2025/01/by-the-people-turns-6/.

A "transcribe-a-thon": By the People email bulletin, Feb. 21, 2025, https://mail.google.com/mail/u/0/#inbox/FMfcgzQZTMQSXzlWBmFMdtcccXXnrFdF.

Five months later: By the People, "African American Perspectives in Print," Feb. 22, 2025, https://crowd.loc.gov/campaigns/af-american-perspectives/.

Clara Barton's diary: "Clara Barton: 'Angel of the Battlefield,'" Library of Congress, By the People, crowd.loc.gov/campaigns/clara-barton-angel-of-the-battlefield/, accessed Aug. 4, 2025.

I was moved: Clara Barton, diary entry, Dec. 7, 1862, Clara Barton Papers, box 1, Manuscript Division, Library of Congress.

For now, transcription: "Volunteers Type to Preserve History," *Today*, NBC, Mar. 10, 2024, www.today.com/video/volunteers-digitize-documents-to-preserve-history-at-library-of-congress-206069829520.

Christian Mobley, a Cincinnati church pastor: Christian Mobley, phone interview, Jan. 30, 2019, and email, Jan. 29, 2021.

"Women are so underrepresented": Schauber, phone interview.

Transcribing appeals: Jennifer Putzi, phone interview, Feb. 15, 2023.

Jess Atkinson struggled: Jess Atkinson, phone interview, Mar. 8, 2023.

Online or off: Karsonya Wise Whitehead, *Notes from a Colored Girl: The Civil War Pocket Diaries of Emilie Frances Davis* (Columbia: University of South Carolina Press, 2014), 5.

Diary scholar Suzanne L. Bunkers: Suzanne L. Bunkers, "Subjectivity and Self-Reflexivity in the Study of Women's Diaries as Autobiography," *Auto/Biography Studies* 5, no. 2 (1990):114–23, doi.org/10.1080/08989575.1990.10815457.

Sometimes a diary: Alexander Masters, "What to Do with a Diary?" webinar, Centre for Life History and Life Writing Research, University of Sussex, UK, Dec. 1, 2020.

Four years into: Kathryn Jacob, email, June 6, 2025.

She pointed to: Lucy Florilla Clapp, diary entry, Apr. 29, 1872, A/C588, Schlesinger Library.

She found diarist: Effie McGrew, diary entry, May 1, 1917, MC1087; Ruth Teischman (pseudonym provided by Schlesinger Library), diary entry, Sept. 3 and 26, 1959; all from Schlesinger Library.

"Mother is dead": Henrietta Bellhouse (pseudonym), diary entry, May 1967, Great Diary Project, Bishopsgate Institute, London, UK.

Bellhouse's entries revealed: Bellhouse, diary entry.

A creative writing: Jennifer Sinor, *The Extraordinary Work of Ordinary Writing: Annie Ray's Diary* (Iowa City: University of Iowa Press, 2002), 7, 22.

Typically disregarded: Sinor, *The Extraordinary Work of Ordinary Writing*, 6–18, 184, 196.

"[April] Tuesday": Annie Ray quote in Sinor, *The Extraordinary Work of Ordinary Writing*, 125.

In Sinor's defense: Sinor, *The Extraordinary Work of Ordinary Writing*, 5–14, 196.

Other reading advice: Sinor, *The Extraordinary Work of Ordinary Writing*, 6–7, 14–22, 184.

Sinor's work was: Putzi, phone interview.

Bunkers offers a different take: Suzanne L. Bunkers, "Introduction," in *Diaries of Girls and Women: A Midwestern Sampler*, ed. Suzanne L. Bunkers (Madison: University of Wisconsin Press, 2001), 19–20.

Desirée Henderson echoes: Desirée Henderson, *How to Read a Diary: Critical Contexts and Interpretive Strategies for 21st-Century Readers* (New York: Routledge, 2019), 88–90.

"Feb[ruary] 27/Sunday": Annie Ray quote in Sinor, *The Extraordinary Work of Ordinary Writing*, 66.

I had a similar experience: Iowa Byington Reed, diary entries, Jan. 25–26, Feb. 7, and Apr. 18, 1878, Iowa Byington Reed Papers, IWA; DIY History, Iowa Byington Reed diary, Jan. 1, 1878–May 11, 1879, transcription, https://diyhistory.lib.uiowa.edu/transcribe/145/10151.

As I browsed: Dairy Diary, "History of the Dairy Diary," https://www.dairydiary.co.uk/pages/about-us, accessed July 2, 2025.

By 2025, Detroit: "Capping Off a Historic Turnaround, Detroit Now Leads Michigan in Population Growth," Mayor's Office/Data Detroit, May 15, 2025, https://detroitmi.gov/news/capping-historic-turnaround-detroit-now-leads-michigan-population-growth.

My reading experience with: Myrtle Keppy, list of diaries, IWA, https://www.lib.uiowa.edu/iwa/topical-holdings-lists/diaries/, accessed Aug. 5, 2025.

But I also found: Catherine Babikian, "Morado Vallejo, Martina," Migration Is Beautiful, IWA, https://migration.lib.uiowa.edu/exhibits/show/people/martina-morado-vallejo; Laughlin, Lois (1925–) , Diaries, IWA, https://www.lib.uiowa.edu/iwa/topical-holdings-lists/diaries/#1, accessed June 15, 2025.

Some of the online diary descriptions: Ida "Belle" Bandfield Holden, finding aid, IWA, https://aspace.lib.uiowa.edu/repositories/4/resources/1986; Annette Cech, Diaries, IWA.

Were any of the Iowa diarists: Sarah Gristwood, "'Who Am I Without Him?': What I Learned About Grief from Reading Other Women's Diaries," *The Guardian*, July 13, 2024, www.theguardian.com/books/article/2024/jul/13/sarah-gristwood-secret-voices-a-year-of-womens-diaries-grief.

I did feel: Judith Klemesrud, finding aid, IWA, https://aspace.lib.uiowa.edu/repositories/4/resources/2079; "Judy Klemesrud, N.Y. Times Writer," (obituary) *Chicago Tribune*, Oct. 15, 1985.

Ruth Laughlin, another fellow journalist: Ruth Laughlin, finding aid, IWA, https://aspace.lib.uiowa.edu/repositories/4/resources/2099, accessed Aug. 4, 2025.

Beyond Iowa: Yitskhok Rudashevski: A Teenager's Account of Life and Death in the Vilna Ghetto, YIVO Institute for Jewish Research, Bruce and Francesca Cernia Slovin Online Museum, https://museum.yivo.org/experiences/life-in-the-ghetto/environment, accessed June 15, 2025.

CHAPTER 12: SELF-EXPOSURE

I keep thinking: Becky Edmunds, "What to Do with a Diary?" webinar, Centre for Life History and Life Writing Research, University of Sussex, UK, Dec. 1, 2020.

Hiding, deleting, obscuring: "How Screwed Would You Be?" Reddit, r/Journaling, May 2024, www.reddit.com/r/Journaling/comments/1cl11hx/how_screwed_would_you_be; "How Do You Get over Your Fear?" Reddit, r/Journaling, July 2024, www.reddit.com/r/Journaling/comments/1dxw151/how_do_you_get_over_your_fear.

Ideas shared online: "Where's the Best Place to Hide Your Journal?" Reddit, r/Journaling, May 22, 2024, www.reddit.com/r/Journaling/comments/1cyfrq8/wheres_the_best_place_to_hide_your_journal/.

Using code: DK, ed., *Remarkable Diaries: The World's Greatest Diaries, Journals, Notebooks & Letters* (New York: DK, 2020), 50; Anne Lister, diary entry, Apr. 29, 1832, in "The Real Diaries of Anne Lister," One Gentleman Jack, BBC, bbc.co.uk/programmes/articles/3QT2z16RXhfxSDn1mrbRNVp /the-real-diaries-of-anne-lister.

Both the British: Michael Weishan, "FDR's Secret Code," Franklin Delano Roosevelt Foundation, Aug. 24, 2010, fdrfoundation.org/fdrs-secret-code/.

Beatrix Potter kept: DK, *Remarkable Diaries*, 164–66; Cara Giaimo, "Beatrix Potter's Greatest Work Was a Secret, Coded Journal She Kept as a Teen," *Atlas Obscura*, June 16, 2017, www.atlasobscura.com/articles/beatrix-potter-secret -journal-code-leslie-linder.

Devoted diarist Queen Victoria: DK, *Remarkable Diaries*, 118–19; Maev Kennedy, "Queen Victoria's Private Journals Published Online," May 24, 2012, *The Guardian*, www.theguardian.com/uk/2012/may/24/queen-victoria-private -journals-online.

Abdul Karim also kept: Kristin Hunt, "Victoria and Abdul: The Friendship That Scandalized England," *Smithsonian*, Sept. 20, 2017, www.smithsonianmag.com /history/victoria-and-abdul-friendship-scandalized-england-180964959/; Alastair Lawson, "Queen Victoria and Abdul: Diaries Reveal Secrets," BBC, Mar. 14, 2011, www.bbc.com/news/world-south-asia-12670110.

They are believed: Dorothy Wordsworth, *The Grasmere and Alfoxden Journals*, ed. Pamela Woof (Oxford: Oxford University Press, 2008), 126–27.

Some speculate: DK, Remarkable Diaries, 97.

"On Monday 4th October": Wordsworth, *The Grasmere and Alfoxden Journals*, 126–27.

Does Dorothy's journal: Frances Wilson, "The Ballad of Dorothy Wordsworth," *New York Times*, Feb. 24, 2009, www.nytimes.com/2009/02/25/books /chapters/chapter-ballad-dorothy-wordsworth.html; Pamela Woof, ed., "Note on the Texts," in Dorothy Wordsworth, *The Grasmere and Alfoxden Journals* (Oxford: Oxford University Press, 2008), xxvii; Woof, "Notes to Pages 126–27," Wordsworth, *The Grasmere and Alfoxden Journals*, 265–66.

Scholars also make: Jeff Cowton, "Two Pages from Dorothy Wordsworth's *Grasmere Journal*," European Romanticisms in Association, Apr. 15, 2018, www.euromanticism.org/two-pages-from-dorothy-wordsworths-grasmere -journal/; Dorothy Wordsworth and William Wordsworth, *Home at Grasmere: Extracts from the Journal of Dorothy Wordsworth . . . and from the Poems of William Wordsworth*, ed. Colette Clark (1960; London: Penguin, 1986), book jacket.

Post-wedding: Wilson, "The Ballad of Dorothy Wordsworth."

"No editor can": Arthur Ponsonby, *English Diaries: A Review of English Diaries from the Sixteenth to the Twentieth Century* (London: Methuen, 1923), 5; David Sedaris, *Theft by Finding: Diaries 1977–2002* (New York: Little, Brown, 2017), 6–8.

"You can barely find": Anne Frank, *The Diary of a Young Girl: Definitive Edition*, ed. Mirjam Pressler, trans. Susan Massotty (New York: Bantam Books, 2001), 255–56.
The diary revealed: The Legacy of Anne Frank, NBC, aired Dec. 24, 1967, available at www.youtube.com/watch?v=AWRBinP7ans.
Most of Anne's entries: Suzanne L. Bunkers, "The Complicated Publication History of the Diaries of Anne Frank," in *The Diary: The Epic of Everyday Life*, ed. Batsheva Ben-Amos and Dan Ben-Amos (Bloomington: Indiana University Press, 2020), 155.
After her death in 1945: Anne Frank House, "The Publication of the Diary," www.annefrank.org/en/anne-frank/diary/publication-diary/, accessed June 15, 2025.
Gone were her mentions: BBC History Extra, "Censoring Anne Frank: How Her Famous Diary Has Been Edited Through History," Mar. 9, 2020, www.historyextra.com/period/20th-century/anne-frank-diary-how-edited-hidden-pages-father-otto-what-she-really-wrote/.
Gone were some: Bunkers, "The Complicated Publication History of the Diaries of Anne Frank," 155; BBC History Extra, "Censoring Anne Frank."
As an ambitious: Bunkers, "The Complicated Publication History of the Diaries of Anne Frank," 148–49.
Beyond trimming: Ruth Franklin, "Was Anne Frank Bisexual?" *Ghost Stories*, Aug. 28, 2022, https://ruthfranklin.substack.com/p/was-anne-frank-bisexual; Bunkers, "The Complicated Publication History of the Diaries of Anne Frank," 152–53.
"Like countless": Bunkers, "The Complicated Publication History of the Diaries of Anne Frank," 152–53.
Anne Frank's diary: Bunkers, "The Complicated Publication History of the Diaries of Anne Frank," 147–50.
So did new arguments: Molly Driscoll, "30 Banned Books," *Christian Science Monitor*, Oct. 3, 2012, www.csmonitor.com/Books/2012/1003/30-banned-books-that-may-surprise-you/The-Diary-of-A-Young-Girl-by-Anne-Frank; Emer O'Toole, "Anne Frank's Diary Isn't Pornographic," *The Guardian*, May 2, 2013, https://www.theguardian.com/commentisfree/2013/may/02/anne-franks-diary-pornographic-uncomfortable-truth; Sheena Goodyear, "Illustrator Stands by Graphic Novel of Anne Frank's Diary That Got Texas Teacher Fired," CBC Radio, Sept. 22, 2023, www.cbc.ca/radio/asithappens/anne-frank-graphic-novel-controversy-1.6975989.
Plath's entries: Mortimer Rare Book Collection, "Plath's Published Journals," Smith College, Special Collections, https://www.smith.edu/libraries/libs/rarebook/exhibitions/conway/pubjournals.htm, accessed July 22, 2025.
In 2000: Karen V. Kukil, ed., "Preface," *Sylvia Plath: The Unabridged Journals of Sylvia Plath* (New York: Anchor Books, 2000), ix.
This "exact" transcription: Joyce Carol Oates, review of *Sylvia Plath: The Unabridged Journals of Sylvia Plath*, *New York Times*, Nov. 5, 2000, www.nytimes.com/2000/11/05/books/raising-lady-lazarus.html; Sylvia Plath, *The Unabridged Journals*, 6.

What I question: Donna Ferguson, "Literary Gold . . . or Betrayal of Trust? Joan Didion Journal Opens Ethical Minefield," *The Guardian*, Feb. 23, 2025, www.theguardian.com/books/2025/feb/23/literary-gold-or-betrayal-of-trust-joan-didion-journal-opens-ethical-minefield; Helen Coffey, "If Someone Published My Diary After I Died, I'd Die Again—of Shame," *The Independent*, Feb. 25, 2025, https://www.independent.co.uk/life-style/joan-didion-diary-therapy-notes-to-john-b2703678.html.

Anaïs Nin's sexually: Paul Herron, ed., "Preface," Anaïs Nin, *Mirages: The Unexpurgated Diary of Anaïs Nin, 1939–1947* (Athens, OH: Swall Press, 2013), x.

Rupert Pole: Rupert Pole, "Preface," Anaïs Nin, *Henry and June: From the Unexpurgated Diary of Anaïs Nin* (New York: Harcourt Brace Jovanovich, 1986), viii–ix; Nin, *Henry and June*, 109.

A five-foot-tall: Helen Churko, email, Feb. 2, 2025.

"It felt worthy": Helen Churko, phone interview Apr. 5, 2023.

Should diarists make: Day One journaling app users, reply to author's question posted on Day One Community Facebook page, Jan. 1, 2024; Robert Ryan, phone interview, Feb. 12, 2023; Janet Levine, email, Mar. 20, 2024.

When I asked digital: Day One journaling app users, replies, Jan. 1, 2024.

"Dread" of hurting: Willliam Soutar, in *The Assassin's Cloak: An Anthology of the World's Greatest Diarists*, ed. Irene Taylor and Alan Taylor (Edinburgh: Canongate Books, 2000), xix.

The legendary Iowan: Evelyn Birkby, on-site interview, Sidney, IA, Apr. 8, 2019.

Beyond this, diarists: Marlene Kayen, phone interview, Feb. 13, 2024.

Darla Ewalt of Iowa: Darla Ewalt, phone interview, Dec. 4, 2023.

Nancy Guri Duncan, an American: Nancy Guri Duncan, email, Feb. 2. 2023.

"No descendants": Nancy Guri Duncan, email, May 2, 2024.

"French butchers": Barbara Reed Valbot, diary entry, Aug. 24, 1966, APA.

although the law: Public Information Office, US Copyright Office, email from senior information specialist, Feb. 4, 2025.

When an archive: With an unpublished work, copyright lasts the life of the author plus seventy years. So, for example, only unpublished diaries from authors who died before 1955 were in the public domain as of 2025. But if the diarist or diarist's death date is unknown, copyright lasts 120 years from the date the work was created, so only unpublished works created before 1905 were in the public domain as of 2025. See "Copyright Services: Copyright Term and the Public Domain," Cornell University Library, https://guides.library.cornell.edu/copyright/publicdomain/, accessed June 16, 2025.

It would be "irresponsible": Janet Weaver, then assistant curator, Iowa Women's Archives, on-site interview, June 11, 2019.

But archives don't: Josh Kitchens, phone interview, May 30, 2024.

"How we approach": Janice E. Ruth, on-site interview, Library of Congress, July 17, 2019.

A helpful LOC document: Library of Congress, "Frequently Asked Questions, Donating Personal Papers to the Library of Congress Manuscript Division," Feb. 2025.

Archivists "have both legal": Susan C. Lawrence, *Privacy and the Past: Research, Law, Archives, Ethics* (New Brunswick, NJ: Rutgers University Press, 2016), 71.

"Archivists recognize": Society of American Archivists (SAA), "SAA Core Values Statement and Code of Ethics," approved Feb. 2005; revised Jan. 2012 and Aug. 2020, www2.archivists.org/statements/saa-core-values-statement-and-code-of-ethics.

Although archives often: SAA, "Copyright and Unpublished Material," www2.archivists.org/publications/brochures/copyright-and-unpublished-material, accessed June 16, 2025.

SAA provided some guidance: SAA, "Well-Intentioned Practice for Putting Digitized Collections of Unpublished Materials Online," www2.archivists.org/groups/intellectual-property-working-group/well-intentioned-practice-for-putting-digitized-collections-of-unpublished-materials-, accessed June 16, 2025. Developed by OCLC Research, the document is available at http://www.oclc.org/research/activities/rights/practice.pdf.

Here's the rub: OCLC, "Introduce Balance in Rights Management," Nov. 14, 2010, www.oclc.org/research/activities/rights.html.

Beyond the copyright: Sara S. Hodson, "Archives on the Web: Unlocking Collections While Safeguarding Privacy," *First Monday* 11, no. 8 (Aug. 2006), http://firstmonday.org/issues/issue11_8/hodson/index.html.

I caught up: Sara S. Hodson, phone interview, May 29, 2024; Ellen LeClere, phone interview, May 24, 2024.

"Technology will change": LeClere, phone interview.

Index

Adams, Abigail, 40
Adams, Kathleen (Kay), 61
adolescent diarists, 45–46, 117, 136, 145, 149, 171, 176, 184, 188
AIDS crisis, 67
Al-Banna, Ibn, 14, 134
Alcott, Louisa May, 40, 89
Alex, Tom, 6
Allen, Roland, 14, 112
almanacs, 13
Alzheimer's disease, 73–74, 77–78, 83–86
American Diary Project, 152–54
'Amr, Sami, 134–35
analog diaries, 32–34
Anastas, Benjamin, 94
Anthony, Susan B., 163, 181
APA, Association pour l'autobiographie et le patrimoine autobiographique (Association for Autobiography and Autobiographical Heritage), 148–49, 196
Apple, 25, 30–31
apps, 3, 19, 24–25, 29–31, 33, 34, 37, 61; mood-tracking, 25
Archiquette, John, 172
archives: and copyright protection, 153–54, 197, 199; donating advice, 203–5; exhibits and events, 163–64; inclusion in, 42–43; as memory projects, 152; non-gendered, 159; and post-war reconciliation and reconstruction, 151; and privacy concerns, 153–54, 196–200; purpose of, 146–47; "secret," 131; and social history, 151–52; women's, xiii–xiv, 157–68. *See also specific archives*
Archivio Diaristico Nazionale (National Diary Archive), 2, 141, 150, 154–55
Aristotle, 106
Armstrong, Heather, 70
artificial intelligence (AI), 3, 25, 30–31, 61, 174
The Artist's Way (Cameron), 101
Ashplant, T. G., 151
astrology, 12–13
astronomy, 13
Atkinson, Jess, 175
Auden, W. H., 192
Augustine, Saint, 60
authenticity, 20
authors, 88, 89–92, 93–100, 137
autobiographies, 3, 10, 11, 13, 19, 148
Autobiography Days, 149
autofiction, 97

Bahrick, Harry P., 82
Baines, Kristina, 37
Baker, Douwe, 127
Baker, Ellen K., 64, 101, 112, 113
Baldwin, Christina, 61
Ballard, Martha, 40–41, 165–66
Balota, David, 84
Barry, Linda, 145
Bartlett, Frederic, 79
Barton, Clara, 173–74
Bashkirtseff, Marie, 14, 44, 46, 69, 96
Basu, Shrabani, 189
Beadle, John, 60
Beard, Mary Ritter, 159
Beatrice, Princess, 188
Beauvoir, Simone de, 97
Bechdel, Alison, 54

Bell, Quentin, 90
Bellhouse, Henrietta, 177–78
Bell-Scott, Patricia, 65–66
Ben-Amos, Batsheva, 25, 171
Ben-Amos, Dan, 25, 171
Benedetti, Giacomo, 141, 145, 150–51
Biden, Ashley, 139
biographies, 13, 19
Birkby, Evelyn, 195
Bishopsgate Institute, 147–48
Black women, 42, 46–51, 65–66, 164, 167–68, 171, 179
blogs, 3, 18, 22–25, 26, 27–29
Bloom, Lynn Z., 18
Bogaert, Catherine, 10–11, 20, 69, 136
born-digital diaries, 21, 25
Borns, Joanna, 138
Boswell, James, 38
Bowen, Elizabeth, 90
Bridget Jones's Diary (Fielding), 5, 98–99
Brown, Tina, 97–98
Buford, Lena, 23–24
Bühler, Charlotte, 127
Bühler, Karl, 127
bullet journals, 16
Bunkers, Suzanne L., 41, 43, 45–46, 53, 175–76, 179, 191
Burke, Carolyn L., 23, 41, 70–71
Burney, Frances "Fanny," 38–39, 73, 90
burning diaries, xiv, 106–11, 194
Burns, Jane, 5
Butler, Andrew, 77–79, 82
buyers and sellers of diaries, 136–39, 154, 182, 197

Cameron, Julia, 101
Camus, Albert, 89
Cangi, Natalia, 151
Caramanica, Jon, 93
Caraway, Hattie, 19–20
Cardell, Kylie, 60, 98
Carroll, Lewis, 68
Carter, Kathryn, 41–42, 53
Cash, Eleanor, 156–57
Cech, Annette, 183
censorship, 191–92
Charles III (king), 143
Charlotte (queen), 39
Chaucer, Geoffrey, 16
Chennault, Anna Chen, 164
Chennault, Claire Lee, 164
Chesnut, Mary, 41
child development tracking, 126–27
China, 131–32
Christie, Agatha, 16
Churko, Helen, 28, 101, 194
citizen science, 126–27
Civil War (US), 26, 41, 51, 122, 137, 167–68, 173–74, 181
Clapp, Lucy, 176
Clark, Caitlin, 163
Clifford, Anne, 38
codes and symbols, 125–26, 166, 179, 187–88
Coffey, Helen, 110, 193
Coffin, Alexander Norton, 120–21
Coffin, Mary Caroline, 120–21
collectors of diaries, 136–39
Confessions (Augustine), 60
copyright protection, 153–54, 197, 199
Coscarelli, Joe, 93
Couser, G. Thomas, 68
COVID-19 pandemic, 7, 36–37, 58, 63, 65, 67–68, 112, 143, 144–45
Cowton, Jeff, 190
creatives, 88–89, 92–93, 99–103
Crossman, Richard, 19
"crypt hand," 166, 187
Culley, Margo, 18, 20, 41, 42, 43–44, 46
Curie, Marie, 17

Dabble Me app, 29, 30, 58
Dacus, Lucy, 93
Dagbogsskolen (The Diary School), 100
Dahl, Roald, 16
dailiness, 10–11, 13, 18
Dairy Diary (Milk Marketing Board), 182
d'Amico, Isabella, 29
Darwin, Charles, 16, 127
Davis, Emilie, 167–68, 175, 190
Day One app, 19, 24–25, 30, 34, 194–95

"The Days" (Su), 91
dementia, 73–74, 77–78, 83–86
destruction of diaries, xiv, 106–11, 194
Deutsches Tagebucharchiv (German Diary Archive), 120–21, 126, 145, 149–50, 152, 195
The Diary (Ben-Amos & Ben-Amos, eds.), 9, 25, 134–35, 171
On Diary (Popkin and Rak, eds.), 16, 136
diary contact technique, 140
Diary Discoveries (podcast), 139
diary fiction, 98–99
diary(ies): associated with women, 9; categories of, 9, 117; defining, 3–4, 9, 10–12, 15, 17–20; etymology of, 13; as feminine or feminized genre, 51–55; forms of, 3; as a literary form, 3–4; as a unique product, 3; use of term, xiv, 28. *See also* journals
The Diary Index (website), 110–11
The Diary Keepers (Siegal), 127
Diary of a Wimpy Kid (Kinney), 51–52
diary reading: ancestor's diaries, 121–22; common misreads (storying, snippetotomy, psychologizing), 178–79, 180 ; digitized collections, 171–72, 181–82; experience of, 170–71, 175–84; by historians, 127–36; by prosecutors, 12; research based on, 140; reasons for, , 8–9; xv; rereading old diaries, 104–6, 111–17; as stories, 178–80; strangers' diaries, 136–39; by students, 139; students' diaries, 101; transcription projects, 170, 172–75; uninvited, 124
diary stories, 4–5
diary volumes, 9
diary writing: appeal of, 54; categories of, 9, 117; dailiness of, 10–11, 13, 18; defining, 3–4; digital, 21–31, 34–35; as an experience, 98–99; feminization of, 52–55; formal instruction in, 100–101; found diaries, 122–24; and ideas about the self, 43–44; immediacy of, 12; inclusive nature of, 7–8; and literacy, 41, 165; modern origins of, 14–15; in non-Western cultures, 14–15; ordinary, 178–79; practice of, 3;; reasons for, xv, 8, 44–47, 65–68; as a selective process, 82–83; selfiness of, 10–12, 13, 18; use of codes and symbols, 125–26, 166, 179, 187–88
Dickens, Charles, 110
Didion, Joan, 16–17, 110, 111, 192–93
digital diaries, 29–30, 34–35
digital narcissism, 69–70
digital technology, 3, 7, 21, 35. *See also* apps; blogs; social media posts
digitization projects, 9, 171–72
disability blogs and narratives, 28–29, 68
Dispatches from Quarantine, 145
DIY History, 170, 173, 174, 196
donating diaries, xiii–xv, 158, 182, 195–205
Dostoevsky, Fyodor, 68
Douglas, R. H., 66
Dreyfus, Alfred, 117
Drinker, Elizabeth Sandwith, 38
dual dictation, 34
Dunbar-Nelson, Alice, 48, 51, 89
Duncan, Nancy Guri, 196
Dunne, John Gregory, 17
Dylan, Bob, 16

Edgerton, Betsy, 8, 28
editors and editing, 190–93
Edmunds, Becky, 122–23
ego-documents, 10, 129–30, 146
Elbert, Amy, 122
Elder, Robert K., 153
Elizabeth, Queen, 188
Ellis, Jay, 59
end-of-life diary plans, 194–96
enslaved women, 42, 48
Ernaux, Annie, 103, 148
Estelle, Ruth, 108–9
European Diary Archives and Collections Network (EDAC) (later European Ego-Documents Archives and Collections Network), 146, 147, 174
Evelyn, John, 14
Ewalt, Darla, 120–21, 195–96

Expatriate Archive Centre, 147
expressive writing, 60–61, 63, 64
The Extraordinary Work of Ordinary Writing (Sinor), 178

Facebook, 3, 6, 24, 26, 27–28, 34, 194–95
fake diaries, 139
feminists, 9–10, 43, 46–47, 53, 67, 159
festivals, 2–3, 149, 152, 155
fictional diaries, 98–99
Fielding, Helen, 98–99
Filipović, Zlata, 45, 64–65, 139
Finkel, Irving, 12, 147
Fitbit reports, 3, 26, 126
Fitzgerald, Sarah, 28–29
Fitzhugh, Louise, 52
The Five Minute Journal, 58–59
Fivush, Robyn, 80
Forbes, Harriette Merrifield, 40–41
Forten, Charlotte, 47, 50–51, 178
Fothergill, Robert, 3
found diaries, 122–24
Fowler, Veronica Lorson, 6–7
Francis, Laura, 123–24, 176
Frank, Anne, 15, 41, 45, 52, 117, 130, 139, 176, 190–91
Frank, Otto, 130, 190–91
Franklin, Benjamin, 125–26
Fredericks, Claude, 94
Friedländer, Saul, 132–34

Garbarini, Alexandra, 128
Garfield, Simon, 144
Garner, Helen, 109–10
Gay, Peter, 13
Gelfand, Michele, 140
gender: changing norms, 53–55; defiance of boundaries 45; male-centric history of diary writing, 14, 37–38, 41, 43–44; and stereotypes about diary writing, 36–37, 45–46; use of diary vs. journal, 9, 51–55. *See also* women diarists
George III (king), 39
George VI (king), 142
Gerhalter, Li, 126–27
Giesberg, Judith, 167–68
Gilbert, Elizabeth, 101
Gillespie, Emily Hawley, 19
Gillespie, Sarah, 19
Ginsburg, Ruth Bader, 163
Goncourt, Edmond and Jules de, 18–19, 34, 38, 69
Google, 23–24
Gordon, Ann D., 168
Gordon, Dimitri, 6
The Grasmere Journals (Wordsworth), 189–90
gratitude journaling, 61, 68–69
Great Diary Project, 12, 145–46, 147–48, 177, 182
Greer, Jessie, 171
Grid Diary app, 30
Gristwood, Sarah, 44, 183
Grubgeld, Elizabeth, 28
Gruwell, Erin, 139

Hadassah, 158
Hall, Justin, 22–23
Hamilton, Laura, 49
handwritten diaries, 31–34, 78–79, 150, 171–72, 175. *See also* transcription projects
Hardin, Blanche Ford, 122
Harriet the Spy (Fitzhugh), 52
Hawthorne, Nathaniel, 89
Hayden, Carla, 173
Heart, Rosalie Deer, 112
Henderson, Desirée, 10, 14, 25, 38, 52, 54, 67, 71, 110–11, 113, 179–80
Herron, Paul, 193
Hess, Jillian, 5
Heti, Sheila, 97
Hill, Sarah Welch, 42
Hinding, Andrea, 160
Historical Society of Pennsylvania, 165–68
hoaxes, 139
Hobonichi Techno, 33
Hoby, Margaret, 38
Hodes, Martha, 82–83
Hodson, Sara S., 199–200
Hogan, Rebecca, 44, 53–54
Holden, Ida "Belle" Bandfield, 183
Holocaust, 127–31, 184

Holyoke, Mary Vial, 46
Hooks, Angela, 101
hooks, bell, 45, 110
horoscopes, 12–13
Horowitz, Glenn, 137
household-accounting daybooks, 13–14
How to Read a Diary (Henderson), 10
Hsu, Hua, 61
Huff, Cynthia A., 41, 43, 45
Hughes, Ted, 192
Huisman, Marijke, 152
Hull, Gloria T., 48
Humphreys, Lee, 26, 113

illness diaries, 66–68
individualism, 13
Instagram, 3, 33, 70
Intensive Journal method, 60, 61, 63–64, 112
International Autobiography Association, 4
Ione, Carole, 49–50
Iowa Women's Archives, xiv, 157–58, 160, 161–62, 163, 173, 180, 182–84, 195, 196–97
Israeli-Palestinian conflict, 132–34, 135
Iyer, Pico, 91

Jackson, Joshua Conrad, 140
Jacob, Kathryn, 156, 163–64, 176, 181
James, Alice, 66–67
James, Henry, 67, 110
James, William, 67
Jaouad, Suleika, 67–68, 102
Jefferson, Mildred, 164
Jerkins, Morgan, 51
Jesus, Carolina Maria de, 43
Jewish Historical Institute, 131
Johnson, Alexandra, 102
Journal app, 25, 30–31
journal therapy, 61
journaling clubs, 4, 102
journals: associated with men, 9, 51–52; brands, 33; bullet, 16; defining, 9; etymology of, 13; journaling as self-help, 9, 58–60; paper vs. digital, 32–34; shared, 5–6, 18–19, 33; use of term, xiv, 28; written by parents for children, 6. *See also* diary(ies); diary writing
Julavits, Heidi, 97
Jung, Carl, 61

Kagle, Steven F., 66–67
Kahlo, Frida, 157, 161, 162
Kamensky, Jane, 52, 162
Karim, Abdul, 188–89
Katz, Kimberly, 134–35
Kayen, Marlene, 145, 146, 149, 195
keeping diaries, meaning of, xvi
Kendzie, Michele, 35
Kennedy, Caroline, 76–77
Keppy, Myrtle, 182
Kiesling, Aubrie, 73
Kilson, Robin, 163–64
Kitchens, Josh, 197
Klemesrud, Judy, 183
Koester, Mark, 28, 31
Krishnan, Claudine, 149
Kureishi, Hanif, 29

Landucci, Luca, 14
Langhamer, Claire, 144
Larson, Erik, 144
Laughlin, Lois, 183
Laughlin, Ruth, 184
Lawrence, Susan C., 198
LeClere, Ellen, 200–201
Legros Chapuis, Elizabeth, 148–49
Lejeune, Philippe, 10–11, 16, 20, 26, 36, 52, 53, 69, 135–36, 148
L'Engle, Madeleine, 77, 99
Leonardo da Vinci, 16
Lerner, Gerda, 159–60
letters, 3, 11, 15, 39, 199
Letts company, 14, 53
Leuchtturm 1917, 33
Levine, Janet, 194
Lewis, C. S., 68
Li Rui, 131–32
libraries, digitized diary collections, 171–72, 197–98
Library of Congress, 163, 173, 175, 197–98; *American Women* (resource guide), 163

life writing, 4, 9–10; from below, 151–52
Linton, Marigold, 81
Lister, Anne, 66, 126, 166, 187
literacy, 41, 165
Lohuizen, Elisabeth van, 127
Lorde, Audre, 47
Lounsberry, Barbara, 90

MacLane, Mary, 46, 96
MacNamara Ivey, Sally, 136–37, 139, 153
Madison, Dolley, 163
Makdisi, George, 134
Mallon, Thomas, 52, 117
Manguso, Sarah, 68, 86
Manjoo, Farhad, 29
Mankowski, Kate, 34–35
Mansfield, Katherine, 43
Marchi, Clelia, 141
Marcus Aurelius, 60
Margalit, Ruth, 133
Markoe, Merrill, 93
Marsh, Elizabeth J., 80
Mass Observation, 142–44
Masters, Alexander, 122, 123–24, 176
masturbation tracking, 125–26
materiality, 182
McCammon, Sarah, 83
McClain, Reid, 34
McDermott, Kathleen B., 79
McGrew, Effie, 176
McPhee, Martha, 101
#MeToo movement, 75, 117, 181
Mead, Margaret, 163
memoirs, 3, 11–12, 15, 19, 29
memories: accessibility of, 82–83; accuracy of, 81; archives as memory projects, 152; autobiographical, 81; construction of, 80–81; and dementia, 73–74, 83–86; episodic, 77–78, 84; fact-checking, 74–77; forgetting, 86–87; imaginative reconstruction, 80; process of remembering, 77–79; as reason to destroy/preserve diaries, 106–11; recording, 78–79; retrieving, 79–81, 84, 86; storing, 73–74
menstrual cycle tracking, 125–26, 179
mental health, 65–68, 70, 71–72, 112
Middleton, Charles, 137
A Midwife's Tale (Ulrich), 15, 165
migrants' autobiographical writings, 151
Miller, Henry, 95, 193
Miller, June, 95, 193
Mimran, Alexander, 37
Mintz, Susannah B., 68
Mobley, Christian, 174
Moleskine, 33
mommy bloggers, 70
Montgomery, Mary Virginia, 48, 49, 175
Moody, Joycelyn K., 50
Morrissette, Alanis, 92
Mortified Live, 104–5, 111
Motz, Marilyn Ferris, 45
Mujeres Latinas (Latin Women) Project, 162
Mukhina, Lena, 45
Munro, Alice, 124; daughters of (Andrea and Jenny), 124
Murthy, Vivek, 70

National Literacy Trust, 7
National Museum of African American History and Culture, 171
National Women and Media Collection, 158
National Women's History Museum, 145
Navalnaya, Yulia, 131
Navalny, Alexei, 12, 15, 131
Nederlands Dagboekarchief (Dutch Diary Archive), 4, 126, 147, 152
Netherlands, 127–30
Nicks, Stevie, 92
Nin, Anaïs, 41, 88, 94–96, 109, 177, 178, 193
NIOD Institute for War, Holocaust and Genocide Studies, 130
Nixon, Richard, 76, 85, 106, 116, 117
North, Polly, 147
nostalgia, 32–34
notebooks, 16–17
note-taking, 25, 78–79

Noun, Louise, 157–58, 161–62
Nun Study, 85–86

Oates, Joyce Carol, 99–100, 192
Obama, Michelle, 61, 116
Oberg, Robert J. P., 35
O'Brien, Greg, 85
Obsidian app, 30
O'Connor, Sandra Day, 163
Oh, Sandra, 4
O'Keeffe, Georgia, 159
Ollila, Madison, 32
Oneg Shabbat archive, 131
online communities, 6–7
online diaries, 22–24, 25
online newsletters, 3
online positive affect journaling, 61
ordinary writing, 178–79
Orwell, George, 92

Palestine, 132–35
pandemic journaling, 7, 36–37, 58, 63, 65, 67–68, 143, 144–45
Pandemic Journaling Project, 37, 65, 144–45
paratext, 182
parent's diaries, 126–27
patient diaries, 112
Patton, John, 121
Patton, Pam, 121
Pattrick, Kirsty, 143
Pennebaker, James W., 60–61, 63, 64, 112
Penzu app, 29, 37. *See also* apps
By the People, 173, 174
Pepys, Elizabeth, 42, 44–45
Pepys, Samuel, 14, 37–38, 42, 45, 90, 117, 187
Perceval, Dick, 123
personal blogs, 23–24
personal curation, 198
Phoon, James, 59
Piccolo Museo del Diario (Little Diary Museum), 141–42, 150
Pierce, David, 30, 31
Pieve Santo Stefano, Italy, 2–3, 141, 150–51, 155
pillow books, 15
Pipher, Mary, 46
Plath, Sylvia, 41, 64, 117, 192–93
Podnieks, Elizabeth, 90, 94–95
Pole, Rupert, 95–96, 193
Ponsonby, Arthur, 190
Popkin, Jeremy, 136
Popova, Maria, 5
popular culture, 5
posthumously published diaries, 190–93
Potter, Beatrix, 39, 187–88
Premio Pieve festival, 2–3
preserving diaries, 107–11, 205
Presser, Jacques, 129–30
Pride of Family (Ione), 50
prison diaries, 4, 5, 12
privacy: and archive collections, 153–54; and donating diaries, xv, 196–200; and journaling apps, 29–30; and strangers' diaries, 139; and student diaries, 101
Progff, Ira, 60, 61, 63–64, 112
Prozhito Center for the Study of Ego-Documents, 147
Putzi, Jennifer, 50, 175, 179

Rabito, Vincenzo, 141
Rabus, Achim, 174
Rak, Julie, 3, 16, 32, 54
Ranganath, Charan, 86
Ray, Annie, 178–79, 180
redaction, 188–90
Reddit, 6, 106
Reed, Iowa Byington, 180–81, 183, 196
Reeve, Ann, 181
Remarkable Diaries (DK, ed.), 38
Rettberg, Jill Walker, 22
Rhodia journal, 33
ricordanze (home accounts book), 13–14
Ringelblum, Emanuel, 131
Roediger, Henry, 77–79
Rollin, Frances Anne, 49–50
Roosevelt, Eleanor, 159, 188
Roosevelt, Franklin, 187–88
Ross, Michael, 113
Rowling, Avery, 20
Royalle, Candida (Candice Vadala), 162

Rubin, Laura, 101
Rudashevski, Yitskhok, 184
Ruth, Janice E., 163, 197
Ryan, Robert, 6, 32, 194

Saif, Atef Abu, 132
Sante, Lucy, 8
Sarton, May, 67, 117
Sax, David, 32
Schauber, Kerry, 170, 174
Schlesinger Library, 157, 159, 162, 163–64, 176, 181
scholarship, 8–9, 54–55, 120–21, 128–29, 134–36
schoolgirls, 45–46, 117
Schumann, Clara, 18
Schumann, Robert, 18
sea journals, 40
search engines, 24
The Secret Diary of Adrian Mole, Aged 13 3/4 (Townsend), 99
Sedaris, David, 100, 190
Sei Shōnagon, 15
Self, Will, 124–25
self-help, journaling as: benefits of, 65–68, 72; expressive writing, 60–61, 63, 64; gratitude journaling, 61, 68–69; harms of, 68–71; historical, 59–60; Intensive Journal method, 60, 61, 63–64, 112; journal therapy, 61–65; marketing of, 58–59; shadow work, 58, 61
selfiness, 10–12, 13, 18
self-tracking, 125–26, 179
The Shadow Work Journal (Shaheen), 58, 62
Shaheen, Keila, 58, 61
Shapiro, Dani, 108
Shapiro, Myra, 27–28
"Shell Ladies Project," 147
Shelley, Mary, 39, 117
Siegal, Nina, 127–29, 130
Sies, Jennie, 181
Simons, Judy, 45
Sinor, Jennifer, 178–79
Small, Scott A., 79, 86
smartphones, 24–25, 27–28
Smith, Barbara, 46–47
Smith, Keri, 102
Smith, Mary Louise, 158, 162
Smith, Patti, 15
Smith, Paula Vene, 12, 31, 48, 50–51, 101
Smith, Zadie, 93
Smithsonian Institution, 144, 171; "volunpeers," 173
snooping, thwarting, 187–88
social history, 151–52, 183–84
social media posts, 3, 18, 21–22, 25–28, 69–70, 113
social networking sites, 3, 6, 24, 27–28, 32, 34, 58, 70
Society of American Archivists (SAA), 153, 154, 198–99, 204
Soeting, Monica, 3–4
Sontag, Susan, 11
Sophia Smith Collection of Women's History, 159
Soutar, William, 195
spiritual writing, 13
stationery stores, 32–33
Stattler, Rick, 137, 139
Sterling, Dorothy, 47–48
Steur, Ina, 127
Steves, Rick, 100
Stewart, Martha, 5
Stoic app, 61
Stone, Lincoln Ripley, 137
storytelling, 74–77, 79–81, 104–5, 111, 180
strangers' diaries, 136–39
Strickland, Alison, 112
Su, Adrienne, 91
suffragists, 159, 181
Swift, Taylor, 92–93
symbols, use of for self-tracking, 125–26, 166, 179

technologies of the self, 32
Teischman, Ruth, 176
Tellaroli, Paola, 155
therapeutic effects, 61–68
Thoreau, Henry David, 38, 117
TikTok, 3, 5, 24, 28, 32, 58, 61
time-keeping devices, 13
toilet-paper diary, 156–57, 181

Tolstoy, Sophia, 43
Tomka, Peter, 32
Townsend, Sue, 99
transcription projects, 170, 172–75
Transkribus, 174
travel blogs and diaries, 5–6, 27, 172, 184–85
Truitt, Anne, 108
truth, 20, 83, 129
Tull, Eileen, 104, 111
Turjman, Ihsan, 134–35
Tutino, Saverio, 150
12th May Diary Day, 106, 142–44
Twitter (X), 3, 24, 27, 29

Ulrich, Laurel Thatcher, 15, 165, 172
United Kingdom, 7, 12, 142–44, 145, 147–48, 177, 182
Updike, John, 137

Vakulenko, Volodymyr, 131
Valbot, Barbara Reed, 196
Vallejo, Martina Morado, 182–83
Vance, J. D., 36
Van der Boom, Bart, 129
Venuto, Francesca, 151
Vermeer, Leonieke, 125–26
Victoria (queen), 39, 117, 188
video blogging, 29
volunteer transcription projects, 172–75
Vorreiter, Maycie, 34
Vuijsje, Ies, 129

Walker, Alice, 48, 73, 91–92, 102
Warsaw Ghetto (radio series), 131
wartime diaries, 9, 26, 41, 92, 127–35, 144, 151
Washington, Mary Helen, 49
Webb, Beatrice, 39–40
Wells, Ida B., 48–49
Westover, Tara, 68–69
Wetherall, Tyler, 91
Whitbread, Helena, 166
Whitcomb, Wendy, 27
Whitehead, Karsonya Wise, 167–68, 175
Willen, Sarah S., 37, 145
Williams, Tennessee, 89
Wilson, Anne E., 113
Wilson, Frances, 189
women diarists: American, 42–44; archives, xiii–xiv; Black, 46–51, 65–66, 164, 167–68, 171, 179; and class, 41; feminists, 9–10, 43, 46–47; historical, 38–41; lesbian, 166; menstrual cycle tracking, 125–26, 179; pandemic journaling by, 145; publication of, 42–43, 47–50, 165–68; reasons for writing, 44–47, 65–68; schoolgirls, 45–46, 117, 136; socialization of, 53; stereotypes about, 36–37, 45–46; subversive, 45; travel diaries, 172, 184–85; undervaluing of, 41–43; writing themes, 45–46
women's archives, xiii–xiv, 157–68
women's history programs, 159–60
Women's History Sources (Hinding), 160, 165
Women's Rights Collection, 159
Woolf, Leonard, 89–90, 126, 190
Woolf, Virginia, 41, 64, 88, 89–90, 108, 117, 126, 178
Wordsworth, Dorothy, 39, 90, 189–90
Wordsworth, William, 189–90
working-class diaries, 41
World Center for Women's Archives, 159
World War I, 134–35, 144, 171
World War II, 127–31, 144, 151, 172, 184
Wreck This Journal (Smith), 102

X (Twitter), 3, 27, 29

YouTube, 3, 32, 138

Zaman, Taymiya R., 107–8
Zapruder, Alexandra, 145
Zirkle, Kate, 152–53, 154
Zola, Emile, 34

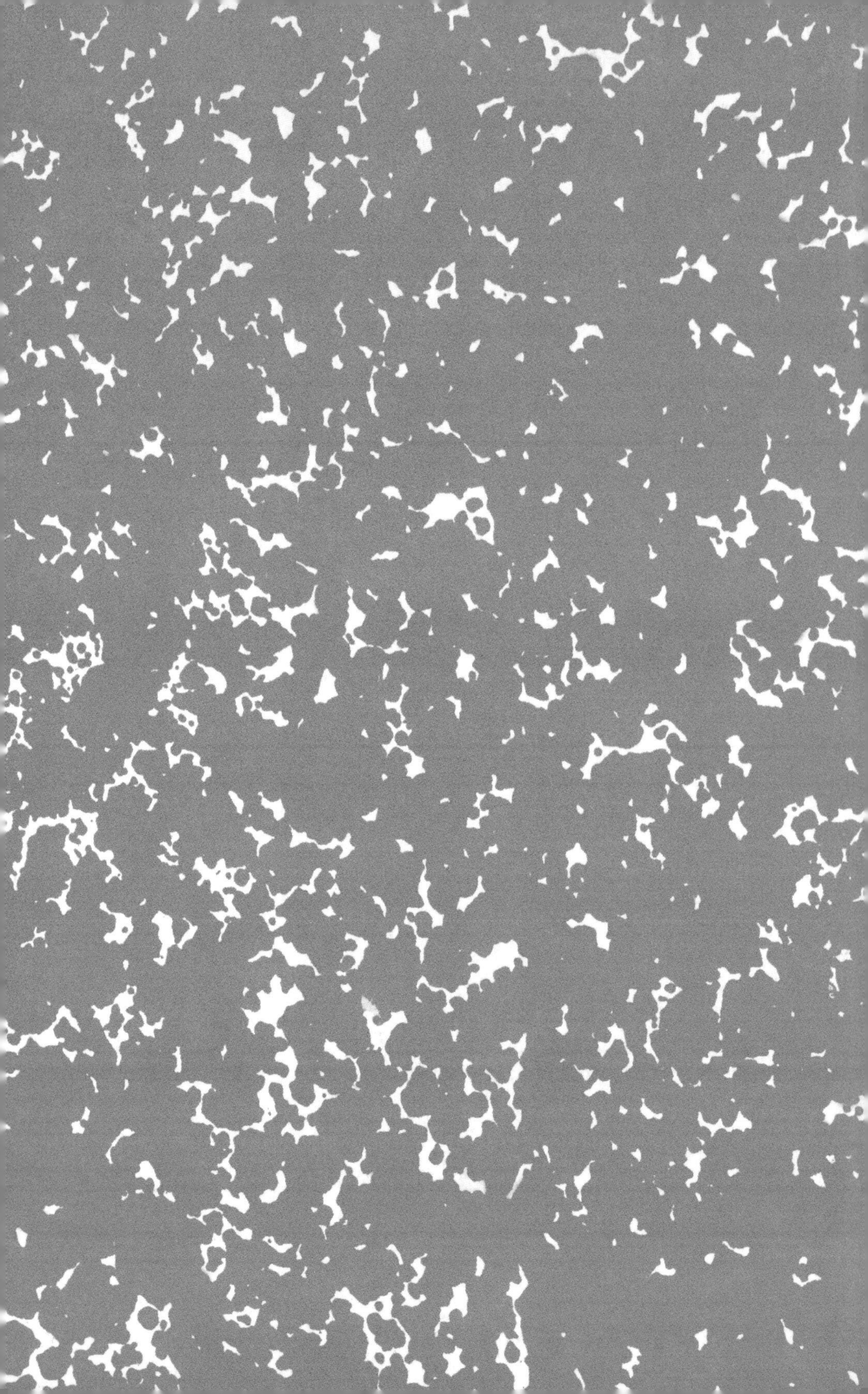